MADELEINE (LIBRARIES)

Brian Hall was born in 1959. His books include *Stealing from a Deep Place*, *The Impossible Country* and, most recently, *The Saskiad*. He lives in upstate New York, with his wife and two daughters.

ALSO BY BRIAN HALL

Fiction

The Dreamers

The Saskiad

Non-Fiction

Stealing from a Deep Place:
Travels in Southeastern Europe

The Impossible Country:
A Journey Through the Last Days of Yugoslavia

Brian Hall

MADELEINE'S WORLD

A Biography of a Three-Year-Old

VINTAGE

Published by Vintage 1999

2 4 6 8 10 9 7 5 3 1

Copyright © Brian Hall 1997

The right of Brian Hall to be identified as the author of
this work has been asserted by him in accordance with
the Copyright, Designs and Patents Act, 1988

First published in Great Britain in 1998 by
Martin Secker & Warburg

Vintage
Random House, 20 Vauxhall Bridge Road,
London SW1V 2SA

Random House Australia (Pty) Limited
20 Alfred Street, Milsons Point, Sydney
New South Wales 2061, Australia

Random House New Zealand Limited
18 Poland Road, Glenfield, Auckland 10
New Zealand

Random House South Africa (Pty) Limited
Endulini, 5A Jubilee Road, Parktown 2193,
South Africa

Random House UK Limited Reg. No. 954009

A CIP catalogue record for this book
is available from the British Library

ISBN 0 09 926835 3

Printed and bound in Great Britain by
Cox & Wyman Ltd, Reading, Berkshire

FOR CORA,
with apologies for this book being about Madeleine

AND FOR MADELEINE,
with apologies for the same reason

ACKNOWLEDGMENT

Since this book is about my own impressions of Madeleine's development, it necessarily limits itself largely to my interactions with her. I should therefore make it clear here that my wife, Pamela, took care of Madeleine about sixty percent of the time, I about forty percent. If those numbers seem improbably precise, you should see the schedule we worked out. Pamela had a dissertation to finish and a book to write, both of which tasks she accomplished on time, while I was constantly late on my various deadlines and more than once asked Pamela to adjust her schedule in order to bail me out. I owe my career during this period to Pamela's discipline, before which, in gratitude and admiration, I prostrate myself.

O

∾ 1 ∾

WE KNEW almost nothing about her before she was born, not even her sex, so we must have referred to her as "it," although I can't imagine that now.

She was quiet when Pamela moved, and active when Pamela was still, particularly after we had crawled into bed. Perhaps the motion comforted her, as Pamela's rocking or my pacing would later, and her kicks and somersaults as we lay in bed were protests. Or perhaps the motion cowed her, and our bedtime was a chance to be bold. She would also stir, sometimes violently, when I played the piano or sang with my lips pressed against Pamela's stomach. The same doubt assailed us here: was this pleasure or indignation? Or was there no more feeling involved than when a pupil constricts at a bright light?

Fetuses often suck their thumbs, or their whole hands, sometimes so hard they raise a blister. Is this because they need comforting? (Do they suck their thumbs when their fathers sing to them?) If so, why do they seek it in this way when the primeval comforter surely is food, and nourishment has always come to them through their navels? Or are they merely practicing, strengthening the sucking action for the day when they will need it?

Do fetuses dream? If not, why do they have REM sleep? If so, what could they be dreaming of? Their thumbs, perhaps, the perfect shape of them. Or the rhythmic boom of the cosmos, the first music of this first sphere. Or a muffled dog's bark and the mother's adrenaline that jolted them, too, something to fear already, something to make them suck their thumbs while they dream.

Do fetuses send dreams to the mother? It is considered a bad sign when a pregnant woman dreams of her baby waving goodbye and retreating into the darkness. Pamela and I had naturally wondered about the baby's sex, and Pamela as an adolescent had taught herself conscious dreaming, so three times during the last trimester she called on the long-unused technique as she fell asleep, and pulled the question down with her like a trapped bubble. The answer, each time, was immediate and clear: boy. Perhaps fetuses don't know what sex they are.

On a September evening two days after Pamela's due date, I was picking vegetables in the garden and as I walked back toward the house I saw a fat moon rising over the sugar maples. I remembered having read somewhere — *The New England Journal of Medicine? The National Enquirer?* — that once a month, at the full moon, there is a spike in births. Early the next morning Pamela's water broke. She labored lightly through the day and night and on through the following morning until, at midafternoon on the day of the full moon, it got serious. Since we had planned a home birth we didn't have to compete for a birthing room in the presumably swamped hospital, but had midwives with us in the dining room, where Pamela rocked in a rocking chair, lowing, hour after hour. She has a high tolerance for pain and she didn't much need me, but I sat next to her, stroking her hard, squared-off stomach with a circular motion she said was comforting, and though I am not a mystical sort, I thought of the pregnant moon, pregnant Pamela, the chair rocking back and forth like the ebb and flow of tides, the tides of her contractions, the tide of seawatery amniotic fluid, the high tides far away along seashores on this full-moon night.

Madeleine was born just past midnight. The room had been heated to eighty degrees, so it would not have felt cold, but what a chilling void it must have seemed. Perhaps it felt like free fall, to have the hugging walls slide back and her arms and legs spring out, jerking like antennae searching for a surface. But free fall is weightless, and she would have felt instead a new heaviness, a lost buoyancy, as though for nine months she had been falling, falling, and now she had landed.

Laid on Pamela's stomach, she churned her arms and legs and slid on her grease toward the breast. She gave a predator's glittering one-eyed squint up at her mother's exhausted face and chomped down on the nipple. Now, at last, she could vent this primal urge on the organ for which it was designed, the Platonic ideal of her thumbs. Nothing came out. But perhaps she didn't know anything was supposed to come out; she knew only that she must suck. She presumably did not know that the real purpose of this first, dry chewing was to make the uterus throw off the placenta and clamp shut over its massive wound before the mother bled to death.

What could she hear? Water remains in the newborn's ear, easing the transition to the sharper sounds outside the womb. She could probably already recognize Pamela's voice, and perhaps mine, but the midwives' steadily rising argument — Pamela was bleeding too much, this was frightening, the uterus would not shut down because the bladder was full but Pamela was too numb to urinate, they should call the doctor, no they shouldn't — probably didn't even register as background noise.

How well could she see? Not across the room, not to the door through which one of the midwives was hurrying toward the telephone. A newborn can focus between eight and ten inches away, the distance from breast to face. Adrenaline grants her an hour or so of alertness and calm, a heightened awareness that will not return for days, and this is the window celebrated in recent years as an opportunity to bond with the maternal face, the one clear image in the little circle beyond which vague shapes flutter and murmur. But the maternal face was replaced by a bearded one, as Pamela was coaxed into the shower, where warm water on the abdomen was supposed to help her urinate. Madeleine didn't seem to care. She stared into my eyes. Her face was squashed, her eyes Uralic, her skin pink and blemishless. Perhaps she concentrated. I could not. I listened to the shower, and fatigue and the sight of so much blood made me feel faint, and I was distracted by fierce admonitions to myself to bond! bond! since bonding would be especially important if I ended up raising this baby on my own. (Actually, new research had already suggested that the whole bonding-at-birth idea had been greatly overplayed, but I was suffering from the usual pop-scientific lag of about a decade.)

From the shower, gasps of relief. It had taken an hour. A few minutes later, the steady bleeding stopped.

The new family got into a fresh bed. Midwives and relatives faded away. It was three A.M. The only sound in the room was one Madeleine had surely never heard before: her own gummy snorting, as loud as a warthog.

❧ 2 ❧

HER WORDSWORTHIAN clouds of glory seemed literal: tiny nibs of white-blond hair marked out a hurricane whorl on her red scalp, and her irises were storm clouds of dark blue-gray. Her pupils were enormous. As windows to the soul, they were thrown wide open, drawing me toward them for a look, a trip, a fall through. I am not being fanciful. Since your pupils dilate when you see something you like, and since we all love to be liked, this is probably the genes' way of seducing the parents, of preventing them from abandoning this alarming burden somewhere in the forest.

As for Madeleine's point of view, one can only guess, in the first weeks, at the mix of volition and reflex. Placed on her stomach, she "swam," kicking her legs and flailing her arms. Attagirl! I might think, or I might hurry to relieve her of what could be distress. But all newborns do this automatically, like wind-up toys. Is it a dying remnant of life in the womb? Or a much deeper genetic signpost, pointing back to our ancient aquatic existence?

She would grasp anything that touched her palm and be unable to let go. Look at newborn monkeys, developmentalists say, who must grip their mothers' hair to ride on their backs. A human newborn has such a strong grip she can hang from a bar. You might think the purpose of that startling hard squeeze on your index finger is to strengthen the grip even more, but in fact it's getting weaker by the day.

In the so-called Moro reflex, a newborn who thinks she is falling will shoot out both hands, spreading fingers to clutch at the air, and then pull her arms tight against her chest. An idea almost inevitably intrudes: branches! The hairy, pea-brained, pre-australopithecine babe is falling out of the tree and it spastically spreadeagles to catch branches in its strong grip. If a human baby, in falling, happens to be holding a pencil in one hand, only her other hand will shoot out. Evidently, she thinks the pencil is a branch. But if the baby is holding her thumbs, this satisfies her as well as the pencil does, and neither hand reaches out. Newborns frequently hold their thumbs. You could argue this supports the theory. If the hands are reaching for branches, then branchlike objects are comforting, and babies hold their thumbs all day for the feeling of security it gives them. You could equally argue it undermines the theory. I see primeval babies plummeting down through the forest understory, blissfully holding their thumbs.

The swimming reflex, the grasp, the Moro — all are remnants, somewhat mysterious, of larger urges and larger questions spanning eons and species, out of which the baby sails. They disappear before our eyes as she individualizes, as she slowly coalesces out of Life into her own life.

At twelve and a half weeks, when it is less than two inches long, a human fetus will turn its head to the right if its right palm is touched, or to the left for its left palm, open its tiny translucent mouth, and suck. When I held Madeleine to my shoulder for a burp in the dim predawn of the first and many subsequent mornings, she would work her way from my neck to my cheek to my chin, a mountain climber rounding the corner of a cliff face, her eyes closed, chuffing all the way, leaving a trail of incipient hickeys. Like the true mountain climber, she had no choice: I was there.

Later, when I watched her grip the air and bring two fists to her open mouth, the word "mammotropic" would come to mind. She was perfectly capable by then of distinguishing a face from a foot and a breast from a brick, and yet when she got hungry she did not look around for Pamela or the breast, she simply tried to stuff whatever was near into her mouth — my shirt, the table edge, empty air — and kept doing it until the breast came within reach. Like the hands grabbing for the invisible branches in the Moro reflex, this rooting seemed blindly opportunistic, and dubiously suggestive of some deep past when each mother (of whatever species we were back then) had thousands of babies, paying attention to none of them, and they all sucked promiscuously, and if one happened to find a breast, it survived.

And yet it was in the nursing that Pamela and I got our earliest sense of Madeleine as an individual, as something more than a mere bundle of irrepressible urges. When we compared her with the babies of our friends (all of whom seemed to be having babies at the same time we did; or did we just lose our other friends?), she seemed by far the most avid nurser. She had an idiosyncratic way of attaching. She would dart her head forward and fasten on the nipple with a sudden bite, vigorously shaking her head as though, catlike, she were trying to break the breast's neck. Later, when the rooting reflex abated and she was capable of turning away from the nipple after a couple of sucks to see what else was going on, she seemed partly to do this because it allowed her to start again with another attacking bite and shake. She already had amusements.

All newborns seem preprogrammed to be attracted to the human face, but only some of them will respond to your stuck-out tongue by sticking out their own tongues. At my repeated attempts, Madeleine only furrowed her brow and slightly tucked her chin. Puzzlement and mild concern? Actually, books *say* newborns focus on the human face, but whenever I held Madeleine she would usually stare, if she looked at me at all, at the top of my head, or over my shoulder. Developmentalists coolly explain that babies like edges. New Agers have their own interpretation: babies can see auras.

Like many parents, I found it almost impossible not to imitate her expressions back to her. This seems an odd instinct, since surely Madeleine was supposed to be learning her expressions from me. As long as she was smiling, everything was fine. She was happy, I was happy she was happy, and either she was happy I was happy she was happy, or more likely, she was confirmed in her original happiness by the fact that I was happy she was happy. Either way, it was a closed circuit of intense satisfaction to me, and of sufficient interest to her to induce her to stick with it for a minute or more. Unfortunately, along with smiling back at her, or crossing my eyes back at her, I would unthinkingly look startled back at her. This particular feedback loop would immediately spiral into a screech. She would startle at something trivial — say, my bumping a drawer on the changing table — and on seeing my cartoonish wide-eyed "Oh!" would infer that her worst fears were true (that she was hurt? that I was hurt? was there yet any distinction between "she" and "I"?) and would instantly break into wailing.

She stared intently at round things, presumably because they looked like breasts. Or perhaps because they looked like faces. If I turned while holding her, she would shift her head to keep the round thing in view. If I kept turning, she would twist her neck as far as it would go, then whip around to the other side. I had never appreciated how many round objects there are in our lives: doorknobs, watches, plates, saucers, tops of glasses, bottoms of glasses, crackers, cookies, cucumber slices, deodorant roll-balls, lightbulbs. I could stand anywhere, and after a second or two she would focus on something round, lean toward it, lock on. Someone gave us a padded-disk squeeze-toy with concentric circles and a bull's-eye, black on white. She adored it. Perhaps the central black spot was an eye, with concentric eyebrows. Or perhaps it was a nipple, creating its own magnetic field, an emanation of "suck here" lines. The globe on the piano was either a winningly friendly fathead or the gloriously overswollen breast of her dreams. Above her changing pad, a mobile of black-and-white patterned disks (our impression that black-and-white objects were part of an educational craze for newborns was confirmed by this gift's brand name: Stim-Mobile) made a whole crowd of faces, jostling for an admiring view, or perhaps it was a happy return to the days when the baby had eight teats to choose from.

Madeleine also stared up a lot. One of the midwives said she looked at the ceiling because its blankness provided relief from overstimulation. (I suppose I could have solved that problem by getting rid of the mobile.) But I wasn't convinced. I suspected the smoke alarms, which were round with nipplelike test buttons, or the circular plates holding up the ceiling lights. We eventually discovered that she loved to hold yogurt lids, and it occurred to me that they were both round *and* blank. Like me with my brandied evening coffee, did she prefer her stimulants soothing?

But there was more to her looking up than the ceiling. She also looked "up" when lying on the bed. That is, she arched her back to look along the mattress, away from her feet. Often when we held her she pushed the back of her head hard against our palms until she ended up prone in our lowered arms, her head hanging upside down. She was trying to roll, which fetuses accomplish in the womb by throwing their heads backward and to one side. Unbuoyed by water, she could no longer do it. In the cramped womb she had been free, whereas now, in this limitless space, she was chained by gravity. Success in her new world was months away. But every day, every hour, she tried.

So as I paced with her or carried her around doing chores, she was always twisted in my arms, looking backward. In her wide-eyed, solemn gaze I imagined I saw sadness, but with a mature resignation. I seemed always to be carrying her away from the object of her greatest desire.

∾ 3 ∾

THE SOUND of conversation was comforting. Both Pamela and I talk a lot, but since I could hold Madeleine indefinitely without getting tired, she would usually be in my arms, and she would never lie quieter, never slip more easily into sleep than when she was leaning back against my chest while I droned on and on. Once she was asleep, nothing conversational — cross-talk conducted at a roar, barked agreements, finger-jabbing pontificating — would rouse her, or even cause her to stir. In marked contrast, two soft sounds invariably made her startle and whimper. One of them was clearing my throat. The other was any kind of rustling. Balling a plastic bag next to her crib would disturb her more than dropping a pot lid.

I happily settled on a theory: to Madeleine, the conversational roar was the sound of the tribe, filling the void, keeping the predator at bay with noise around the fire. The rustling — so quiet, so stealthy — was the predator itself, creeping up over dead leaves and twigs. And my throat-clearing was the very growl of the beast. Men tend to talk in high voices to their babies. As a fake tenor in pickup choirs, I had a well-developed falsetto anyway, and I derived a (perhaps significantly) deep satisfaction from wah-wahing old songs to Madeleine an octave above where they belonged. One theory I've read holds that men do this instinctively in order to sound more like the mother, who is, after all, the vital parent at this stage. But perhaps we do it in order to sound less like a saber-toothed tiger.

Like adults, babies find white noise soothing. Light-sleeping lawyers in city apartments have to buy white-noise generators because they no longer have a parent around to hold them close and say "Sshh." That instinctive shush is our homemade white noise, an effective blocker of distressing sounds like throat growls and leaf rustlings, or the baby's own cries which, when she hears them, frighten her all the more. Perhaps it also recalls for the baby the hiss of water in the ears in the womb, or the muffled whoosh of the mother's circulatory system. Lovers go to Niagara Falls partly because the negative ions thrown off by falling water sharpen the libido. We went to Niagara Falls when Madeleine was six weeks old for a more prosaic reason: I had an assignment. But for Madeleine, evidently, the stimulant ions couldn't hope to compete with the sound of the world's largest white-noise generator, and she slept for almost three days straight.

Or perhaps it was the lousy weather. Madeleine had a keen barometric sense. On low-pressure days, she would swirl, cloud-like, down into a cozy depression of her own. We had noticed the correspondence at home, when on rainy days her nap lasted all afternoon, but it was only at Niagara Falls that we saw a reason for it. There, we were forced to venture outside despite the weather, as in the prelapsarian arboreal days, and she was down in the Snugli on my chest, the only warm and dry member of the family. If she had woken, she would have fussed, and that would have forced us to bring her out into the spitting sleet.

Once you settle on the primate-memory model — the idea that while parents are driving to the doctor or the supermarket, honking at other members of the herd, their baby in the back seat is crossing the veldt, fearing carnivores and lethal weather — you can amuse yourself devising reasons for all sorts of things. The most terrified we ever saw Madeleine in the first months was when I put her in her car seat on the morning of the first snowfall and unthinkingly set about scraping ice off the windshield. The black scraper blade was a paw, clawing at the fragile saplings hiding the mouth to her cave. My allergic sneezing was so common she eventually got used to it, but to my blowing my nose, never. The white tissue was some small but insanely aggressive animal, a proto-wolverine, which with greedy snorts was devouring my face.

For these fears, or the pain of gas, or the obscure misery of fatigue, she could be soothed by pacing. The rocking chair worked well enough, but walking worked better. From the kitchen through the dining room to the living room was about thirty feet. Refrigerator to piano, back to refrigerator. I walked to California on that quarterdeck in Madeleine's first year. She would almost immediately quiet down and look up and watch the smoke alarm sail to the rear, then the round plate of the ceiling light. Then the plate would come back, then the smoke alarm, then the smoke alarm again, then the plate. (I'm tempted to see in these comforting disks passing overhead a root of the popular passion for flying saucers, filled with aliens who are almost all face, and knowledgeable beyond our understanding.)

Parents tend to pace or rock their babies at the heart's rate of seventy per minute. Although I am left-handed, I always carried Madeleine in my left arm, thus forcing myself to do chores with my clumsy right hand, and I have since read that for both right- and left-handers, four out of five parents carry their babies on their left side, where the heartbeat is loudest. So surely pacing calms because it's a return to womb rhythms, physically and aurally. But I am reluctant to abandon my model. When the primate family set out on a journey, it was at its most vulnerable: in the open, in the unknown. Babies who cried when their parents walked out into the world betrayed their location to saber-toothed tigers and proto-wolverines.

Plate . . . smoke alarm . . . plate . . . An unmistakable increase in her mass — no, I don't believe it, but I swear it's true — would tell me that she had fallen asleep. A dream might boil across her face, opening eyes that floated in opposite directions, stretching the corners of her mouth into practice smiles or whimpering grimaces. Dreaming of . . . ?

❧ 4 ❧

WHEN I first held Madeleine up to a mirror, she ignored her own reflection and stared at mine. I tried to direct her attention to her image, but she merely glanced at my pointing finger and back at me. At this stage she took in everything with the same wide, bright-blank eyes, all reception and no transmission, so interest could be gauged only by the length of time she stared at an object. My face was noteworthy and hers was not, which suggested to me that she already could recognize my face, and in the confused swirl of her world settled on it as a familiar island. Perhaps she also knew that engagement with this face brought results, like getting picked up and carried to the breast.

The third or fourth time we stood in front of the mirror, she made a discovery: me, my reflection, me, my reflection. Two of me! I imagined surprise. But why should she have been surprised? Why not ten of me? Why not two faces for all the people in the world, one with breasts and the other with arms to carry her to them?

One might wonder why babies would be surprised by anything. But some expectations do seem to be hard-wired. Newborns turn their eyes in the direction of a sound. Apparently, they have an *a priori* expectation that aural and visual cues will match. Perhaps Madeleine was not surprised by there being two of me but by the fact that the mouth in front of her moved, whereas the voice — "Look! Two of me!" — came from off to one side.

After six weeks of loving parental beams evoking blank stares, Madeleine's first real smile was bestowed on her uncle Jon. The smile may originate as an appeasement gesture, and Jon, strange looking anyway, was grotesquely flapping his tongue and rolling his eyes at the time. An alternative theory hit upon by the wounded parents was that Jon's bald pate made him look especially like a big breast.

But faces were clearly acquiring their own appeal quite apart from their mammary qualities. High on our kitchen wall were four vegetable faces — two Arcimboldo reproductions and two modern imitations — which, in their exuberant spikiness, looked nothing like breasts and were not even (I would have thought) obviously faces, and certainly not *human* faces, yet one morning I realized Madeleine was staring fixedly at the first in the row. I lifted her above my head, and she drank in this assemblage of fruits and grains in profile, with a zucchini nose and whole-wheat pasta hair. After a moment, as if she were in a gallery, she shifted her gaze to the next in line, to which I moved her, and she focused correctly on the two cherries on either side of the Bosc pear. Then on to the next. This became a morning ritual I could not forgo, and indeed had to repeat so many times that I took to resting my arms by letting the refrigerator top take Madeleine's weight while she gazed adoringly at the last portrait, a cabbage with pearl-onion eyes lidded in snow peas. In one of those ecstasies that seem entirely reasonable to the parent but are powerfully emetic to everyone else, I referred to the faces as Mr. Zucchini-Nose, Mr. Pear-Nose, Mr. Radish-Nose, and Mr. Squash-Nose, and over time Madeleine came to recognize the names.

At around two months, she began to prefer her own reflection in the mirror to mine. Perhaps she had now grown familiar with her own face and liked its simpler, more ideal features, its exaggerated eyes. Or perhaps it was still less familiar to her than my face, but as the world around her grew less intimidating, she was beginning to prefer novelty. Certainly her interests were expanding beyond mere faces (love me!) and breasts (feed me!), as she perhaps began to assume the bare fact of her survival and wondered what else there might be.

For example, color. The black-and-white Stim-Mobile and bull's-eye squeak-toy were suited to those first weeks when her eyes would float in opposite directions — her hands flapping in panic as the already bewildering world doubled on her — and she needed a sufficiently stark edge over which to throw an ocular grappling hook. But at two months, Madeleine could track a moving object. She no longer cared about people's auras. Among her earliest possessions was a small yellow terry-cloth duck with a printed wing of blazing red. That wing fascinated her. It was so bright it seemed to float off the body of the duck. She would arch her back in the fold-up travel bassinet that was her bed for the first four months and stare up at the red wing in the corner.

One morning I was peering in at that avid stare. Something momentous was happening. Her right arm was twitching. It jigged her hand up and flapped it down again. The hand fluttered at the end of the questing arm like a fish on a line, struggling but unable to control where it would be yanked next. It fetched up against the cloth side of the bassinet and stuck there. The autonomous wrist joined the fray and commenced wiping the hand up and down the wall in an attempt to drag it free. When this maneuver succeeded, the force of the effort shot the arm above the head. Madeleine arched her back farther and focused again on the wing. The arm jerked. The hand whipsawed. It fell short and far, like artillery finding its range. At last it glanced off the duck, nudging it out of reach. The arm lay still and the hand softly flexed and unflexed, as though gasping for breath.

Interaction! Agency! Surely our hands are our most important discovery before speech. Madeleine was no longer a passive viewer, a mere receptacle. The world was different for her being in it. *She had moved the red wing*. And a more profound discovery was now possible. She and the world were distinct from each other. Her hands — these fascinating wiggly objects that floated into her field of vision even more often than the face with the breasts and the other one with the arms — could be commanded. They, like the two obedient faces, apparently belonged to her. The red wing did not. It would not move until the hand touched it. And when the hand did touch it, Madeleine could see the boundary of self: Madeleine touched not-Madeleine.

She applied her new talent to old passions. She broke from nursing to lean back and give the breast appreciative pats. She explored the grabbable openings and hairs of the two faces. As she gained more control, she discovered that a thumb in one of the small paired holes and a finger in the other, with a hard pinch of the material between, brought a gratifyingly dramatic result for such minor effort. Perhaps these faces *didn't* belong to her, since they would then hold the holes out of reach and not respond to the most diaphragmatic exercises of infantile will.

When the pacifier was brought close, she would make a clumsy grab and try to stuff it in her mouth, usually twisting it sideways so that the nipple lay along her cheek. Holding it firmly there, she would turn her head to get her mouth on the right part, but since the whole thing turned with her, she would keep turning until the torque in her neck stopped her, whereupon she would drop the pacifier over her shoulder. Plugged in at last, her eyes taking on a sated, distant look, she would keep a finger on the pacifier to prevent its escape, and soon learned to loop the finger through a hole in the plastic wing for added security. Then she would forget the arrangement and, reaching for something else, she would inadvertently pop the pacifier out of her mouth and fling it away.

Glitches aside, that was clearly the point of hands: to stuff things into the mouth. Now when Madeleine was held up to the mirror, she not only beamed at her reflection but reached out to enfold it and drag it in for a few good hard sucks. It is said that babies put things in their mouths in order to explore them, that mouths are more sensitive determiners of shape and texture than fingers are, and I have seen babies for whom this seems to be true. It was not true for Madeleine. She did not put things in her mouth to explore them, but to eat them.

Here was her first great frustration, her first sense of the inherent insufficiency of existence. Here was the universal human desire, in its unsublimated infancy, to consume whatever appealed to her, to erase the subject-object division that these same hands had taught her only weeks before. As adults, we kiss the beloved because kissing, as Desmond Morris and others have argued, is a disguised form of consumption, still apparent in those cultures in which the mother or older sibling masticates food for the baby and inserts it directly into her mouth, tongue to tongue. We say that we "drink in" a beautiful view, and although we capture it with a photograph, we want something more. But we are adults, so we don't reach out our arms and try to sweep the scene into our mouths. The satisfaction Madeleine looked for in a discovered object was literally visceral. Even before she got it in her mouth, one could sense in her arm-pumping excitement — want! want! — an edge of desperation. And then the thing itself: hard, tasteless, milkless. She took it out and shouted objections. She studied it again, felt renewed excitement — want! — tried to eat it once more, then threw it angrily away, looking at us with a clear appeal to resolve this structural flaw in the world. I shrugged, adoring her, and consumed her by taking notes.

Eventually she gave up trying, and by four months was never putting anything in her mouth except the breast, the pacifier, and her own fist, which presumably did not highlight so painfully the subject-object division. If her hands could not be the means of returning her to the paradisiacal days before she fell out of the surrounding world — a process perhaps like precipitation, the gathering drop of selfhood — then she had to accept and refine their real function, that of emphasizing the distinction between herself and the world.

A pointed finger became a concrete manifestation of the attention Madeleine could focus on not-Madeleine. Bending low over the tray of her highchair, she would fix her gaze on a stray droplet of juice and lower her index finger onto it with excruciating care. She would not so much probe the drop as hold it down. Looking at us, she would solemnly raise that finger and guide it into the line between her eyes and ours, as though commanding us, too, to stay where we were.

Fingers tested existence. Meal after meal, puzzled anew, they tried to pick up the pictures on her highchair tray of babies like little princes riding planetary rattles, and argued that her eyes had been fooled. They could annihilate: a single sweep of her hand across the rimless tray and all her lunch ceased to exist. They could transform, enlarging the white roll by the toilet a hundredfold, then making it multiple.

The most rewarding transformations of all — so complete, so unpredictable — could be accomplished with a simple turn of the wrist. Flaps! In *Pat the Bunny*, the blue scrap of cloth was poked up, and Paul's face appeared. In *Where's Spot?* a piano became a hippopotamus, a grandfather clock became a snake, and (to the accompaniment of triumphant parental cries of *woof-woof-woof*) the basket became Spot himself. Create and destroy, create and destroy, a power beyond anything else in her experience. In a sense all books are flap books, because pages themselves are flaps, and Madeleine loved those biscuitlike board books from the moment she could grapple with them, certainly not for any story, nor for mere mechanical progression through the pages, but for any one of the hinged boards, tilting back and forth to change its face. The first time I saw Madeleine amuse herself for ten straight minutes, she was holding a Bicycle playing card and turning it over again and again, from the blue swirls to the three red hearts, with a scientist's quiet absorption. Would the blue always change to red? Once she had satisfied herself on that point, she paused, continuing to gaze at the swirls. Then she flipped the card again, but along a different axis, now bringing the top down instead of the side across. Would it again be red? Yes! Would it be red each time? Yes. Yes. Yes. Yes . . .

Globes and circles retained their importance, but now a whole new class of objects in the house called to her. Drawer handles that flipped up and fell back down. Pot lids that turned over with a cowbell clank. And best of all, doors. To a baby not yet strong enough to lift an orange, these were an amazement, as a single swipe transformed a whole wall.

Along the way she had learned to use both hands together, to pick up an object too big for one alone. Then she discovered she could shift a smaller object from hand to hand. Next, with what I thought was astonishing speed, she learned how to use this technique to hold on to an object while a shirt was being put on or taken off, casually shifting it between sleeves.

From here it was a short step to handing objects to us. Partly this was imitative, since as far as she could tell, the point of our existence was mainly to hand objects to her. Partly it was reassuring, like peekaboo, which appeared at around this time (six months). In peekaboo, the parental face does the worst thing it can do: it disappears. But a few seconds later it pops back, and the child's relief bubbles up in a giggle. When Madeleine raised her dress above her head and waited for us to sing out, "Where's Madeleine?," precipitating a downward fling on "There she is!," it was not she who was hiding, but the whole world, and what reassurances later in life could match that budding realization that the cosmos did not need her constant vigilance to continue existing? (Perhaps this early skepticism is also at the root of infants' distress at something so natural as falling asleep. How can they be sure that their eyelids descending are not curtains coming down on the last act?)

Handing objects to us provided a pale echo of this reassurance. Madeleine would hold up a cracker and stare, mesmerized, as my hand approached and latched on to the far side (I always found myself thinking here of Apollo and Soyuz). She would release, and the object would float away. In control, out of control. But not like the red wing in the bassinet, which was beyond all control. Part of her fascination in our exchange perhaps came from the realization that my hand was a large version of her hand, that the cracker was moving from her control to my control. But she taught us early that this could not be the end of it. No, the point of this experiment (none of these were games) was to provide proof through induction that the object would return to her. This was more a social reassurance than the ontological one of peekaboo. Pamela and I had turned out to be creatures separate from her, but still, we would not take her things away. A more meaningful test, because more challenging, lay just around the corner: throwing things down from the highchair. Would we return them? We would. Would we come across the room to do it? We would. Would we do it again and again? This was good science, a graduated series of tests, a determination of the parameters of natural laws.

The handing back and forth of an object served another social function. We were communicating. Since Madeleine could not yet talk, her way to get me onto the subject of her cracker was to hand it to me. The culmination of this hand-centered sociability was the wave. As I held Madeleine up and chirped "Bye-bye?" and Pamela or some stranger flapped her hands, perhaps it seemed to Madeleine like some sort of handing-off at a distance, a lobbing of invisible bye's and hi's at each other. Only God knew what "bye" and "hi" meant, but that didn't matter; what mattered was that a wave established that she and we were thinking of bye or hi at the same time. Carrying such a freight of potential reassurance, the wave was a serious matter. Out of the corner of my eye I would glimpse a pale flutter across the room and turn to see Madeleine's hands, both held high and opening-closing (like the giving and taking of a cracker), and Madeleine staring at me as gravely as though the continuation of time and the cosmos depended on my response. I would of course wave back, and there we would be, stock-still at opposite ends of the room, waving solemnly at each other.

The baby in the mirror did me one better, since she waved back instantaneously, and as I plucked Madeleine out of her bassinet each morning, she would begin a double-hand wave before I opened the bathroom door, and would lean out, as I passed the mirror, to commune furiously for a brief moment with the other baby before I sailed on through the other door to the room with the changing table, Madeleine still waving over my shoulder.

And if waving meant communing, and was therefore her first lesson in sublimating the desire to consume, perhaps it was no surprise that it also appeared when she ate. As I guided the spoon toward her mouth, was she waving to me to signal that, yes, we were in agreement, I had understood what she wanted? Or was she waving to the food itself, out of some inarticulate need to pay tribute, the unburied seed of a culture's prayers to the corn god, or the saying of grace?

Falling asleep, she would have one hand on the pacifier in her mouth, the index finger looped through its side hole. The other arm would lie behind and stretched up along the head, the index finger inscribing slow circles in the short nap of hair. Those hands formed a cradle, an impenetrable barrier, and they had the entire universe covered, front and back. The index fingers pointed inward from either side, suggesting *I am here*. The two curtains would come down on this act, but the two hands would preserve a space for her until morning, and the two fingers would hold her in it.

♋ 5 ♋

I AM HERE! Long before Madeleine acquired words she shouted it, her face purpling, in burr-edged *annhs!* achieved by clenching her diaphragm and forcing the last teaspoon of air from her body. The shouts reverberated through the house. She would pause for a moment to listen to that glow, pleased to have echo-located herself, before howling again, louder.

I am here! I wondered if Dr. Seuss had had that shout in mind when he wrote *Horton Hears a Who!*, in which the entire population of microscopic Whos, living on a dust speck, have to yell in unison, "We are here! We are here!," to prevent the skeptics in Horton's circle from boiling their tiny world in a kettle of Beezle-Nut oil. It is a little hidden Who-child, discovered and snatched up by the Mayor of Who-ville and carried to the top of the town's highest tower, who contributes the crucial, threshold-crossing noise, a self-assertive Whitmanesque "YOPP!" — a song of himself, shouted literally over the roofs of his world.

For Madeleine, immersion in language began in rituals of rhythm and song and only later calmed into utilitarian prose, a progression reflected in the maturation of national literatures. Don't all parents sing to their babies? Madeleine's first sound of my voice was as a bad Placido Domingo, crooning "Un Dì Felice" through the uterine wall. Later, Pamela rocked her to sleep with lullabies: "I Gave My Love a Cherry," "Shenandoah." I preferred pacing to rocking, and ballads to lullabies: "Barbara Allen," "Henry Martin," and an obscene sixteenth-century number entitled "The Bonny Black Hare" (don't ask), which I had to remind myself, a couple of years later, not to sing anymore. The daily diaper-changing song was "Somewhere over the Rainbow," since its melody was emitted, in crinkly chord clusters, by the wind-up mobile of plaster animals (made by Uncle Jon and, he helpfully informed us, colored with toxic paint) that had replaced the Stim-Mobile over the changing table. Other numbers in the revue were: "Little Girl, Little Girl (on the Changing Pad)," sung to the tune of "Cinnamon Tree," from *Man of La Mancha,* and "Yes, It's Bath Time," to the tune of "Suppertime," from *You're a Good Man, Charlie Brown.*

But songs were only a fraction of it. Virtually every time I spoke to Madeleine I used a voice that seems to come unbidden to parents, a rhythmic, rhyming chant, as though I were summoning her spirit or coaxing a new one out of myself. The altered cadence must be useful to the infant, a signal that these words, hopping and bopping out of the background chatter, are meant for her. I found myself speculating about this one day after I had spent five minutes bouncing Madeleine in my arms and asking her, in a dotted rhythm arranged in bars of 2/4: "Who's this little | ba-by with the | stuffed-up | nose?"

The theory, anyway, lent some dignity to the endearments for Madeleine that popped out of my mouth without my ever having consciously formulated them. Picking Madeleine up, I would say "yes oh yes oh yes" or "oy oy" or "ooda ooda." (One day I caught myself muttering a comforting "ai ai" to the laundry basket as I hoisted it.) We had sometimes called her the Bun when she was in the womb, as in "the bun in Pam's oven," and at birth the moniker had lengthened naturally into Honeybun, or Hon-bun, which later exfoliated into Hon-bun Humbledy Bum, at which point it was futile trying to keep out the Bumble Bee tuna jingle of my childhood, and I went the whole nine yards: "Hon-bun Humbledy Bum Bum Hon-bun Bum," and so on.

Pamela relied less on rhythm in speaking to Madeleine and more on pure ardor. She called her Sweetest Girl, Love Child, Love Bug, Buglet. She was counterbalancing my simple-minded doggerel with simple-hearted Homeric epithets. We didn't know it at the time, but we were filling stereotypical complementary roles, since mothers tend to soothe their babies and fathers tend to stimulate them. The mother strokes, the father pokes. The mother hymns, the father rhymes.

I thought more about this when Madeleine began to speak in clear syllables. All over the world, babies begin with the same basic repertory of utterances. This initial vocabulary, reasonably enough, consists of the easiest sounds to produce: the vowel sound *ah;* the labial consonants *p, b,* and *m;* and the tongue taps *t* and *d.* It is no coincidence that the core family words "mama," "baba," "papa," "dada," and "tata," which occur throughout the world, are constructed out of these sounds. But individual babies vary as to which of these sounds they use most, and Madeleine's preference was unequivocal: "Da!"

She would say it upon spotting an object, a terse, tense sound, as though exclaiming "There!" — a word that is, in fact, a relative of the Germanic *da.* Once we had handed the object to her, she would emit a "Da-da-da-da," a ripple of satisfaction descending like a sigh. As she lay in her crib, just awake from a nap, she would say "Da da?" with a contemplative upward drift, and it would sound so uncannily as though she were addressing me that I would only half jokingly answer, "Yes, honey?" and hover for a moment on the edge of a surreal expectation, until she tripped back down the scale: "Da da da da." I am constrained in my use of verbs here, because there isn't one in English for what Madeleine was doing. She wasn't babbling, because she wasn't saying "ba ba." Nor was she gurgling. Or murmuring. Or cooing. Why does English have no "daddling"? Was Madeleine's preference for "da" so unusual?

That point about "mama," "papa," and so on being nearly universal words for the core family has been frequently made, but I had never seen anyone go a step further and speculate as to why the *m* sounds refer in most languages to the mother. (The father is assigned variously among the other sounds, and the word for "baby" sometimes bears no resemblance to any of them, suggesting that parents don't need so urgently to believe that the baby is talking about herself.) Could this be connected to the observation that mothers tend to comfort their babies, while fathers stimulate them? "Ma," with its initial phoneme conceivably rising out of a moan, the lips pursed as though around an absent nipple (an absence adults also commemorate when they emit an *mm* at the thought of good food), struck me as a needy sound, whereas "da" and "pa" — declarative, plosive — were excited ones. To my admittedly biased eye, Madeleine seemed an exceptionally happy baby when compared with her peers, almost never crying and engaged to an unusual degree with the world around her. It was easy to convince myself that it all made sense. With no need of the solipsistic "ma" (me!), she could confine herself to the assertive "da" — not only "there!" in the Germanic languages, but "yes!" in the Slavic.

Crypto-sexist speculation aside, the bare fact remained: Madeleine said "Da." And with this first sonic tool she beat out a rhythm, a treble-drum accompaniment to parental song — da! da! da! — complete with arms and legs jigging in synchrony, the very motion that, as soon as she learned to crawl, would result in a back-and-forth, butt-high bounce, and when she learned to walk, would become the true stiff dance that toddlers break into at the sound of music, the Mexican-bean jumping that dissolves their parents into surprised laughter, even though the kids have been attempting something like it ever since birth.

Madeleine's next step was to discover that vocalization — this stick with which she tapped objects, or beat out a rhythm to beat back not-Madeleine — could also be used to communicate, as her hands, in waving, were learning to do. Perhaps it made sense, then, that her first understanding of the call-and-response possibilities of sound seemed to come in conjunction with the hand. When Pamela, one day, hummed to her while dribbling an index finger over her lips, Madeleine picked it up almost immediately. Now, from across a room, she could make me stop whatever I was doing to wave to her with one hand and dribble my lips with the other.

Once the breakthrough was achieved, her repertory of sounds grew quickly. The hoarse "I am here!" shout, which was originally intended for the world at large, a comforting assertion, was redirected at us, and retuned as a complaint: "I am here (and I'm hungry)!" "I am here (and you're not paying attention to me)!" She worked up a gravelly weasel noise that was less grating, more neutral. From the complicitous look on her face as she caught our eye, inviting us to join her, it could well have meant "We are here," rather than "I am here." Then there was a softer sound, a thrummed gurgle in the throat like a dove's call, which was affectionate, appreciative: "You are here." She could produce this one with her mouth in an open smile, and when I held her she accompanied it with a lean into my face, hands around my neck, the smile landing on my chin. As a tactic designed to keep us from abandoning her in the forest, it was extremely effective.

Soon she learned to form a real kiss, but did not use it to kiss us. Instead, she squeaked her lips in our direction and waited for us to squeak back. But as soon as she learned the Bronx cheer — the punch line to a fart joke of Pamela's that was just about right for a six-month-old — it became her favorite, perhaps because of the spray of spittle that shot out like sound made visible, and the cohering of it in a pendulous drop on her chin that made us hurry toward her with a tissue. This sound, too, was intended to call up the same in us, and we were usually happy as fools to oblige.

To the parents this is all a game, but the fact that the baby also laughs does not prove it's a game to her. Surely for the baby it is real language and a whole language, expressive of all the concepts she knows: I am here, I am here (and I'm hungry), I am here (and you're not paying attention to me), we are here, you are here. Her laughter is also language, a response to the parent's call: we are happy to be here, we are relieved to be here. And the intent stare that accompanies the baby's call, the disconcerted look that comes with the failure of response, suggest that this is not merely language but the word that calls into being the thing it names, the primal chant in which nomen and numen are one. We are here because we say we are.

At six months, Madeleine loved this: I would touch my head to hers and sing a tone. She, wide-eyed, concentrating, would match it. The tone would vibrate through both our heads. I would nudge my pitch up or down and a pulse would begin, as the two nearly identical sound waves throbbed in and out of phase. Madeleine, imitating me, would adjust her note as well. If we eased the pitches further apart the pulse quickened into a blur, if we brought them back toward each other it slowed, to a run, a walk, a wary standstill. Everything was combined here: pitch, rhythm, communication, touch. The slow pulse in our heads was like the heartbeat in the womb, that first music of that first sphere, but this was music of two spheres, social instead of solipsistic, the rhythm in each impossible without the other. We were there.

∾ 6 ∾

AT NINE MONTHS, this was Madeleine's world:

In the submarine glow of the night-light she wakes with gas pain, kicking the bars so hard her crib bangs against the wall and emits a strangled sound like a metal rod being struck: *Irrnngg!* Then a desperate gabble in the otherworldly voice of a Pentecostalist speaking in tongues: "Ah ga ba!" I pick her up and she writhes in my arms, flinging herself backward, kicking against my chest as though she could push herself away from this pain, vault into a better place. I murmur "Ooh ahh," sounds of mere presence, low like sleep, and for a moment she goes still. I pace and sing, "There were three brothers in merry Scotland . . ." She squirms and ratchets the scream higher. I carry her into the living room. She gasps for breath and shrieks higher still, higher, I think, than I've ever heard it, and half asleep and half panicked I imagine the gas building in her abdomen until she explodes in my arms. "The lot it fell first upon Henry Martin, the youngest of all the three . . ." Piano, refrigerator, piano. In the shuddering silences she curls against me, seeking protection under my chin. Her wide eyes stare out, haunted, waiting. It comes. She kicks. "Engg!" I turn her stomach-down along my forearm. Worse. I lift her high and tip her, head down, and listen for the soft puttering of farts, a beautiful sound, but nothing comes. I lay her on the couch and bring her knees up to her stomach, one after the other, a bicycling motion. "With broadside and broadside and at it they went, for fully two hours or three . . ." More screams. I pick her up again. Piano, refrigerator, piano. "Bad news, bad news to old England came, bad news to fair London Town . . ."

The first time it was this bad, we woke up the doctor. We were guessing intestinal blockage, or a perforated colon, with no idea that it would go on for months, four or five terrible nights alternating with two or three better ones, and now I just pace, or Pamela rocks, and we tip and turn and bicycle and sing and wait, and after an hour or so Madeleine falls asleep again, but precariously, so we don't try to put her back in her crib but bring her into bed with us. When she cries for a nursing at around five, the breast is right there and I sleep through it, and later, in sunlight, she wakes happy, safe between us, her face unlined and her eyes showing no memory of the night.

I change her while Uncle Jon's mobile sprinkles the rainbow tune all around. When her shirt comes off, she rubs her stomach with evident pleasure, and I wonder why she should delight in her soft skin as much as we do. "Fat tummy," I observe, and she makes soft blowing sounds through her lips: "Pehhh pehhh." Of course she may have learned it all from us, the patting and smiling, the sibilant whistles of pure gratification. Am I seeing perfect pleasure or a perfect mimicry of it? How many of our passions begin with such mimicry, masks that grow like sod into our faces?

If she has a rash, I pat her dry gently but she still whimpers. She cries as I apply the cream. I think about this pain. How does she know I am not inflicting it on purpose? When she was four days old I held her for the PKU test, and she was looking placidly into my eyes when the pin punctured her foot and the midwife pinched the flesh to force out the blood. Her face dissolved, but she continued to stare up at me, I imagined in horror, wailing a newborn's version of "Please stop!" while I cooed and let the torture continue. How could she know? Pheromones, perhaps, or the size of my pupils, or the electrical conductivity of my skin, which increases with distress? Surely nature had made some provision for this, to preserve the family and the species. Surely.

Now eye drops. Her right eye is infected again, a frequent occurrence owing to an undersized tear duct she inherited from me. When she was only a few weeks old we used an antibiotic ointment, and it was easy to hold open a lid and smear it on. But soon she started to fight. The ointment was painless, but perhaps she didn't trust me after the betrayal of the PKU test, or the several vaccinations, when I had also held her with such convincing protectiveness and — jab — Oh honey, it's all right, it's OK, I'm right here — jab — Oops, there's another one, I'm right here, don't worry. So as soon as she was strong enough to fight, she fought, clamping her eyes shut and twisting her head away. We switched to drops, and for a while it was easier again. She would look ardently into our eyes, paying no attention to the dropper sneaking closer at an oblique angle. The drops are also painless, but of course disconcerting, and now I can administer them only by dint of remorseless trickery. I hide the dropper behind my back and hold up something she has never seen before. "Ooh, what's that?" I say unctuously, despicably. I whip out the other hand and in one smooth motion squirt a drop in the innocent, upturned eye.

Right. Madeleine is much too smart for that. She figured out a long time ago that any attempt to engage her on the changing pad was a diversionary tactic, any object presented, no matter how intrinsically interesting, was a decoy. The simplest, deepest things I would want to encourage in her — trust, curiosity — have been compromised for the sake of clearing a little pus out of her eye. When my hand shoots out she's ready for it and flings up an arm, deflecting me, and now twists away, hands rubbing both eyes. Since apparently I will not protect her, she will do it herself. I coax, I wheedle, I lie, I wait. She peeks out and I fire. Nose, forehead. At least I'm keeping the infection from spreading.

I wind up Uncle Jon's mobile again, to divert her while I rinse the diaper. The music tinkles, the little plaster animals rotate: blue shark, orange rabbit, yellow tuna, red bear, green turtle, black seal. All smiling, chubby, endearing. I carry her to breakfast. Her plate has a red A with an alligator, a blue B with two balloons, a yellow C with three crayons. Up the sides of her bottle are stacked more A's, B's, and C's, jauntily tilted as though kicking up their heels. Her sippy cup has an iconic cow.

Her hands and feet rotate like radar dishes as the spoon approaches. She hums happily when she eats, and she eats a lot. Parents of other babies have expressed envy, then surprise, and ultimately have been reduced to a shocked silence at the sight of Madeleine eating. She grabs the spoon and tries to feed herself. She tips it just millimeters before it reaches her lips, pouring the food down her front and mouthing the empty spoon. She pokes at the splatter on her tray, smears it in a straight-arm arc. She tries to pick up the babies riding the rattles. She pokes her index finger in the face of the sippy cup's cow, making its startled goggle eyes seem fleetingly apt. She enjoys the bang of the cup hitting the tray, the slosh of the bottle hitting the floor. She grows more excited until she is shouting at me. Is she starving, or so stuffed that another spoonful will make her vomit? One moment she's shoving the spoon violently away, the next she's hauling it into her mouth. Is she trying to hold the food in front of her to get a good look at what she needs so much? Or is she merely confusing attraction and repulsion, her synapses going haywire in the electrical storm of excitement?

I clean her up and set her among her toys on the floor, positioning pillows on either side to keep her from tipping sideways. She has a stacking toy of six disks that decrease in size through the rainbow — red, orange, yellow, green, blue, violet. Madeleine can slide the disks off the pole but can't get them back on. Instead, she turns them over and back like playing cards, and throws them to hear the good crack when they land. She loves it when I turn them on edge and spin them. They look like glittering balls, dancing in intersecting circles, and when they collide they bounce away with sudden force, gone flat again, sliding to a stop. She holds them on edge, but they don't turn into balls for her, they merely fall over. She has plastic keys on a ring: a green key with one notch, a red key with two notches, a blue key with three notches, and a yellow key with four notches. She has a terry-cloth rattle with a red A, a blue B, a green C. She has plastic links of red, blue, yellow, and green that can be fitted together into a chain that clicks when she shakes it. She has an award-winning toy made of six rods in rainbow colors held in floating tension by black elastic cords to form an icosahedron. She has another award-winning toy that looks like a model of an alcohol molecule: a blue ball inside two red rings, connected by a yellow flexible cord to a smaller red ring. It came with a sixteen-page instruction manual explaining its myriad educational, recreational, athletic, and moral purposes: the development of hand-eye coordination, color recognition, tug of war, "legercises," parent-child bonding, the fostering of world peace, etc. Madeleine uses it to practice her gross motor skills. She grabs the small red ring and waves, and the heavier end whips around on the yellow cord like a bola and slaps her on the head.

She wails, and I pick her up. I get the boo-boo bunny out of the freezer, and the cold little bunny nose kisses the spot. Madeleine grabs the bunny and fingers the terry-cloth eyes. We look at a book together. In *Pat the Bunny* she pats the fuzzy bunny. She pokes up the blue flap of cloth hiding Paul's face in peekaboo. The stiffer flaps in *Where's Spot?* give her trouble. I flex the page to pop the flap slightly open, but when she reaches for it, fingers ready to curl beneath the edge, her thumb hits the flap a split second before her fingers do and pins it to the page. She pulls back her hand and the flap pops ajar. She reaches again, and her thumb pins it shut again. I get into wrestling matches with that thumb. Her board books are alluringly plump, like stuffed wallets. They're all trademarked: Chunky, Wee Pudgy, Pudgy Pal, Super Chubby. I can't imagine why no one has published a line of Fat Tummies™. In *Color Me Bright,* each page is an animal and a color: red birds, an orange tiger, a green frog. In *Baby's Zoo,* toddlers cuddle goats, chicks, sheep, rabbits, and so on. Even in a complex picture, like the opening bedroom shot in *Goodnight Moon,* with its red balloon and telephone and fireplace, its comb and brush and bowl full of mush, Madeleine points straight to the animals: the rabbit in bed, the three bears in chairs, the cow jumping over the moon. She scratches a finger across their tiny eyes. Life greets life.

Animals everywhere, and rainbow colors, and numbers and letters. There is even a real animal, Wolf, an aged, sweet-tempered dog, half German shepherd, half Bernese mountain dog, who officially lives in the two rooms upstairs with Pamela's sister but spends most of the day collapsed on the kitchen floor, his jowls puddled on the cool linoleum, or barking at the Great Nothing and whining to be let out so that he can protect the property. Madeleine's first close encounter with Wolf was a sorrowful lick in her eyes at one month that made her cry, and his senile barks frighten her, but she loves him whenever he's not looking. Safe in the sling against my chest, she'll reach out beaming to shyly touch his bright brown hair, but as he turns to sniff her, his spruce-branch tail wagging, she draws in her hand, giggling, and hides her face against me.

Time to change her diaper. The rainbow tune tinkles, and the blue shark and orange rabbit, the yellow tuna, red bear, green turtle, and black seal smile down at her. I rinse the diaper and put her on the floor, on her stomach. She arches her back and tips her head to the right to pull herself over. Until recently her outstretched right arm would get pinned and she would have to clamor for a rescue, but now she neatly folds the arm under and rolls onto her back, twitches all four limbs, and proudly shouts.

I rip out two magazine pages and crumple them so that there will be no straight edges to cut her. I spread them out again and let her hold one in each hand. She will lie happily for several minutes, jerking the pages up and down, looking like one of those strange flying machines in the old newsreels, squat fuselages with flimsy wings, bouncing risibly but never rising off the ground. She loves the paper for its rustling, which was precisely the sound that most terrified her as a newborn. This seems a clear example of conquering a fear by becoming the thing feared, as animistic peoples will ritually take on the role of a predator. Now she is the rustler, and rustling no longer disturbs her sleep. (How this imaginative incorporation would have helped the pre-australopithecine baby survive, I'm not sure.)

Nap time. Pamela appears from the study for nursing. Madeleine reaches for her earrings, which have been a source of fascination for months. As soon as she touches one she looks at the other, then reaches across to touch the second and looks back at the first. Back and forth, five, six times. It appears that her breast worship has grown more sophisticated, progressing from all round objects to the more abstract notion of paired ones. Moreover, she has had to work hard to recognize false dichotomies — the doubling of the whole world that was only her eyes drifting apart, the second me that was only an image in a mirror, the red-winged duck on the floor that was not a twin of the duck in her crib but the same duck, which had merely fallen from the crib to the floor. But these earring twins are real, and they are examples of a pattern that she is beginning to sense is fundamental, either in the world or in her brain: the two sides of the playing card, the legs at either end of the table, the eyes on either side of the nose. Perhaps she can already dimly sense the less tangible pairings that will inform her life: inside and outside, up and down, big and small, want and don't-want — all the multiplying couples begat by that original pair, Madeleine and not-Madeleine, that shattered her holistic paradise.

Eventually, she deigns to nurse. She pats the breast approvingly — "da, da!" — and strokes it as she falls asleep. When she wakes, it's time for lunch. The hands and feet rotate like radar dishes broadcasting a homing beacon to the spoon. A drop of juice on the tray needs to be held down.

Another diaper change. The shark, rabbit, tuna, bear, turtle, and seal smile down at her. While I rinse the diaper, Madeleine sits by the changing table and pulls the bottom drawer in and out, a transformation as dramatic as a door swinging. She gives it a good shove and I see what is about to happen, but it's too late. She catches a finger in the gap. She looks up at me, frozen, her finger pinched, her mouth open. She knows she has made a mistake but instinctively looks for my reaction, to gauge its seriousness. The pain hits as I open the drawer and she bawls, opening and closing her fingers, trying to flick off the hurt as though it were an insect biting her. Pamela is there, too, and Madeleine twists from my arms and reaches for her mother, but after I hand her over she twists again to reach for me. She wants us to remove this insect, and since the one holding her apparently can't do it, perhaps the other will.

She soon calms down, and I take her outside to the back yard and sit her in the grass while I hang a load of diapers to dry. She pulls up grass, looks at it in her fingers, throws it, pulls up more. She can do this for a long time, almost as long as it takes me to hang the diapers. Toward the end, I hold her in the sling and she laughs when the diapers hug her, pushed by the wind into her face.

Inside, I sit at the piano with her in my lap and play lullabies and ballads, and "Somewhere over the Rainbow." In the lullaby book are pictures of bears and horses, ducks, cows, and cuckoos. Madeleine rocks violently, throwing herself back against my chest, which means she is interested. Her stare, alternating between the keys and my face, is grave, too puzzled for a smile. I suppose there is no genetically encoded predisposition toward this kind of singing. She slaps at the keys, too weakly on the old stiff action to produce a sound, and looks to me for explanation. I press her fingers on the keys but she wants to do it herself, and no sound comes, and she rocks, now agitated, edging into anger.

Hoping to wash the dishes, I put her on the kitchen floor, where she happily contemplates cleaned white plastic yogurt lids, gently placing them on the empty containers and even sometimes succeeding in snapping them into place. She reaches for another lid and pitches forward, banging her head on the floor. Wails. So much pain, so often! Impossible to know how bad it is. The survival value of screaming in apparent agony over even minor discomforts is obvious. How can the baby know what is serious, what is not? Her only job is to summon the parents, who will decide. I decide she is tired, and put in a request for the breast.

By the time she wakes, we're coming down the home stretch. She pulls grass while I take in the diapers, then sits with her stuffed animals. There's a furry raccoon and a terry-cloth dragon and a monkey made out of two socks. She rubs a finger back and forth over the bulbous eyes. The monkey is her favorite because the limbs are thin enough to grasp easily, and since they are long and supple they pleasingly exaggerate the motion of her hands, turning little twitches into impressive palm-frond swayings. A hand-puppet cow talks to her in a motherly drone, which excites her a bit too much, and her shouts are that stew of stratospheric delight and dread that regularly washes over babies in the months before they are able to compartmentalize pleasure and pain, one here and the other there, like a left and a right earring. Her other animals do a jig toward her and she flails — want! want! — but as soon as she takes them into her hands they go limp, and with a smiling wince or wincing smile she throws them aside.

Dinner, with the red A and the blue B and the yellow C and the one two three and the startled cow and the unreal babies and the spoon guided in along the homing beacon. Then an evening walk in the sling, past the chicken run to the neighbor's pond, with Wolf running ahead, and the sight of Wolf running always makes her bounce in the sling and laugh with a purer delight than anything else we know of. Life greets life. Wolf turns at the laugh and comes to sniff, and she hides against my chest, and Wolf turns again to run on his crippled old hind legs, and the pure delight breaks out again.

Then back home and a diaper change, the shark and the rabbit and the bear and the others singing the rainbow tune, then she sits in my lap in the rocking chair with Dexter the Dinosaur, who Learns All About Numbers! on page after blindingly colored cloth page. Dexter waves from behind a shocking-pink 1 and leans against a royal-blue 2, and there is one ocean liner and two trucks and three ducks and four puppies. Everything is chubby, everything smiles, the eyes are huge, the hands are waving. Animals everywhere, and colors and numbers and letters. Colored numbers and numbered animals, letters standing for animals, and animals painting letters in cheerful colors. No wonder our earliest memories are of a world more colorful and more alive. Madeleine's world is a menagerie, a rainbow, a schoolroom, where a cow's head springs disturbingly to life on the end of an arm, and everywhere she turns there are smiles demanding smiles and waves demanding waves, and behind the bright, chubby, clacking keys stands some bright toy designer who sees an opportunity, in a baby chewing on a yellow key, to teach the little sucker about 4, to make her feel 4 with her fingers so that the idea of 4 will be as tactile as the chubby key, as bright as the yellow plastic. Her finger in the drawer, her head against the floor, the diapers hugging her, Wolf running, the piano not playing for her, the disks not spinning for her, the dancing animals going limp in her hands, yellows and blues and ones and twos — the pile has been growing all day, and it tips over. Too much, too exciting, too new, too frightening. Filled too full, Madeleine spills. She sits in my lap in the rocking chair and cries.

She cries on and on, until she's empty. She sucks on her pacifier and an index finger inscribes a slow circle in the velvet nap on the back of her head. Pamela is at her aerobics class. I have a bottle of expressed milk. This is the one time of day I rock instead of pace. Madeleine pats the bottle as she does the breast. She pulls it out of her mouth to hold it up and give it an appraising look. Perhaps it has A's, B's, and C's, or fluffy sheep saying *Baaa*, or a cheerful train carrying pastel zoo animals so cloyingly chubby they are nearly indistinguishable from each other. She pops it back in. I rock. "Well met, well met, my own true love . . ." It's a contest to see who can stay awake longer. I've sung these ballads so many times I can sing them in my sleep. The woman is in her robe of glittering gold, and as she moves the robe throws off flashes of light, she is flat and hieroglyphic, she has turned into a Gustav Klimt painting, bending down to pick up her baby and kiss it goodbye, and I wake in the middle of a line: ". . . stay right here with my house carpenter, and keep him good company."

Madeleine is asleep. I lay her in the crib. The night-light glows. When Pamela gets back we crawl immediately into bed. Drifting, I am brought awake by Wolf, who is spooked by the silent house and warns off the Great Nothing with a gruff bark. Madeleine stirs and cries out in her sleep, and as I drift off again I wonder what she might be dreaming of, and it becomes my dream: a friendly dog sniffing close and suddenly snarling in her face, the hidden beast unmasked, the parental face smiling reassuringly, it's all right honey, and disappearing behind the hands and not coming back.

❧ 7 ❧

BY LEARNING how to rustle, she had conquered rustling, but she could not growl, and growling still scared her. She knew something was down in the basement, something large that, like her, hummed when it ate, masticating its food with an unreasonable amount of saliva, then swallowed and panted faster and faster, so eager was it to get its teeth into more prey, and she could only look at me, dismayed that I treated it so cavalierly. I had already damaged my credibility on this score by my mistake with the coffee grinder. Setting her on the dining room floor and running the grinder in the kitchen, I had tried to reassure her that everything was all right by turning away from the machine and smiling at her through the doorway. But perhaps this reinforced her suspicion that as a protector I was well meaning but incompetent. There I was, clowning around, oblivious of this monster behind my back. (With our second daughter, Cora, I would keep my eyes fastened on the grinder, and she feared the sound much less, seemingly aware that I was in control, my hands firmly around the little bastard's throat.)

The radio on top of the refrigerator was altogether different. Instead of growling, it sang, or spoke in voices trained to be maximally alluring. The round speakers at either end of the unit were large and wide-set, like a baby's eyes. If I let her too near, she would attempt a hug and drag the radio off the refrigerator, leaving me juggling her in one hand and the radio in the other, trying not to drop either.

When the music ended in applause, she clapped her hands. At first I was surprised. How did she know that this rainy static was the sound of a thousand hands clapping? I realized I must have once clapped my own hands at the sound, as a way of engaging her. She probably had no conception of the nature of applause, she just knew now that when she heard it she was supposed to clap, and clap she always did, if necessary dropping a toy to do it. As yet she had little idea of refusal, of any great tension between her will and the world's, or her will and ours. Imitating the world, she reflected its perceived reliability. Combs touched heads, so when she got hold of a comb, she touched it to her head. Shirts puddled around the neck, so she pulled cloth across the top of her head and down to her nape, over and over. The fact that she had no hair to comb, or did not end up wearing the cloth, was irrelevant, and probably unnoticed. It was the actions themselves that mattered, rituals in a pure sense, empty but far from meaningless, just as, when she and I tossed back and forth an "ah," the meaning was all in the tossing.

Well, not quite all. She tended to reserve "ah" and "eh" for these antiphonal bouts, perhaps because they were most compatible with the open-mouthed smile that accompanied them. "Ma" had indeed turned out to be a sound she used when mildly upset or tired. For getting through spasms of pain, she preferred "ga" or "gla." If the pain was particularly bad, she drew it out into a high, tense "glleee!" At around ten months, she realized that parental vocalization involved a lot of tongue use, so she began addressing us in long sentences of clotted linguals, complete with declarative, interrogative, or exclamatory intonation. She would lean forward and stare earnestly at us as she relieved herself of one of these stem-winders, seemingly convinced that she had at last found the key to our language. Fortunately, whatever it was she wanted was still easily discernible by other means: the pointing of her finger, the smell of her diaper.

Also at ten months, she finally figured out how to roll from her back to her stomach, and three seconds later corkscrewed straight off a bed. The rolling came so late that it was only another month before she was crawling. Like most babies, she went backward first, not intentionally, but as a natural consequence of pushing up with her arms and shooting out her legs. She had no control over where she went. She would arc and angle backward over the floor like a balloon deflating in slow motion, and would end up stuck in a corner. The spaces underneath armchairs were quicksand. Once she got her feet in, any move she made only worked her farther in, until nothing but her head was sticking out.

Blind, developmental processes seemed to be at work again. No matter how tired she was at night, she would squirm in our arms, doing thigh exercises. When she finally fell asleep and we transferred her gingerly to the crib, she would come half awake and push herself up, sobbing with exhaustion, and begin a slow lurch backward. When she collapsed, we would stroke her back and sing, until she heaved herself up again, like yeast dough, like the undead, brought to a simulacrum of life by some cosmic power. She would collapse once more, her eyes down on the backs of her hands, praying, trying to block out the power, then churn up again and at last drift off on her hands and knees, and settle, slowly settle, still on her knees, her elbows bowing outward, her cheek coming to rest on her knuckles, all in slow motion, like a ship sinking to the ocean floor.

Forward motion required the discovery of shifting left and right hands and knees independently, a fairly complicated feat that she eventually mastered by watching her principal playmate, Theodore. At first, she even imitated his habit of crawling with the right leg stuck out to the side, the weight on the foot, giving a peg-legged hitch to her motion. Perhaps that extra lurch initially explained the bobbing and swinging of her head as she crawled, but it continued after she switched to a normal crawl, and grew so histrionic I was convinced she was doing it because she knew she was cute. No doubt we had told her so, but this was the first self-consciousness I had noticed, and it prompted me to wonder where she had learned such a conventional image of self-satisfaction — eyes closed, mouth in a pursed simper, head ducking as though to rhetorically ask, "Adorable? Me?" — since no adult would display it except in parody. I searched for inherent reasons for this body language. Perhaps the closed eyes aided the inward focus. And the bobbing head? The ego's love song to itself brimming over into dance? Or perhaps we *had* parodied it to her, sincerely thinking she was adorable and (since we couldn't tell her in words) calling up from our common cultural storehouse of body-language tropes — slapping a knee for humor, patting the stomach for satiety, and so on — this saccharine mime's version of adorability. Like my mirroring of her expressions when she was a newborn, this was a feedback loop of somewhat greater subtlety, and the tip of an iceberg of feedback loops, I'm sure, that were too subtle for me to notice.

It seemed reasonable that her self-awareness would increase with crawling, since mobility represented an enormous advance in Madeleine's control over her world. As a babe in arms, she was necessarily a fatalist. Not able to transport herself, she couldn't much appreciate the element of choice in the parental transport system, so when a desired object receded into the distance, she might be unhappy, but she didn't seem to blame us. (Whereas, since she understood hands, if an object was taken away from her, she was outraged.)

Now that convenient delusion was ending. If we would not bring her to the desired object, then she would get there on her own, perhaps wondering why we chose to make it difficult for her. A number of times as I carried her around the house she burst into tears, seemingly for no reason. I kept checking her clothes for hidden thumbtacks or Velcro scrapes or a trapped biting ant. Then I realized what it was: if I got within a few feet of the front or back door, she thought I was taking her outside — grass! — and the outburst would come with my first step in the wrong direction.

A number of other developments conspired with her new mobility to create a crisis. First, for some time she had understood "object permanence," so she knew that when we removed something from her sight it did not cease to exist. Second, with an increasing store of information about colors, shapes, and other qualities, she could better discriminate between objects, so she increasingly recognized a substitution for what it was: a tawdry trick. Third, her love of novelty was mounting daily, partly because her growing confidence offered more room for her curiosity, partly because her ability to chase down and pick up an object had already begun to pall (childhood is full of these midlife crises), and she was restlessly searching for something that would deliver the same high as those first thrilling safaris. Fourth, her grip was now accurate and quite strong, her throwing arm good, giving her the ability to maul or break a wide variety of things. Fifth, her imitative urge made her most want to hold what we held most: wallets, keys, and other losable objects of considerable practical importance.

In other words, just as she was making the heady discovery of the richness and accessibility of her domain, we seemed bent on denying it to her. Now I really *was* carrying her away from the object of her greatest desire. Or I was putting it in a place that I could reach and she couldn't, a bully's tactic. Or I was hiding it, and then breaking the sacrosanct peekaboo rule by not producing it again. I had once been a face so obedient she thought it belonged to her. Then I was hands that were autonomous but trustworthy. Now I was an agent dedicated to opposing her.

I don't mean to make light of this. To Madeleine, it must have been a shock. Her first year was a series of falls from paradise: first from that well-watered garden, the buoyant womb; then from the oversoul, plummeting down into individuality, as Madeleine recognized not-Madeleine, and in recognizing it, walled it out; and now this, the shattering of the union of her will with ours, the loosing into the world of discord. This was the sin of disobedience — my disobedience, Pamela's disobedience. Madeleine searched the garden, wondering where her beloved creatures had gone, and when she found us, we were naked.

❦ 8 ❧

FOR HER FIRST birthday party, Madeleine wore a long necklace of dried lima beans painted purple. She loved necklaces because, unlike shirts, she could get them over her head. This one was her favorite because the light, dry beans made cheerful clicks.

Theodore came to the party. The son of friends of ours, he was two months younger than Madeleine, and smaller, physically more active, more focused on things and less on people. When Madeleine was six months and Theodore four, we would stand them up to face each other, and Madeleine would flap her arms and grunt with the desire to get her hands on him, while Theodore would stare slightly down, deadpan, unmoving, tethered to the ground by a rope of drool.

But it was Theodore who crawled first, and would later walk first. His head was a geyser field of blond hair, and his dimples and upturned nose gave him a gamin, mischievous look, which was entirely appropriate. When he saw something he wanted, he headed for it, paying no attention to the alarmed shouts of his parents, and when they took it from him, he didn't appeal to them or accuse them, but cried into the empty space, as though the object had disappeared of its own accord. Madeleine and he could not yet be said to play together. The most we could hope for was that they would play near each other. To Madeleine, Theodore was like the baby in the mirror, a thing to get excited about but not really to interact with, and to Theodore, Madeleine was either invisible or a moving target, holding something he wanted.

I am looking at two typical photographs that happen to come from Madeleine's birthday party. In the first, Madeleine and Theodore are sitting next to each other. Madeleine is looking at

Theodore. Theodore is not looking at Madeleine. In the second, Pamela is holding Madeleine, who is crying. Theodore is nowhere to be seen. Did he hit her on the head? Wrest something away from her? I can't remember.

We had talked up the birthday to Madeleine, but it meant nothing to her. What mattered was her necklace, and Theodore, and her first dessert, an apple bundt cake, with a single short, fat candle filling the hole in the middle. This was the first lit candle she had ever seen, and the mercury blob of flame was perhaps a laughing eye. She smiled at the candle and hid her face, as she did with strangers. The four adults singing in unison was an amazement, as though we all had become one person, channeling the voice of the air in the room. We tried to show her how to blow out the candle. She pursed her lips, but did not exhale. Did we want her to kiss it? She pursed her lips again while we blew, and the eye winked out. This disconcerted her, but she forgot everything in the apple cake, a revelation, a whole new world of possibilities opening before her.

"From Theodore!" we all said, while Theodore went after the electrical outlets and Madeleine puzzled over the bright paper and ribbon. I unwrapped the present for her. A fabric house sewn by Theodore's mother, with Velcroed windows that you pulled open to reveal a smiling kitten, a smiling fish, a photo of smiling Madeleine. And from us, as it happened, something similar: a flap book about peekaboo, with photos of Madeleine pasted behind the flaps.

Who knew what all this was about? Who cared? Flap after flap, she called herself into existence. Madeleine smiled at smiling Madeleine. Da!

1

❧ 1 ❧

PARENTS OFTEN talk about their child's first word, but Madeleine's language, like her personality, had no identifiable beginning. Madeleine was talking for months before we understood her, broadcasting her interests in polysyllabic train wrecks while we pedantically repeated the simple words we thought she ought to know. At some moment, from opposite sides, we reached common ground, but neither of us had crossed any appreciable boundary to get there.

Embedded in the scores of "da-da"s she uttered every day were one or two that I began to suspect had mutated into "Dada." Perhaps it was only my impression, but she seemed especially likely to say it (a statistical analysis was called for here) when I entered the room. I conferred with Pamela. It was hard to see the trees in the dense forest of all those *d*'s. Still . . . Her eyes would turn toward me, her arms would pump: "Dada!" Was this, then, her first word?

But did she mean me? Or any man? Or any man with a beard? Or the beard itself?

Did it count as a word if she misused it?

Or did she say it when I, rather than Pamela, hove into view merely because during this period I was working on a complicated article and she saw less of me, so she was doubling her standard indicative "da" for emphasis: "Oh, *there* you are."

And speaking of da, she often said it now while pressing her index finger into some favorite image in a book. I thought I could detect a glottal stop budding at the end of the vowel, the shadow of a *t*: "Da(t)!" That! Was *this* her first word? But perhaps it was trivial to count words like "Dada" and "that" (as I had not, come to think of it, counted the early da that could be taken as the germ of "there"), since they probably derived from random baby noises in the first place and were therefore not learned from us, but vice versa.

Then there was "engg duh." Pamela claimed Madeleine would say it when reaching for something, and that she was trying to say "want that." Inferring "want that" from "engg duh" seemed a bit of a stretch to me, and anyway, I couldn't hear the engg duh in the first place. Pamela kept saying, "There, that time it was clear," but all I was hearing was the usual knotted, parti-colored string. When I did occasionally wonder if I had heard something, it sounded more like "give me," but Pamela assured me I was hallucinating. Pamela does have a much better ear than I do — I spend movies leaning into her, whispering "What did he say?" — but this is my book, so Madeleine did not say "engg duh," and even if she did, it did not mean "want that."

All right, then, how about "wuh"? Wolf had moved away to Seattle when Madeleine was ten months old, and although she now looked blank when we said "Wolf" to her, perhaps some dim memory of him sharpened her interest in a book about a dog called *Carl's Masquerade*. Carl was a rottweiler, a beast like Wolf, who turned out to be gentle: he rescued a baby (unnamed, but obviously Madeleine) from her confining crib and carried her lovingly on his back through dark streets to a costume ball, where, amid bright colors and balloons, they danced. The first time we had looked at the book, I was droning on as usual, naming things and describing the action, when I pointed to Carl and emitted a gruff "woof!" As Madeleine turned from the page to stare at me, intrigued, I realized why parents everywhere do this, and why so many books are designed to give them the opportunity to snort, neigh, bleat, low, crow, cluck, chirp, bark, and roar. I had made animal noises to her before, but by now she was thoroughly familiar with the tone of my voice, and that chesty "woof!" (conscientiously drained of growly elements) must have stood out from the confusing jumble more dramatically than any rhymed or repeated word. It was a handle, and she hung on. After two or three readings, she was pointing to Carl and saying "Wuh!"

Parental excitement! Command performances! But the question remained: what did she mean? Was "wuh" the sound a dog makes, or did "wuh" mean "dog," or was "wuh" the particular name of the rottweiler in the book? Any memory Madeleine might have retained of Wolf would have clouded the issue, since Wolf's own bark did not sound like "woof," while his name sounded a lot like it. Further potential confusion lay in the fact that we had also called Wolf a dog, as we called Carl a dog, and Madeleine couldn't be expected to understand the difference between specific and generic names, and "wolf" was also a generic (we had a book about a wolf, too), and Wolf wasn't a wolf.

Then Madeleine pointed to a little white terrier with its tongue hanging out in *Color Me Bright* and said "Wuh!"

Parental amazement! How could she know that this silly pipsqueak and the dignified Carl, and perhaps the half-remembered Wolf, were all dogs? Had I said "woof" once while pointing to the terrier and just didn't remember it? Or was there some common morphology to dogs that we adults couldn't see, some ineffable doggy quality about all canine breeds?

Then Madeleine pointed to a tabby cat in her book *Baby's World* and said "Wuh!"

Parental puzzlement. Did "wuh" mean any animal? Did it mean "fur"? Did it mean "I am pointing"?

Then Madeleine stopped saying "wuh" altogether.

Parental disarray.

Perhaps to conceive of a word as having "meaning" for Madeleine was misleading. She was hard-wired to imitate us, and in doing so, she associated certain things with other things. Combs and hats went with heads. At the sound of a car engine, Madeleine started waving. Perhaps, at first, she merely associated "wuh" mechanically with dog, with no inkling of the nature of the relationship. Subsequently, she associated "wuh" with parental approval, and so, naturally, she began using it more often. Then "wuh" seemed to lose its ability to evoke our approval, so she dropped it. Perhaps the word never "meant" anything, just as pulling herself up to stand (which was also associated with certain objects, like the coffee table, and which also elicited parental approval) did not mean anything more than itself.

For eons, babies have survived by imitating their parents like good soldiers, not reasoning why, so shying away from the scorpion and snapping the yogurt lid on the yogurt container are equally imperative. Before the child is sophisticated enough to think of words as symbols, they are objects like any other, and Madeleine followed by rote the arrangements we repeatedly laid before her. When she heard "tummy," she patted her stomach. When she heard "foot," she looked at her foot. I could as well call these her first words. To disqualify them merely because she couldn't say them herself would be to suggest that the vocal cords are more fundamental to language than the brain is, or that deaf-mutes have no language.

Much of this early passive vocabulary was centered around food, body parts, and animals. The vital interest of the first subject is obvious. The second has both a sensual, ticklish immediacy and a convenient ubiquity: there was nowhere I could be with Madeleine where there weren't at least two noses to poke at. As for animals, she seemed to have an inherent interest in all life forms, which she recognized by motion if they moved and by eyes if they didn't (so that the radio was alive, whereas, when she could eventually talk, she would point to a picture of a child with its face averted and ask, "What's that?"). This inborn fascination was probably a spillover from interest in the parent, which was so vital that nature supplied it in spades, with no strings attached, and its superfluity was apparent in other animals as well, such as the ducklings and goslings that, having been imprinted to Konrad Lorenz, padded filially after him.

Three generations ago, I suppose, most American babies and toddlers stared entranced at real horses, pigs, sheep, and goats, and marveled at the outlandish sounds they made, but today the majority have to make do with books, which cater ceaselessly to that wordless kinship. Madeleine hardly saw even cats in the flesh, since I was allergic to them, but in *Soft as a Kitten* she could stroke a patch of artificial black fur, and in *Moo, Moo, Peekaboo!* a kitten inspected the milk pail, and in *Carl's Masquerade* there was a woman in a cat costume, and in Sandra Boynton's *A to Z* the letter C was being cleaned by cats, and on page after page of *Baby's Peek-a-Boo Album* a cat looked through a window or slept in a rocking chair or eyed a bird, and of the fifteen animals on the "Pets" page of *Baby's World,* seven were cats.

I'd be curious to know what percentage of children say "cat" as one of their earliest words, given the abundance of live ones in urban and suburban settings and the conspiracy of books (I would be willing to bet that cat owners are overrepresented among children's book authors and illustrators). Certainly Madeleine passed a milestone — I use this term in order to bypass the problem of the first word — one October morning when she was thirteen months old, watching the cat of some friends pick through leaves in their yard. "Madeleine said 'cat,'" someone casually observed, and Pamela said, "No, she doesn't talk yet." Then Madeleine repeated it quite clearly: "Ca!" Until that moment it had been inaudible to her parents, for whom her sidling approach had been too gradual. Perhaps she had been saying "Ca!" for some time, and our lack of histrionics had fortuitously prevented her from mistaking the sound for an all-purpose tool for eliciting approval. Unlike "wuh," "ca" remained steady. Whatever it might mean, she knew it was supposed to be said upon seeing a cat. And it was fascinating, and a bit puzzling, to see how early she understood that a two-dimensional, scentless, and often stylized picture shared an identity with the much larger live animal it represented. The largest cat in all her books, an orange tabby, was also the most realistic, being a photograph, and the real cat in the leaves that day had been an orange tabby. But Madeleine would also say "Ca!" upon seeing the sketched black-and-white cat in *Baby's Peek-a-Boo Album,* which to me looked like a pig with whiskers, and Sandra Boynton's cats looked like gophers. But I had probably pointed to these and called them cats a dozen times by now.

One by one, the words started to come. In her books, dogs ran a close second to cats, and pretty soon she was trying again, this time saying "Daw!" She said it with an explosive *d* and a honk of a vowel, and I wondered if she thought it represented the bark — not this cautious woofing business, but the real sonorous article she occasionally heard in town, a sound that frightened her and therefore cried out for her to appropriate it.

She had the cow on her sippy cup, and several cows in books, and a stuffed one with a calf whose Velcro nose latched on to its mother's udder, and some real ones a mile down the road, all deserving attention because all had big eyes and bigger breasts, and the real ones foghorned *m*'s and *n*'s, the first for "motherly" and the second for "nasal," which was the wonderful quality of the ring in her head when her mouth (*m*) was busy nursing (*n*): "Cah!" (This was a more rounded sound than "ca," which had the same broad *a* as "cat." It was, in fact, exactly the right vowel for "cow," if you couldn't manage diphthongs and left off the final *oo*.)

She ignored big stationary things such as trees and buildings, but was entranced by big moving things, which might be predators (saber-toothed tigers) or protectors (parents), but either way demanded attention. Most attractive were the ones that helped her conquer fear, the beasts that turned out to be gentle, like Carl the rottweiler. The modern big game replacing the occasional elephant that the baby on the veldt might have gaped at were trucks, which rumbled by on the road outside, reassuringly not stopping, apparently looking for something else, and the yellow earthmovers that manifestly *were* gentle, picking up or patting down dirt as slowly as her own hand when I held it and stroked it against my face, saying "Gentle, gentle," to teach her not to hit me when she was excited. "Tuck!" she said (happily not recapitulating her father, who, as a little boy with a loud voice and a passion for trucks, would point out the windows of crowded stores and bellow "Fuck!").

The only real animals she saw daily were the neighbor's chickens, which frequently flew the coop and went pecking down our driveway, so that we woke in the mornings to their clucks and whirs outside our window. Here was her two-syllable triumph: "Tik'n." That *k* was as swallowed as an Arabic *q*, a glottal slam that neither Pamela nor I could reproduce, and we wondered where she had picked it up and why she felt she needed it when, as we knew from "ca" and "cah," she could produce the normal

American version. Then it occurred to me that she was accurately reproducing the chicken's cluck, just as her "daw" was something like a bark. I was beginning to understand that I was observing the origins of language, in which nomen and numen really were one. Madeleine wasn't learning a symbolic code, she was taking pieces of the real world in her mouth and shaping scale models of them in sound, models that, like voodoo dolls, gave her power over their referents. Since many of the words I was feeding her — more than I had realized — were descendants of this ancient onomatopoeic impulse, she had only to adjust them slightly to achieve the sounds she might have come up with on her own. She was taking Pamela's and my language back to its roots in sympathetic magic.

❧ 2 ❧

" 'HERE ARE Paul and Judy. They can do lots of things. You can do lots of things, too.' "

Madeleine now had *Pat the Bunny* down cold. When I opened to the first interactive page, she didn't bother to wait until I'd read the words — "Judy can pat the bunny; now YOU pat the bunny" — but shot out her hand to give the suggestion of a stroke to the fake fur, then pawed at the book, urging me onward. I would read faster — "Judy can play peek-a-boo with Paul" — but she would have already fingered the scrap of blue cloth, and as I hurried on to "now YOU play peek-a-boo with Paul," she would be prying open the next page. Some sense of authorial due, or plain anal compulsiveness, kept me trying to read the text. "PaulcansmelltheflowersnowYOUsmelltheflowers," I muttered in the background while she popped the sketch up to her nose and back down, next! On to the mirror, Judy's book, Mummy's ring, done! From beginning to end, the book took less than a minute. With a little more practice, we'd be able to read it twenty times before breakfast.

Madeleine's response to the mirror in the book was revealing. On our first reading she had clearly understood it, which was to be expected, since she already loved the bathroom mirror and the bedroom cheval glass (which I had had to tie to the ceiling to prevent her from adoringly pulling it down on top of herself). But now when we reached this flimsy little chrome disk she would perform a hurried mime of her initial ecstasy, pulling the book to her unfocused eyes and grimacing. One day I was watching her crawl across the floor, and *Pat the Bunny* happened to be lying in her way, open to the mirror. As her face slid into view beneath her, she cried out in delight and dived on it, open-mouthed, leaving her bottom hanging in the air: a kowtow to herself. Clearly, then, it was not overfamiliarity with the mirror itself that had drained it of meaning, but the ritual of reading. *Pat the Bunny* was our liturgy, and when I opened it with her on my lap and began, "Here are Paul and Judy," I might have been intoning *Introibo ad altare Dei*. Madeleine crossed herself, murmured, and genuflected her way through it, serenely confident that her observances were serving some unknowable higher purpose.

Madeleine in the past weeks had been confronted with her first crisis of boredom. By now she had the physical world pretty well under control, being able to crawl to any part of the four downstairs rooms, pick up any object, examine it, turn it over, throw it. But what else? She knew she could not eat it. And although she had yet to speak the words, she probably had sufficiently mastered the differences between purple and green, hard and soft, smooth and rough, to render those qualities unenthralling purely for their own sakes. She had no conception yet of make-believe, of storytelling, so objects could not speak back to her beyond a predictable jingle or squeak. When she slapped them, they didn't slap back. We had no pets, no other babies. At times, after she'd picked up a dozen bright toys in quick succession and then looked up at me, whimpering, I was convinced she was wondering, with a touch of fright, Is this it? Is this all? Her yearning arms were an appeal: Take me away!

Books were an escape. Not because she understood their contents, but because the physical interactivity — the finger in the hole, the touch against the nose at the required moment — was an externalized version, a practice run, for the mental interactivity of following a story, which would come later. It was no coincidence that at this time she was also becoming receptive to songs with accompanying hand motions, like "Itsy-Bitsy Spider." She couldn't manage the thumb-to-index-finger swiveling that indicated the spider going up the waterspout, so she merely touched her two index fingers together, making a tepee, and her "out comes the sun" gesture looked suspiciously like the upflung arms of "How big is Madeleine? Sooo big!" But accurate or not, once she had learned the moves, they were irrepressible. I sang, she did her routine. Her smiles, her eyes looking to make contact with mine, suggested this was not simply a question of my ringing the bell and watching the dog salivate, but included a large element of social reassurance. (I think the Pavlovian aspect *was* there, however. Two months after she learned the song, Madeleine saw her first real spider, and while she gaped at it, oblivious of my presence, her two index fingers floated together to form a tepee.)

Everything comes back to the desire to incorporate the world, an urge of which Nietzsche's supposedly fundamental "will to power" is surely a mere displacement. The newborn's dance of arms and legs in synchrony with the parental voice serves to bring that voice into the domain of her body, and Madeleine's "reading" of *Pat the Bunny,* like her performance of "Itsy-Bitsy Spider," was a form of dance. Unable literally to consume the book, she could at least embody it through prescribed pokes, scratches, and bye-bye waves. This had to do for now, but the more satisfying incorporation of her surroundings — actually taking things into her mouth, by naming them — was already, bit by slow bit, replacing it. The most satisfying incorporation of all — reversing her fall out of the world by bringing the world back into her head, through imaginative play — would come next.

The days of her inspecting books on her own were over. They were no longer flaps packaged conveniently together like keys on a ring, but an activity that required my or Pamela's services as ringmaster or priest. Like a ventriloquist's dummy, the book seemed alive, sitting on my lap and speaking to her in my voice. Since it was a projection of me, its dependableness was a manifestation of my own and thus, whereas Madeleine valued novelty in other things, she demanded constancy in books. The bright, jingly toy, no matter how bright or jingly, was good for about ninety seconds, but a book sufficed, over and over and over. The reassurance that this emanation of myself, *Pat the Bunny,* would invariably unfold from peekaboo to flowers to mirror to Mummy's ring was a minor variation on the fundamental theme: the reassurance that I would not put the book down, walk out the door, and never come back. And here, as in so many cases, I could see in Madeleine's bald and concrete desires the seeds of my own more layered and metaphorical ones. Didn't I, too, wish that objects could be more alive (that is, more engaging) and people more dead (that is, more dependable)?

The gaudy charms of the flap books and the scratch-and-sniff books tended to make them equally attractive. But as Madeleine advanced enough to appreciate the subtler interactivity of merely pointing and listening, she exhibited strong preferences, and her first favorite was *The Very Hungry Caterpillar*. I had more than enough time, during forced-march rereadings, to ponder its appeal.

The Very Hungry Caterpillar had large, simple pictures in bright colors, not great blank fields of color but textured terrains, encouraging Madeleine to rub them, to test the woody grains to see if they were real. It began with an egg on a leaf in the moonlight, and the egg was small and round and white, like a hole in the leaf, and Madeleine would poke it, as though she might put her finger through the hole, or at least get a little bit of that clean white light on the end of her finger. The moon was big and round and white with a sketched-in face, and Madeleine beamed at it for the usual reasons. More than that, the egg and the moon formed a pair, small and large, like pairings Madeleine had recently become enamored of as we practiced words for body parts and clothes — her small hand and my large one, her shoe and my shoe. Perhaps she was beginning to divine behind these correspondences the larger wonder of child and parent, the first glimmering idea of herself as a small version of us, as she had seen kitten and cat, puppy and dog. Here was a baby egg and a mammary mama moon.

On the next page a leonine sun came up, tremendously big and bright orange, filling the page, with smiling eyes and rays like a spiky mane. The egg had hatched into a little green caterpillar (a male, according to the text) whose existence was ruled by one hard urge, an imperative Madeleine could readily understand — to eat. On Monday he ate an apple, and Madeleine loved apples. The apple stood alone on a page only two inches wide, with a real hole bored through it. On Tuesday he ate two pears, and pear juice regularly ran down Madeleine's arms and dripped off her elbows, and the pears stood all alone on a four-inch-wide page, and the hole in the apple lined up with the hole in the first pear. On Wednesday he ate three plums, and the three plump purple plums stood alone on a six-inch-wide page, and the holes lined up. On Thursday he ate four strawberries, and on Friday five oranges, and Madeleine marveled at the way the holes lined up, and the pages got wider so that the last fruit of each day stuck out beyond the previous day's page, and when all the pages were down you could see one apple, one pear, one plum, one strawberry, and one orange, all in a line. The little green caterpillar crawled away from the last hole at the back of each page, as though Madeleine might catch him actually gnawing one of the holes if she opened the book at the right time, and her fingers fit through the holes like little peach-colored caterpillars, just as she jammed her fingers into real fruit when she ate it, reveling in the wet pulp and the running juice.

She couldn't count yet, but my voice took on more urgency with each day as the line of food stretched longer. One apple. Two pears! Three plums!! *Four* strawberries!! *Five — OR-ANGES!!* And yet, day after day, no matter how much he ate, "he was still hungry"! Saturday opened into a two-page spread, an orgy, a bulimic binge, of chocolate cake, ice cream, pickle, Swiss cheese, salami, lollipop, cherry pie, sausage, cupcake, and watermelon, and as I read through the list, amazed and appalled, Madeleine always laughed conspiratorially. This was the sort of eating she could do. Sunday was rest, recovery. The caterpillar ate a green leaf the size of a shovel pan, and felt better. Now he was a BIG, FAT caterpillar, filling the page with his juicy chloro-phyllous green, and Madeleine knew all about fat, too, because we called her that all the time, convulsively squeezing her, as I squeezed her each time I read this page. He spun a cocoon and when he came out — another two-page spread — "he was a beautiful butterfly!" The huge, colorful wings studded with magenta eyes stood one on each page, so that as I trumpeted "Butter-fly!" (imitating Pavarotti, running up the hill) I could flap those wings around the spine of the book, until the book rose off my lap and flew away, the word become flesh, while Madeleine made an echoing gesture, a quick finger flutter on a roving fist, and yelled, "Mö! Mö!" which I was beginning to realize meant "More!"

∾ 3 ∾

PICTURES, words, and the objects they represented were becoming entwined, confused as to which Madeleine learned first. She responded to the apple in *The Very Hungry Caterpillar* presumably because she had eaten real apples. She pointed to the real orange tabby cat and said "Ca!" because cats had already been marked out for her attention in books. I wondered at what level of sophistication or abstraction she recognized a correspondence between the apple on the page and the apple in her hand. Did she know that the former was only a picture, and was she learning to pretend it was real for the sake of the enjoyment of reading, thus achieving her first step toward make-believe? Or was the apple on the page also real, but somehow inaccessible, like the dishes in the glass cabinet, which she knew were real but always turned out, when she reached for them, to be two-dimensional?

"Remember Wolf dog?" we asked her when going through the photo album, and she petted the photograph and said "Woof!"

Unlike the approximately life-size pictures of the apple, Wolf here was only two inches tall, so surely she understood he was not real. And if she understood that, was her petting correspondingly metaphorical, a signal that she would like to pet the real Wolf if he were present? Or was the photo in some talismanic way really Wolf, and she was radioing comforting pats to the absent, full-size dog? Or had Pamela or I at one time patted the photo ourselves, and she was merely imitating us, and it could have been a photo of a gnu or the Dead Sea Scrolls for all she knew or cared? (I suppose I might have gained some insight into this through experimentation, but the idea of possibly confusing Madeleine just to satisfy my curiosity was repellent.)

"Butterfly" was first that brilliant drawing, as big as a bat, lifting off my lap. Then it was her flapping fingers, following the book, a motion that grew more dramatic with repetition, eventually comprising a violent swing of both arms and a body twist that, if I didn't grab her, would take her right off my knees, like the book, but unfortunately not in defiance of gravity. Then it was also the sound in the air, that word she couldn't reproduce, which had a flutter of its own. Only months later, when spring came, did "butterfly" also come to mean the real insect, and only after we had pointed one out — so much smaller, so much less brilliant — and unlocked its nature with the magic word. That first time, it was the word and not the insect that made her swing her arms and twist, and perhaps the second and the third time, too, but the final circuit was eventually closed, the four avatars revealed as one, so that she could see the insect, cry out "butterfly!," perform her jig, and look for the book, in any combination or order.

Except that Madeleine could not pronounce "butterfly." As usual, I failed to discern any attempt on her part to say it, but relied on Pamela, who thought she heard some *b* sound, *ba* or *buh* or *bö* (the last being the German *ö*, or the French *eu*). This made my job harder, this long lag of tongue behind brain on Madeleine's part, and ear behind brain on mine, and the necessity of trusting Pamela, whom I sometimes suspected — probably peevishly — of overzealousness. How many words, every day, did Madeleine urgently direct toward me that I simply could not distinguish in the rippling run of *ah, cah, bah, bö, dah, dö, mah*?

"Nana" was pretty clear, and at first it meant "food." The nutritive value of the *n* sound had long been established by the word "nursing" and was later reinforced by "banana," which was her first solid food, and her favorite. For a while, I think her "nana" was a synecdoche, understood to mean "banana" but also used to refer to all food (as in, "Let us peel nana together" and "Man does not live by nana alone"). Bananas hung in a high basket by the kitchen door, and thus, reaching in the direction of that basket meant "I'm hungry," whether or not there were bananas there and whether or not she specifically wanted a banana. (These gestural codes were continually spawning and dying off. Only those already used by us, or adopted in besotted imitation of her, survived.) The missing "ba" in her banana was only to be expected, and would happen to other unstressed first syllables. All day long we taught her words by saying, "This is a-SHOE, a-CHAIR, a-NOSE. SHOE! CHAIR! NOSE!" Evidently, all words had detachable unstressed first syllables. "This is a ba-NANA," we said.

"Mama" and "Dada" had already suggested to her that longer words could be finessed by repeating syllables, and "nana" confirmed it, so Madeleine began to put together a mini-lexicon of double-barreled nicknames for things she couldn't pronounce. Now that "nana" meant banana, she needed a different word for nursing, so she called it "nö-nö." (That continental vowel again.

My guess is that all English-speaking toddlers, defeated by their language's treacherous diphthongs, start off sounding like Europeans, a process an Anglophile might characterize as philology recapitulating phylogeny.) She had never babbled "ba-ba" as a baby, but now that she consciously tried to learn the word "baby" from us, to apply to herself, she said "baba." "Caca" meant coffee, which manifestly needed a word because of its constant presence at the end of my arm. Pasta was "papa." Pasta was such a favorite that, like banana taking over the entire food chain, it monopolized all initial use of the syllables "pas" or "pos." When I mentioned the post office, or unwisely said that something was possible, Madeleine was sure I meant pasta, and she would chant "Papa! Papa!" hoping I might produce from behind my back a steaming bowl. The reign of pasta meant that another important feature of her oral life, her pacifier, could not be called papa, so she fell back on "tata." And intimately connected with her tata was her "yaya," her lambskin, on which she slept. (She meant it to be "lala," but all her *l*'s came out as *y*'s.)

Since these were words Madeleine had made up, Pamela and I only gradually came to recognize them (Pamela usually first, and me grudgingly afterward), and viewing them more as useful codes than triumphant acquisitions of real language, our response was appreciative but undramatic. This was not the case whenever she managed to conquer the correct pronunciation of a word. When "apple" one day sprang out of her head fully formed (on closer listening, it proved to be more like "appuh," but I'm quibbling), it got such an enthusiastic reception that, like "wuh," it went on the road and came to stand for all roundish foods — tomatoes, pears, oranges — and eventually other round things, like wooden balls, and even unround things (as long as they were red), like the hearts on that year's Valentine's Day cards. Since it was partly the accurate pronunciation that excited us, we didn't go mute just because Madeleine started assigning it to the wrong things, so unlike "wuh," it dug itself in deep. Confident that she already had the word, Madeleine ignored our corrections, or perhaps misinterpreted them. She already knew that this hard red thing was an apple, and thus our repeated "Ball! Ball!" must have meant "throw it" or "bounce it," and she would happily throw it or bounce it, and call after it "Apple!" and we'd shout "Ball!" again and she'd proudly pat her tummy, perhaps wondering if "ball" meant "good girl" or "good throw."

But pears were so loved that eventually they had to have a word of their own. It was sometimes "peh" and sometimes "pö," which was understandable, since the adult pronunciation, deconstructed, is something like "peh-ö-r." I imagine that fruit, because of its juicy sweetness, dominates the early food vocabulary of most children, and if you looked at a list of any kid's first twenty words, you would be able to infer from the fruits what season she was learning to talk in. Madeleine's "pear" and "apple" gave the game away.

Similar to food in fascination was clothing, and for similar reasons of bodily intimacy. She swallowed food, clothes swallowed her. I've already mentioned the necklaces that she loved to pull over her head, and she now acquired a word for necklace: nana. She seemed utterly unconcerned that "nana" already meant banana, thus destroying my theory that nursing had become "nö-nö" precisely to avoid this confusion — although I will lamely try to salvage it here by speculating that since nursing and bananas served related functions, they needed separate words for the sake of clarity, whereas there was no danger Pamela or I would try to feed Madeleine a necklace.

On the "My Clothes" page of *Baby's World,* Madeleine would always point to the shoes first. She tried to pronounce the word, saying "sheez," and occasionally "shit," while making no attempt to say "shirt" or "pants" or "dress." Shoes were attractive, I think, because they looked like faces, with either close-set beady eyelets or the two large, surprised eyes of strap shoes, and mouths as comically agape as mine was whenever Madeleine pulled up her shirt to show me her tummy (I was imitating a cartoon character accosted by a flasher, and since Madeleine imitated me, the exposure of her stomach made both of our jaws drop and all four eyes bug out). Even if all clothes in a way swallowed her, the association was most compelling with shoes, which sat in a hungry line like goslings in her closet. Their eating of her feet was a jolly echo of Pamela's and my eating of her feet. (Madeleine so loved having her feet eaten — this deepest of all fears coaxed out and neutralized — that I eventually cured her of her fear of the vacuum cleaner by having the machine suck on her toes. Anything that tried to eat her feet, she reasoned, could not be all bad.)

Socks were fascinating, too, because they were the first item of clothing she could take off. Babies love to suck on their toes, and they have sweaty feet, so they have two reasons to get the socks off, and it turns out to be so easy, since their feet hardly have heels. Naturally, this gets them interested in trying to put the socks back on, and just as Madeleine would pull a shirt across the top of her head and down to her nape so that it wrapped her like a stole, she would drag socks up and down the backs of her legs as though she were polishing her calves. One of her puzzles involved putting the jigsawed monkey down into the cavity where an identical monkey was pictured, the lion on the lion, and so on. Consequently, when we dressed her, she wanted to put the second sock on the first one. She couldn't pronounce s, so she neatly solved the problem by calling her socks "shoes" — that is, "sheez" or "shit" — and as with "apple," she serenely ignored all attempts on our part to correct her.

"Shit" had its own history. I stubbornly and stupidly resisted adopting into my own vocabulary the words "poop" and "pee," because they sounded silly to me. I had grown up in a house with a large sign on the kitchen wall that said "Fuck Housework," and unless I thought my interlocutor would be offended, I called shit "shit" and piss "piss," because to me those were the real words and everything else suggested embarrassment and shame, or worse, a covert titillation, such as you find in those books of bathroom humor that snigger about little kids "tinkling." Pamela warned me and I ignored her, and for some reason it wasn't until the first time Madeleine pointed into our toilet and said "Shit" that I realized I had made a mistake. Suddenly, belatedly, I could see it: I had set Madeleine up for shocked responses from many people (many more than would have been shocked by my saying the word), and their shock would do precisely what I had wanted to avoid — it would make Madeleine think there was something shameful about shitting. So I coughed and said, "Poop, hon. Poop."

It was a long struggle. Her attachment to "shit" might have been increased by the fact — if she was aware of it — that she pronounced it almost perfectly. I knew I was sunk if I betrayed any desire for her to change, because that would have intrigued her, and her interest would naturally have attached itself to the word. So she pointed to her shit and said, perfectly, "Shit," and I pretended not to hear her and doggedly muttered poop, poop, poop, all day long until the word stopped sounding silly to me and became merely a synonym. If I could change myself, surely I could change Madeleine. Poop, poop, poop. I sounded like a tugboat. And after a long hesitation Madeleine adopted it, first using it interchangeably with "shit," then gradually preferring it, until at long last "shit" dropped out of sight and Pamela heaved a sigh of relief.

Then one day I was slicing a banana for Madeleine's breakfast and she looked over from her highchair and cheerfully sang out, "Shit!" As I was long used to doing, I ignored it, but wondered, as I sliced, what had caused the word to come back. She called out again, "Shit!" I cut another slice, and then realized: the wet hiss of the blade through the banana, the sharp retort as it hit the cutting board. The knife, like Madeleine, pronounced it perfectly: *shit, shit, shit.*

Ω 4 Ω

I LOVED these glimpses of a language more alive than mine, words spawning straight from sound waves like single-celled life forms wriggling out of primordial ooze. Of course we also taught Madeleine the standard onomatopoeic words, tacked down and tabulated, like "bang" and "bump" and "ding-dong," and the various animal sounds, but these, too, she would occasionally liberate into wider meanings. One morning I was hit so fast with a stomach bug that I didn't make it to the toilet, but fell on my hands and knees in the dining room and belted out a river of vomit. I hadn't puked since I was a kid, and the huge noise of an adult diaphragm in full bucking revolt amazed me. Madeleine happened to be sitting on the floor three feet away and saw it all. I thought the sight of her father collapsing and puking his guts out might upset her, but no. Later she pointed at the spot on the floor and said, laughing, "Daddy — daw! Woof woof!" On my hands and knees, for her amusement, I had imitated a dog, and had finally barked as loud as a real one.

"Moo" was not only the sound cows made, but, as one of Madeleine's first words, it also meant moon.

I had always heard that babies loved the moon, and once we

had Madeleine it became obvious why. If cheap plastic smoke alarms on ceilings are powerfully attractive, how much more so that beaming face in the sky, softening the darkness like a night-light. Obeying the cliché, Madeleine reached for the moon in her first months and then appealed to us, hoping we might hand it to her. Of all her quaint infant illusions, this struck the deepest chord in me, some old echo of my own childhood. In the silver light out in the yard, I felt sorry for both of us that I could not bring the moon close. We say that love on a face shines, and the shine of the moon still feels like a certain kind of love to me, a love that in the quiet of the night, in the unprying light, seems patient and tolerant. In other words, a parental love.

Or, as another cliché has it, maternal love. I have already written "mama moon" in this book, and what with the moon's menstrual cycle, the connection is understandable. But the im-plied dichotomy makes me uncomfortable. The sun, to Made-leine, wasn't a face but a spiky piece of nastiness poking her eyes through the car window as she sat helplessly strapped in her car seat, twisting her neck, sputtering. This was a bit too much like God the Father, Whom Moses was allowed to glimpse only from behind, since a frontal view of Him would have burned the old guy to a cinder. Far from hoping we would bring the sun close, Madeleine shrieked until we shut it out, hanging a towel from the rearview mirror or trapping it in a rolled-up window. Driving into town, I was half out of my seat with one hand on the wheel and the other shifting the towel at each turn. This predator was persistent.

Madeleine's books showed friendly suns, but I don't think she connected them much with the real sun, since the last thing we wanted to do was encourage her to look at it. In any case, there were far more moons. As with cats, an unintentional but de facto conspiracy was operating here, since so many books for young children attempt a crude hypnosis by telling a story about falling asleep. By the last page the illustrated tyke or furry animal is dead to the world, and the hope is that your kid is, too, but of course she's not — she's happily pointing at that beatific last-page moon.

For American children, the lunar ur-text is *Goodnight Moon,* which was a favorite of Madeleine's, as it has been for millions of children. In the great green room with the red balloon and the telephone, where the little old lady is waiting for the bunny in bed to fall asleep, there are not one but two moons, a full one shining through the window and a crescent (over which a cow is jumping) in a picture on the wall. Nothing happens in *Goodnight Moon.* Various objects in the room are picked out and wished a good night. Nothing changes except for the clock on the mantelpiece, which moves in ten-minute increments from 7:00 to 8:10 P.M. (ha! amateur hypnotists, dream on!), and the full moon, which bit by bit heaves itself above the windowsill until, at the end, with the room dark and the old lady gone and the little bunny fast asleep, it shines entire through the window, a protective presence, "her watch keeping," as the lullaby goes (whereas presumably the sun is out with the boys). An irony here is that babies get moonstruck. Far from lulling Madeleine to sleep, the real full moon called her to the window, and as her own moon face stared up wide-eyed into the light, she would be filled with an edgy, unearthly energy that sent her crawling around the house, chattering and climbing the bookcases and refusing a lullaby or the crib until far past her usual bedtime.

During the day, she could pick the moon out of the blue sky far better than I could. "Moo!" she would call, reaching up from the sling in which I carried her, and I would turn, "Where?," and have to follow her pointing finger. There it might be, ghostly crumbs of a crescent mostly lost in tree branches. And since she also said "moo" for the sound a cow makes, I wondered if the two were connected in her mind. Maternal cows, maternal moons —

or by her way of thinking, I hoped, parental cows and parental moons — and that picture on the bunny's wall of the one leaping over the other, a conjunction so incongruous that it hinted at some secret correspondence.

But her ability to locate the moon so easily was not the sign of a mysterious infantile lunacy. She could do the same thing with airplanes. "Ah-pai," she called them, in an inspired conflation of "airplane" and "up high," and could pick out even the jets at thirty thousand feet, even the ones without contrails, X's so small in the grainy blue that I would lose them again after she pointed them out to me. She came to recognize the accompanying sound, and I could be with her in town amid a Jacuzzi of noise, cars passing and kids shouting, and from the sling she would announce "Ah-pai!" and at the next lull, listening hard, I would catch the faint rumble. She was not infallible. The wind thrumming through an old antenna on top of our house could fool her, and we would pass a breezy evening politely thanking her for a series of false alarms.

She was proud, of course, and may have felt she was performing a service. The first time she had done it we had made the usual astonished noises, so naturally she assumed that reports of incoming were important. Reinforcement came in a song that began, "Baby-bye, here's a fly, we will watch him, you and I." In our songbook, a drawing by Maurice Sendak showed a little boy pointing at a fly crawling up a wall, while an adult crouched and embraced him appreciatively. When I saw a fly in the house I would sing the song, and Madeleine and I would both point. This combination of index fingers — our tools of control — and chant was clearly a ritual to domesticate these bits of chaos that had invaded the house and provoked parental anger by buzzing about and tripping through arm hairs in the early morning. The airplanes crawling across the blue ceiling of sky were also flies, no farther away than the moon (that is, about the height of the smoke alarms) and equally in need of supervision. Later, when I admitted to Madeleine that I killed flies — to my surprise, she didn't seem to mind much — I would stand ready with the swatter while she pointed to the insect as it caromed around the room. I was constantly losing it, and she never did.

❧ 5 ❧

THEN, inevitably, there was the word that she first pronounced "nay." For some reason she had trouble reproducing the long *o*, and she had heard me once or twice utter the Norwegian *nej* (halfway between "nay" and "nigh"), because my only previous experience with saying no to young children had been when I worked on a farm in Norway, where there was a three-year-old who required a *nej* about every thirty seconds.

So "nay" it was, with its charming, if accidental, Old World air. I first heard it one day when I was carrying Madeleine downstairs after a rare visit up to the study. She said it so quietly, so politely into my shirt, with a small shake of her head, that I almost missed it, and when I took her down anyway, she didn't cry.

But her fascination with the word, and with the momentous idea behind it, grew. Instances of Pamela's and my disobedience were daily growing more outrageous. Madeleine had gotten very good at slamming doors, so we bought rubber wedges to hold them open, because we were worried she was going to crush her fingers. Moments after we installed them, Madeleine discovered she could no longer swat her bedroom door shut. She knew we had done this, and knew that the bright yellow thing, hooked high over the top hinge, was responsible, and knew also that we could take it off anytime we wanted. She wanted us to do just that, and she pointed up, her request perfectly clear and reasonably framed, yet we would not. This was not like the various small objects that, over the past weeks, we had immediately removed from her grasp. In this case, we had allowed her to fall in love with this activity, we had given her a good long time to grow dependent on it — and clearly there was no danger because she had never hurt herself — and now we had taken it away. The shock of this made her cry, and she was more shocked to discover that even her shock did not budge us, and the horror fed on itself until she spiraled upward into her first genuine fit of rage. Now she threw herself at the world. For the first time she put everything she had into it, screaming, bawling, and pounding her fists. She was terrible, she was towering — and she was inadequate. It would be difficult to overstate how devastating a lesson in powerlessness is a child's first tantrum, how immeasurable a drop from the belief, cherished so recently, that the world was an external manifestation of her will. And through it all, Pamela and I, suddenly strangers, as in some nightmare when a loved one doesn't recognize you, kept sounding this monotonous knell: "No."

Perhaps she didn't understand, but she was hard-wired to imitate us, and she would copy this, as she did everything else. She had long been interested in the pissy water of the diaper pail, but had always accepted that it was to be left alone. This had not been obedience, but a lack of conception of a choice. Now we had taught her the choice, and she exercised it, sometimes obeying, sometimes not. She would hold some article of clothing over the pail while I wrung out diapers and ask, in her new, hard-won pronunciation, "No? No?" I loved the intonation she brought to the word, a high flutey avidity, rising sharply into dog-whistle range at the end, so that it always sounded like *No?!* She was not only asking for confirmation that she was not supposed to drop whatever it was into the water. She also wanted confirmation that this fascinating bifurcation of obedience/disobedience did indeed exist, that there was this strange, wonderful word "no," and she was using it correctly.

"Yes, no," I would say, or "Right, no," nodding my head and shaking it, confusing even myself. And when one day she went ahead and threw her white knit cap in the dirty water, I lunged after it, and for the first time in her life I addressed her with real sharpness: "No!" She stared at me for a moment, wondering. Then she cried. What had she done? The two of us had been investigating discord together, hadn't we? I had been answering reasonably, lovingly, and had suddenly revealed the snarling beast.

This no was indeed a puzzle. It frightened her, and so of course she wanted to incorporate it, to tame it, to make it *her* no. Like most young children, when she got too excited in contemplation of us, she patted us too hard in the face, and we brought her hand softly to our cheeks, saying, "Gentle." She learned the word, and repeated it with a pitch-perfect imitation of our caressive intonation — "Genh!" — and copied the gesture, but in the time before she knew about discord, she had not realized the word and gesture were a criticism of her hitting. She would stroke us and say "Genh" and then hit us again, both actions being simply elements in her repertory. But now she knew, and if I was lying down, she might sit by my head and pull her hand back behind her ear, elbow forward, ready to let loose and really whap me, and ask in that endearing, flutey tone: "No?! No?!" Aware as I was that we were investigating this phenomenon together, that as a research subject I could not necessarily expect gentle treatment, I would stare at that elbow, those inquiring eyes, and try not to flinch as I agreed, "No."

She came back to this again and again. She would suddenly stop a game with us, a puzzle, a book, to draw back her hand:

"No?!" Her fascination went beyond the nearly inconceivable proposition that there were things in this world, her oyster, that she was not supposed to do. On another level, the very idea of hitting us, of hurting us, had to be revisited constantly. It had to be accommodated, as later the idea of death has to be accommodated. In later months, whenever Madeleine accidentally hurt me I was always aware, while hopping around on one foot or cupping my groin, that my main responsibility was to comfort her. It frightened Madeleine, and angered her, that I could be hurt. How much more frightening, then, was the thought that she could deliberately hurt me.

The knowledge the Edenic apple conferred was nothing inherent in the fruit itself, but the practical knowledge acquired by the act of eating it: the awareness of free will. You *can* disobey. You *can* breach the walls of the garden and be yourself the agent of chaos. So in raising her hand to hit me and asking "No?!" she was seeking repeated assurance that, though not impregnable, I was at least vigilant. As she had once turned over the playing card twenty times to see if the obverse would be red each time, she wanted to know that this law would always hold: I would protect her from herself. She had thus turned the shock of discovering there were things we would not let her do into a kind of comfort.

❧ 6 ❧

FOR THREE MONTHS, we thought Madeleine would start walking any day. Holding each of my index fingers in her hands over her head, she loved to walk around the circle formed by the dining room, our bedroom, the bathroom, and her room. I would get a stiff back from leaning over her and want to stop before she did. I didn't realize that I tended to end the game in the same room in which we had begun — deriving some sense of order, I suppose, from having completed a certain number of laps — until Madeleine started refusing to reenter that room, in the hope of prolonging the game.

If Pamela and I sat on the floor no more than three feet apart, Madeleine could sometimes be coaxed into shuffling between us, but she wasn't really walking. At no point did she even try to achieve balance, but instead fell toward us, throwing out her arms. Clearly this was not a bid for independence, but a celebration of its opposite. She seemed in no hurry.

Theodore was already walking, but if anything he was an advertisement against it. He trundled on stiff legs, looking like Frankenstein's monster, and in order to turn he had to jerk to a standstill and slowly teeter into a new direction. He fell like a giant, too — hard. He would cry briefly, then get up and stump off again. His specialty was hitting his head. He would outrun his feet and go down like a smokestack, knees, chest, and nose whacking the floor in turn. He'd leap on the inviting mound of a paper bag, which would turn out to be empty and would collapse beneath him, guiding his body through a perfect arc to bring his forehead into ringing contact with the metal grate of a hot-air vent. His face was blotchy with bruises.

He had always been reckless. He would swing anything swingable to see what would happen when it hit anything hittable. The shouts of his parents as they ran toward him, or their remonstrations as they picked up fragments, still seemed to raise in him no more than a mild curiosity, as though he were watching elephants in the zoo going about their unfathomable business.

If Theodore was a small Goth who had somehow got through our city gate, Madeleine was one of the citizens. She would watch him and periodically look toward the grownups in alarm.

She wanted to obey the law. She mulled things over. She hung back. Even now, when she reached for some new object, she would pull back her hand as I brought it close, unsure, waiting for guidance. Theodore could smack his head in some rash maneuver and smack it again five minutes later attempting exactly the same thing. Madeleine slipped once in her yellow plastic bathing tub, and since Pamela caught her she didn't even fall, but for the next few weeks she whimpered every time we lowered her into the bath.

Madeleine's caution, her consciousness of rules, might strike some as stereotypically feminine characteristics. Perhaps they were, but she got them from me. I was always the one hovering and worrying, thinking up elaborate and (Pamela assured me) improbable scenarios by which Madeleine might get hurt in almost any situation. Pamela was the one who took shortcuts across other people's yards, while I went the long way around, angry at her, half expecting divine retribution to descend in the form of a snarling dog, or at least a shouting homeowner. I usually carried Madeleine when we all went out together, so it's plausible she learned to read danger in the wide world through the tensing of my body. Since I had grown up with dogs, I wasn't afraid of them, but I was worried about what they might do to *her*, and perhaps as a result, Madeleine was afraid of dogs. I hate loud noises — my earliest memory is of hiding my face in the grass and crying during a fireworks show when I was almost three — and Madeleine covered her ears and cried whenever I flushed a toilet in a public bathroom.

Every dinner, I pointed out the various items on the table that were hot. I warned about hot water, hot radiators, hot asphalt, hot coffee, hot lightbulbs, hot oven doors. I pointed to the fire in the fireplace of the great green room in *Goodnight Moon* and said "Hot," just to keep in practice. Consequently, when Madeleine put anything in her mouth that was more than two degrees above room temperature, she panicked and spit it out. "Hot" was one of her earliest words, pronounced with careful precision, as befitted something that needed a safe eye kept on it. She exaggerated the aspiration of the *h*, mirroring the stream of *h*'s I blew on her red-hot food, and perhaps also the exhalations of steam that the food itself gave off, or the hot-hot-hot of the coffeepot announcing it was done. Soon it was she who pointed to the fireplace in *Goodnight Moon* and said "Hot." And when we read *Hide-and-Seek Puppies,* she pointed to the doorway of the doghouse and warned me again — "Hot!" — because it had the same black tombstone shape as the *Goodnight Moon* fireplace. I was teaching her to worry about more things than I imagined.

Whenever I left the house, I made sure the stove was turned off. Checking with a glance wasn't good enough. I had to stop and focus. There were six dials on the stove, and it helped me to say the words out loud: "Off off off off off off." I was often carrying Madeleine when I paused to do this, just before going out the door, and soon Madeleine was leaning out of the sling and beating me to it, bouncing her finger in the air as though counting: "Off off off off off!" (She always said it five times, not six. Perhaps it was a consequence of the strong sense of rhythm young children have, since saying five "off"s allowed her to end on a downbeat.) I wasn't so compulsive that I *always* did this, just most of the time, and now if I happened to neglect it, Madeleine would stop me at the door, pointing back, and we'd return to the stove and chant our "off"s together.

Begone, evil spirits! Given a world that needed such vigilance, Madeleine was in no hurry to walk. She didn't even crawl much, but would pull herself to stand against my legs and demand to be picked up, "Ap! Ap!" It was safer to be carried, and the more I carried her, the more she felt, through me, that dangers lurked everywhere. Instead of drinking caution in with her mother's milk, she absorbed it through her father's stomach muscles.

But not walking had its disadvantages, especially when she was with Theodore. He could get to disputed toys faster. When he came near where she sat on the floor, her round head of blond velvet was so inviting, a target at perfect hitting height, literally shining. Like the chieftain in one of the Icelandic sagas, whose unlucky servant, while filling a goblet, happened to position his head precisely for a decapitating sword stroke, Theodore succumbed to temptation again and again.

In January we visited Theodore after returning from a Christmas vacation of a couple of weeks. Madeleine took a long look at him, now quite a competent walker, even if he still occasionally misjudged a doorway, bounced off the jamb, and boxed his own ear against the floor. He had taken to carrying a badminton racket with him everywhere, and perhaps the sight of that weapon going by at the level of her face entered into her thoughts. She was nearly sixteen months old. She stood up. She walked.

Pamela and I looked at each other. Madeleine walked from room to room, her hands triumphantly over her head, her stomach out in that strutting parody of pride that toddlers do. She was now a toddler! She turned corners without falling. She bent down to get something and stood up without falling. From that day forward she always walked, and she never fell. She had been waiting until she could do it in complete safety.

No physical advance for the rest of her life would measure up to this one. Something analogous for an adult would be learning how to fly, and I have often wondered if the nearly universal dream of flying arises from memories of the sheer exhilaration, the triumph of conquering a new dimension, that came to us when we learned how to walk. In my own dreams, I never flap my arms, but float, often at about twice my height, moving forward over the ground, smoothly surmounting fences and ditches. This recalls the crawler who has suddenly attained standing height, stepping over the threshold or the rug edge that used to catch at his knees.

Madeleine flew. The frog pull-toy came out of the closet, and she processed around the circle of rooms, a victory lap, holding the rope above her head like a trophy, the hard amphibian body dangling in front of her, banging against her shins.

But new freedom always brings new fears. She was going around the circle without me. At every moment she could either stop or keep on going. She wanted to follow the rules, but what were they? Could completing three circles be as inadvisable as leaving the house without shouting five "off"s? She had no idea. I stood back, smiling, not helping.

Madeleine had not been afraid of the dark, as far as I could tell, but now that she could walk into a darkened room by herself, she would stop outside the door, point, and flute, "Dar? Dar?" Crawling, she had been hunkered down, quasi-fetal, protected, whereas a walker must constantly keep up enough confidence to expose her soft underbelly. And purely practically, a walker can trip and fall in the dark. (And perhaps, also, this newly acquired word "dar" was a seed around which her fear could crystallize. The name had made darkness a thing that filled a room, a thing that could crawl all over her, whereas before there had been only the rooms themselves, in varying states of illumination.)

"Ap! Ap!" She wanted to be carried more than ever. I liked doing it, so I didn't argue. As a crawler she had progressed to the point of being able to amuse herself for fifteen or twenty minutes at a stretch. As a walker, she took a step backward and wanted attention all the time. It comforts me to read that most children, not just those with a slightly neurotic parent, go through a needy period when they learn how to walk. How do they know we won't let them walk away? Or the most frightening thought: how do they know they're not *supposed* to walk away?

They test us, that's how. The chasing game kids love is a pure draft of reassurance that they can't get away from us even when they try. Madeleine played that, and also a variation of her own design. She had recently perfected her long *i*, and could now pronounce those two crucial words from her earliest, simplest conception of human relations: hi and bye. Exaggerating the mastered diphthong, she would say "Baiee!," waving, and walk around the corner. One second later she would return, tripping toward us with arms wide and stomach out, ready to fall into our embrace as she had done in those securer days when walking was only a game with parents on each side like pillars, and we would shout with delight, "You're back!"

"Back" was obviously a powerful word. Soon she could pronounce it, too, so she would go off with a "Baiee" and instantly return, "Back! Back!" The word, right in her mouth, helped her assimilate the feeling of security even better than our repeated hugs did, and eventually she didn't need the hugs. "Back" was enough. Then she learned an even more powerful form of the spell: "Rai-back!" Right back. When Pamela went off to aerobics, she would be right back. The word "aerobics," too, was rendered "rai-back," and why not? It was the same thing, the test that Pamela passed twice a week, when Madeleine and I, looking out the window at quarter past seven, saw her headlights coming up the road.

❧ 7 ❧

CONSTANCY; object permanence. We would not abandon her, and neither would her things. Her world continued to take on weight, to gel. Helium balloons, she knew, quickly shriveled, soap bubbles popped, and jack-o'-lanterns rotted, but her clothes, after disappearing for days into the laundry, came back. Her shoes in a corner of her closet, her toys in the toy chest, her books on her shelves, waited for her. This was a promise, precariously trusted, checked daily.

Thus began the reign of a book entitled *Baby's World*.

It is no coincidence that "like" means both "similar to" and "derive pleasure from," and in babies the psychology behind this linguistic tie lies naked before you. Babies like a likeness. The more alike, the more they like it. Which is why that kid in the mirror is the best thing around, and others kids are second best, and third best are women, whose comparatively larger eyes and smaller features make them look more like children than men do. The tendency is even more marked in the case of books, since a real object can be explored, but a pictured one can only be recognized.

So the idea behind *Baby's World* was simple: show the kid her own things. Don't draw them or paint them, don't interpret. Forget moons with faces and huge rising suns and brilliant, oversized butterflies. Set up the object and photograph it straight on, against a white background, like a mug shot. Forget stories, forget action, forget verbs. Beneath the toy car, print "toy car." (While you're at it, forget serifs.) Beneath the crib, print "crib." This was post-Warholian, Richard Avedonian, eye-glazingly boring. The book's subtitle was *A First Picture Catalog*, and I shuddered to think there might be others.

On the cover was a cute baby. "Hi, baby!" I said several times a day, seven days a week. Madeleine waved and said "Haiee!" "What a cute bay-bee!" I sang, and Madeleine confirmed, "Baba!" On the title page, a girl crouched over an open book. "Hi, Cecilia!" I said, having named her at random months ago. "Haiee!" "She's reading a book," I said. "Buk!" You could see on the open page of Cecilia's book pictures of her own baby things. The infinite regression of this hall of mirrors hazily implied something about the human psyche that I didn't want to think about.

Now a double-page spread, entitled — what else? — "Me." A naked little boy on the left, a naked little girl on the right, with their various body parts labeled. "There's Nigel and Amaryllis," I said. Amaryllis's tummy got the first pat. Then Madeleine raised her shirt and stuck out her own stomach, like a puffer fish, so far it startled me for the hundredth time. She cradled it and crowed and we bugged our eyes out. Nothing gave her a sharper sense of her own importance, her crystallizing position in the world, than the sight of that Round Thing, that breastlike object, that belonged to her. Then she lifted my shirt and we compared. I pointed back to the naked kids. "Nose!" "No!" "Eye!" "Ahh!" "Back" had opened to Madeleine a whole new world of final k's, so now she could say "cheek" and "neck." Nigel's penis and Amaryllis's vagina were neither named nor visible, an absurd omission, but sadly predictable.

Next came "In My Room." Madeleine always pointed first to the aerial view of the baby on the changing pad. "Poop!" she said. "You bet," I said, while she sniggered. Then the mobile, a word she wasn't attempting yet, and finally the crib, in which Cecilia was playing with a teddy bear. "Look at that happy girl in her crib," I enthused. Sneaky, ineffectual propagandizing. There were other objects on the page, but none of them looked enough like Madeleine's stuff to make her interested in them.

"My Clothes." The line of shoes across the bottom of the page was photographed from above so that they resembled a children's chorus in full cry. I suppose they were singing "Shoes!" Madeleine sang back "Sheez!" I pointed to the socks.

"Sheez!"

"No, socks."

"Sheez!"

"Sssaaawwwks."

"Shheeeeezzz!"

Madeleine slid off my lap and fetched her corduroy booties. Climbing back up, she planted them next to the corduroy booties in the photograph. "Sheem!" she said. Same!

And so it went. In "My Toys," there was another case of "sheem," a stubby blue plastic airplane that looked like her purple one. We spent the most time on "Things to Eat," where Madeleine recognized everything, except the cherries, which she called apples, and the glass of milk, which she called an egg, reasonably enough, since it was photographed from straight overhead. "In the Garden" and "Sand Play" were passed over in puzzled silence, as we were in the depths of upstate New York's long winter and Madeleine remembered nothing of outdoor games, or grass, or warm sunshine. Perhaps she thought the kids were playing on an exceptionally dirty floor. "Bath Time" brought us back from science fiction with three sheems on one page, and the book closed with "Going to Bed," which was Cecilia's job. More tendentious unction from me, somewhat undercut by the last photograph of poor Cecilia standing in her crib, patently unready for sleep, looking up at the camera with a grim, abandoned expression.

I knew there was a whole class of books like this one. The oddness of them was most striking in the simple ones, the board books with a single item set starkly on each page: a key, a rattle, a shoe. Surely these minimalist *opera* were a consequence of the modern mania for "education" in its most formal, sterile sense. The fewer books that even well-educated parents read themselves, the more they venerated the Book as the sign and source of intelligence in their children (reading was becoming like drawing and singing: an enjoyable activity that children would drop in junior high school as they came to realize only kids did it), and so you had parents "reading" to babies months before they had any conception of narrative, or make-believe, or abstraction, or indeed anything but key, rattle, shoe. But why bother to take a full-color photograph of a key, print it in a book, and show it to your kid when you could just hand her the key itself? Wasn't this defensive book-boosterism in fact teaching the kid to value image over reality, passive viewing over interaction, which was the perfect thing to deliver her as early and securely as possible over to television?

Madeleine's first taste of plum was an exciting experience. But it was made more exciting by her realization that this was a *plum*, the thing she had seen for months in *The Very Hungry Caterpillar*. She ran to pull the book off her shelf and opened it to the page with the three violet orbs. She lined up three real plums to match, and then ate all three, bubbling ecstatically through the juice in her mouth, "Sheem!"

Real food, real toys, real clothes, I gave to Madeleine and often retreated, hoping she might occupy herself for a while so I could get the dishes or the laundry done. But books had the imprimatur of my constant presence. Like Holy Scripture, they spoke to Madeleine in the voice of her two gods.

She loved *Baby's World,* and I never refused to look at it with her when she asked. We lifted the lid and there were her things, day after day, exactly the same: codified, controlled, convenient to the index finger that held them down in turn. She evidently needed this validation, this reassurance. But it did unsettle me that she was thus learning, so early, to value the representational over the real. I had imagined that unmediated Wordsworthian bliss would survive the second birthday, anyway. I had imagined that the oft-cited distancing effect of literacy would not precede learning to read. That it would not precede learning the *alphabet*.

Half an hour ago, I told Madeleine I had to go up to the study to finish this chapter. She hung on my leg, not wanting me to leave, and I had to get Pamela to engage her attention elsewhere so that I could make my getaway. It did not escape me that I was fleeing the real Madeleine in order to spend time with this portrait of her.

❧ 8 ❧

To see a drawing of a plum and know it's not a real plum, and get excited anyway, is an early form of make-believe. Sheem! she said, and we nodded happily, Yes. But the truer answer was No, they were not the same: one was fructose, water, and carbohydrates, the other was wood pulp and printer's ink.

Madeleine as a baby had been awash in wild imaginings, delusions, projected fears. It was only as she began to grasp, within her tight lit spot of expertise, what was real and what was not that she could turn the loose cannon of her mind toward intentional delusion, projecting hopes instead of fears (but fears, too, digging channels for them to drain the swamps), filling the mute world of her dependable things with voices, with the verbs that were missing from *Baby's World*.

I had been watching out for the beginnings of make-believe

GALWAY COUNTY LIBRARIES

ever since her first birthday. At fourteen months she pushed a wooden car around the floor and said "Brrm!" Aha! I thought. But once again, the evidence was tainted. When I had first given her the car, I had pushed it around myself and said "Brrm." (All self-respecting researchers, throw up your hands.) It occurred to me to wonder if I was viewing the learning process backward, anyway. I had assumed that she would eventually accomplish the conceptual leap from toy car to real car, and that she would then express that understanding by making the toy car act like a real car. But perhaps it went the other way around: I gave her the wooden car; she had no idea it represented the large object in our driveway; I moved it around, saying "Brrm"; she imitated me; after several days or weeks of making the little wooden thing act like a car, she gradually came to associate it with the real car. Body taught mind, rather than vice versa. Rote learning was absorbed until it became indistinguishable from insight.

She hugged her stuffed animals, but that didn't mean she was pretending they were alive, since she also hugged pillows and fluffy balls. Earlier, when I had made the animals dance around and kiss her stomach, she had believed they really *were* alive, but by fourteen months, although she still giggled and fended off the furry snouts, she would always look at me when she wanted more. It seemed that she was no longer fooled; she just enjoyed getting tickled, and if I liked to do it with a firefly glove on my hand, well, that was my business. One of her cows mooed when it was turned over, and her reaction of anxious surprise suggested she knew perfectly well the thing wasn't alive and she didn't appreciate it pretending otherwise — a textbook case of the Freudian uncanny.

These and other animals had come as gifts over the months and seemed to provide Madeleine with plenty in the hugging department, so it had not occurred to us that she had no human doll. Then one arrived from friends in Norway when Madeleine was fifteen months old, and it immediately vaulted past the others to become the favorite. The doll represented one of the Olympic mascots for the Lillehammer winter games, her tag told us, a nine-inch-tall jerkin-clad Viking girl named Kristen. She had a round face of polyester fabric with printed features: oversized blue eyes, an elfin smile, a virtually nonexistent nose. Her abundant yellow yarn hair was gathered in two braids as short and thick as a wrestler's thighs.

At first Madeleine played no discernible games with Kristen, but she stared at her face for much longer periods than she had ever done with her animals. She took the doll to bed with her. She sat in her crib sucking on her pacifier and doodling an index finger around the back of her head, staring silently at those friendly blue eyes. That combination of pacifier and index finger still served to soothe her to sleep, but she also seemed to use it to comfort herself in the face of her own momentous thoughts.

For Christmas two weeks later her grandmother gave her another human doll. This one had a cloth body in a sleep suit, abundant blond polymeric hair, and a plastic face with eyes that opened when you picked the doll up. The blue pupils were constructed like reflectors. Kristen was bumped to second place. Madeleine communed long and deep with this new face, sucking the pacifier and twirling her finger, but also bringing the finger down again and again to press a glittering eye open or shut. Kristen looked like a young girl, but this one was proportioned like a baby, so I pointed and said "Baby," and Madeleine agreed solemnly, "Baba," and stared on.

I didn't have to wonder for long. On the night we flew home from Christmas, the temperature was twelve below zero and the winds were at nearly gale force. In the deserted airport terminal we chased Madeleine around, in no real hurry, bit by bit getting her clothes off and diaper changed and pajamas on. Madeleine was carrying Baby, as we had taken to calling her. We were explaining that these preparations were necessary because she (Madeleine) would surely fall asleep on the long car ride home. A few moments later she laid Baby gently on the floor and put her finger to her lips: "Shh." Baby was sleeping.

I had not shown her this, nor had Pamela. Perhaps one of her grandparents had. But whether her action was imitative or inspired, eventually the distinction must be considered trivial. In artificial-intelligence research, a computer is presumed to have become sentient when its responses are indistinguishable from those of a sentient being. Baby was asleep, and we needed to be quiet. Madeleine's world had woken up and begun to speak.

Babies like a likeness because they like what they know and they know very little. Madeleine's world first spoke to her in her own voice. Baby was the figure in the mirror, doing what Madeleine did. She slept; she ate. Regarding clothes, Madeleine had three interests: things that went around the neck, things that went on the feet, and things that lifted to reveal tummies. Baby had a small tie-on bib, which Madeleine was forever wanting to get on and off, appealing to us for help. Unfortunately, the purple booties were sewn on, as were Kristen's rust-colored felt shoes. (Kristen's jerkin, however, could be raised enough to get a deeply satisfying glimpse of flesh-pink polyester.) Even though Madeleine could hardly be expected to understand why we couldn't take the booties off, she resigned herself to it with a quickness that surprised me. But I should not have been surprised, since the defining aspect of make-believe is the winking acceptance that there are things one must gracefully gloss over. As I realized later, I had thought the sewn-on booties would upset her because I knew it was possible to make a doll with removable booties.

Madeleine didn't know this. As far as she knew, the fact that Kristen's and Baby's booties did not come off was as necessary a compromise with dumb reality as the fact that the two dolls didn't walk around and take off the booties themselves.

At sixteen months, Madeleine was with us in a toy store when she spotted a two-year-old boy holding a doll. This doll was only six inches long, with an almost spherical head, full cheeks, and wide-open blue eyes. Unlike the hirsute Kristen and Baby, it was bald. It could not have looked more like Madeleine if it had been modeled on her. I only determined this later, however. At the time, all I knew was that one moment Madeleine was placidly holding my hand and the next she was charging a strange boy (something she had never done before) and yelling "Baby! Baby!" The poor kid went up on his toes and clutched the doll to his neck, fixing his alarmed eyes on this juggernaut of desire. Fortunately, the store had a box full of the dolls, and the one that we bought immediately became the new center of Madeleine's attention. Later I pondered the fact that Madeleine had yelled "Baby" and not "Baba." This might have been a coincidence. Perhaps she had mastered the correct pronunciation sometime in the past week and I simply had not noticed it. But given her instantaneous reaction at the sight of this miniature Madeleine, in a store full of dolls to which she had paid no attention, the properly pronounced word sounded like a revelation. By God, she recognized a real baby when she saw one.

So now there was a triptych, with Bald Baby in the center and on either side her prophets, Big Baby (now called) and Kristen. Madeleine would sit with the three of them in the plastic bathing tub while I dragged them around the circle of rooms, or she would put them in alone and direct me to give them a ride. Madeleine carried Bald Baby everywhere. Her small cloth body was easy to hold in one hand, and Madeleine enjoyed an occasional contemplative suck on the smooth round head of soft plastic (which made her look a bit unnervingly like Kronos eating his own children). With a good deal of tugging and tweezering finger work, Bald Baby's sleeper was removable, and the only thing Madeleine liked better than putting it on was taking it off again. I assumed off always eventually won out over on, because it felt more intimate to Madeleine, more secure. She had probably already come to associate underwear or nakedness with home, and in the coming months would strip all her favorite dolls as far as she could. Bald Baby, lying around in her unremovable underwear, was not only clearly a good friend of ours, she also was evidently not about to go anywhere.

During Madeleine's baths, in the big tub with me or Pamela, Bald Baby sat on the rim and watched, and was later dropped into the plastic tub, pulled out, dropped again. Before Madeleine ate, she stuffed Bald Baby into the mouth of an upright cardboard cylinder (part of a building set) so that only the doll's head, arms, and feet stuck out. "Hai-ch'," Madeleine explained. Highchair. Apparently, Bald Baby functioned somewhat like a voodoo doll in reverse. Instead of causing things to happen to Madeleine, she confirmed what had already happened. Not only could Madeleine look from her own highchair to Bald Baby on hers and think, "I am here, I am eating," but she could do to Bald Baby what we did to Madeleine. Of her several incorporations, this internalization of authority was perhaps the most important to her self-constructing sense of self. Certainly it was the one she would practice most assiduously, or rather, compulsively, in the months to come. (When she learns the word, perhaps she will call it her conscience.)

Naturally I couldn't know whether Madeleine had really just made a conceptual breakthrough or had merely progressed physically to the point where I could infer her thoughts from her actions. Whichever was the case, soon after I noticed her breathing life into her dolls, I saw her do it to other things. Perhaps it had taken a mirror image to unlock her empathy, but once unlocked, empathy obeyed its own logic and flowed everywhere. She pushed raisins around on her highchair tray, saying "Brrm," and I wondered whether she was imagining they were cars, like the one in our driveway, or wheeled wooden blocks, like the one she had in her toy chest, or both. She jumped the raisins over little puddles of milk, and here I recognized a moment from a book we had just read, in which two rabbits were jumping over daisies.

Now books could come into their own as windows to the wider world, storehouses of images and ideas that Madeleine could absorb, ponder, tinker with, and reproject onto her own narrower circumstances, lighting them up in new colors. This enormous broadening power was the upside of literature's distancing effect. *Baby's World* remained important — for months to come she would frequently return to it for a few clustered readings, to recharge her sense of groundedness in the real — but she began to move beyond it, back to her old board books with new understanding, and forward into the lives of new characters.

We had been given a book called *Will's New Cap*, a simple story about a boy who was proud of his new cap with its smart-looking visor. He went to buy a newspaper for his mother, and when it started to rain on the way home, he broke into a run. The rain softened the visor until it drooped down in front of his eyes, causing him to trip over a curb and scrape his knee. He braved it out until he got home, but as soon as his mother opened the door he collapsed on her, crying. She bandaged his knee, gave him a soda, ironed the visor dry, and everything was all right.

In the first weeks of owning the book, we had read the story two or three times to Madeleine, and it had seemed to hold only average interest for her. She now let us read books from beginning to end, and dutifully gazed at each left-hand page before the right, but it was impossible to know how much she understood as she sat there quietly, index finger and pacifier working. Then one night Pamela reached the page where Will fell down, and Madeleine burst into tears. The reaction was so sudden and strong — a real face-crumpling wail — that Pamela thought Madeleine had perhaps bitten her own tongue. She and I conferred and thought it improbable that a sixteen-month-old, even if she was our sensitive, preternaturally intelligent Madeleine, would cry in sympathy for the sufferings of an illustrated character. We waited two nights and tried the book again. When Pamela got to the picture of Will falling down, Madeleine once more dissolved into tears. Pamela said, "Poor Will," stroking the fallen figure, and Madeleine, still crying, also reached out to stroke him. (Interestingly, the sight of Theodore falling and crying had never provoked her to tears. But then, Will had never hit Madeleine on the head.)

After this, Madeleine frequently pulled *Will's New Cap* out of her bookcase and handed it to us. For a while, she wanted us to skip the offending pages, and would whimper if she caught a glimpse of the prostrate boy as I flipped past. But with each of these bowdlerized readings she was assured that Will did in fact get home to his mother, and so, within a few days, our readings entered a third phase. I would start at the beginning and read through to the fall (which I had begun to think of as the Fall). We would pause in somber contemplation. Madeleine would not cry, but both index fingers would be furiously describing arabesques on her head and the *tch tch* sound of her pacifier would fill the room. "Ouch," I would finally say, reading the text, and Madeleine would echo me, "Ow." Then she would urge me forward three pages, to the picture in which Will reached his mother and cried, and she would point and say "Mama," looking up at me as if to reassure me, as if to say, "See, he's OK." (Thus had she already extrapolated from the lesson of Bald Baby. She was taking on the parental role and comforting herself far more effectively from this internal position of mature wisdom.) Then we'd flip back to the picture of Will on the ground ("Ow") and back again to the mother ("Mama") several times, until her storm of feelings abated. Having achieved our catharsis of pity and terror, we would put the book away.

The empathy issue aside, Madeleine's reaction to *Will's New Cap* was the first clear indication that she understood a narrative. Perhaps not the buying of the newspaper, or why Will had to run, or the ironing of the hat afterward, but the central knot: Will fell down! And understanding that a picture can represent an action, a movement, is much more sophisticated than recognizing a plum. Somehow she had learned to accept that he was running on the left-hand page, even though in reality he was motionless. And since the drawing on the right-hand page showed him lying down, the fall itself, the crux of the matter, occurred only in her mind.

Watching her burgeoning imaginative life, Pamela and I wondered about nightmares. She sometimes woke at night, crying hard, but apparently not from pain. We listened for some word, we asked her, but she had not yet said anything, she only cried and clung. We had no clear proof that she dreamed at all.

Then the first confirmation came, in a startling way. I had been reading a grim picture book myself, Art Spiegelman's *Maus,* and one night, after I had brought Madeleine into our bed, I was dreaming of the cover sketch for the second volume: the swastika with its superimposed head of Hitler depicted as both cat and skull, and below, the crowd of haunted rodent faces behind barbed wire. In my dream the faces of the mice faded away and were replaced by babies' faces. Starving, haunted babies stared at me through the wire. Frightened and upset, I woke up. I lay still in the dark. The room was quiet. Perhaps five seconds passed. Then Madeleine stirred in her sleep and cried out. In the darkness she called out a word distinctly, three times: "Cat!"

❧ 9 ❧

MADELEINE'S WORDS at nineteen months sketched out a portrait of Madeleine's world, a guide to what was important to her.

"Ba-bö" was diaper. When I opened hers up, if there was poop I bugged out my eyes and dropped my jaw the way I did when I saw her tummy, and I announced "Poop!" and she joyfully shouted "Poop!" and rocked back, flinging up her legs to hold her feet. "Wawa" was the water in the cup, and "bukreh" was one of the wiping cloths that I indecorously called butt rags. With her new diaper on, Madeleine flushed the toilet herself, waving her poop goodbye.

Her fascination with poop was in full flower. Poop *was* her flower, her own daily bloom, shouting its version of "I am here!" Opening her diaper, I called out poop or pee as I might say "It's a girl" or "It's a boy." Two wolf pups came out of a zippered tummy of a mama wolf that Madeleine had been given for Christmas, and poop came out of her tummy. I recalled that when I was a kid we called farting "laying an egg."

Poop was Madeleine's daily contribution to the household economy, its importance manifest in the amount of time we spent dealing with it: rinsing the diapers and putting them in the pail, carrying the pail down to the washing machine, transferring the diapers to the dryer, carrying them back up and folding them on the rug, with Madeleine helping to smooth the fabric out after each fold. Preparing them for the drawer, I stacked them in little towers that Madeleine sometimes found too tempting, too much like the cardboard-brick towers I built and she knocked down. The diapers were hers, after all. They were soft like her stuffed animals. She liked to crawl into the clean pile of them. She liked to be a diaper herself, and get carried up from the basement in the laundry basket.

Pamela pointed out that Madeleine never pooped now without telling us. I countered that she could hardly fail to, since she said the word every five minutes. Either she was merely keeping us apprised of her thoughts or she was mistaking farts for poop. She liked farts as well, because their audibility made them sociable — we could all bug out our eyes or snigger lasciviously together — but she hadn't learned the word yet. She had lately been introduced to a potty seat, which she called "papa," and would try it, as long as I dropped my pants and sat on the toilet at the same time. Cackling over this pairing of big and small, she would perch for several minutes. She wanted a magazine in the holder at the side of the potty chair. Then she would get up, "Ha!," to reveal the empty bowl and dance around triumphantly. Later she'd poop in her diapers, as usual.

Madeleine would hold Bald Baby up to me and say "Poop!" and I was supposed to sniff at her crotch and agree. "Ba-bö — aw!" Diaper — off! Madeleine's make-believe had now become sophisticated enough that she didn't always need a prop (although she preferred one), and she accepted from my hand motions that I was removing an invisible diaper, bugging my eyes out at the voluminous, indeed well-nigh incredible contents, sloughing them into an invisible toilet, flushing and waving goodbye. If I tried to put on a new diaper immediately, Madeleine objected, "Bukreh!," and I had to back up, wipe Bald Baby's butt, dry her off, apply some oil. "Ba-bö — *aw!*" Diaper — *on!* I would mime it and hand Bald Baby over with a silent prayer. But usually in vain. "Poop!" Madeleine would announce, handing her back. (The fact that she used "aw" to mean both "on" and "off" facilitated another self-perpetuating game: she was interested in the putting on and taking off of her shoes, and could simply shout "Aw!" at me continually as I went through a number of cycles.)

Her own pee was uninteresting. She didn't seem to know yet when she was peeing, and since it disappeared into the cloth it hardly existed. Pamela's pee was also invisible. But my pee was conspicuous, and fascinating. She would stand by the bowl, staring as it arced down. Since her favorite bathtub game at the moment was to insert her fingers into the braided string that spooled out of a snorkeling Mickey Mouse and delightfully proved to be liquid, I was worried she would try the same thing with my yellow string, but she never did. She had sufficiently learned that poop and pee, though wonderful, were not to be touched. Or perhaps the taboo existed *because* they were wonderful, their power too great. Certainly she had never seen anything as emotional as our reaction when, months ago, she suddenly scooped up a fingerful of her own poop and tasted it, or the flurry of activity that had erupted only days ago when Theodore, whose latest passion was brooms, was discovered off in a corner industriously batting around his own hard turds, which were bouncing like superballs out of his diaper and rolling down his pant legs.

"Ch' " meant chair. Chairs loomed large in Madeleine's mind as the loci of important activities. "Hai-ch' " was where she ate. "Aunh-ch' " (armchair) was where she looked at books with us during the day. "Raw-ch' " (rocking chair) was where we read in the evenings and sang to her. She had measured her physical progress in terms of chairs. Back in her crawling days, her instinctual urge to climb had sent her repeatedly up into her own miniature chair, where she would get stuck, straddling the summit. Later she drafted the full-size chairs into service as makeshift walkers, and pushed them shuddering around the house. Now that she could climb into the rocking chair, we often found her there, blissed out on the motion. We bought a rocking horse, which she also loved, and also called "raw-ch'."

Foods beloved enough to be privileged with their own words had expanded beyond banana, apple, pear, and pasta. "Gr" was grapes, which she could eat as fast as I could cut them in half and hand them to her. "Jö" was juice, "ra-ra" was raisins, "peh" was peas, "bö" was bread.

"Mö" meant "more," and was clearly a powerful word, too powerful to be constrained by one thing. At this stage, most of Madeleine's words were concrete nouns, and the few others she had acquired tended to be taken over by the more easily conceptualized objects related to them, as "up high" had been subsumed by "airplane." "Boo-boo," for example, did mean an injury, but only by analogy to what she seemed to think boo-boo literally meant, which was knee. "Mö," however, roamed freely, perhaps drawing strength from the primal comfort of that m. Food could be mö, tickling could be mö, the mobile over her changing pad could be mö.

She now had the core family words well in hand. At eighteen months, she had switched from "Dada" to "Daddy," as the months of evidence from her ears finally penetrated that inner sanctum of preverbal utterances. Pamela remained "Mama," since that was the word we used. "Baby" had multiple uses. Bald Baby was "baby," and so was Big Baby. Real babies were baby. A small version of some familiar object, such as an undersized vegetable, was baby. Initially, I had regarded this last usage as endearingly anthropomorphic. I pictured Madeleine living in a world of daddy and mama tomatoes, who perhaps sang cherry tomatoes to sleep at night. But it may not have been that at all. Madeleine had begun to be interested in the concepts of big and little, but had been able to express them only in the context of concrete pairings such as "Daddy — *shö!*" and "Baby — *shö!*" It was quite possible that "baby," when referring to a vegetable, simply meant little. If so, here was another example of a concept word getting folded into an object word. The clearest communication between her and us by necessity centered on objects we could point to, and Madeleine had to make do with what she had. She wasn't forming phrases yet, so "jö" (juice) might also mean thirst, or liquid, or sweet, or "Juice is good," or "I'm thirsty," or "There's no more juice," or "Look at me hold my own bottle."

The most important meaning of "baby" was this particular baby, Madeleine. She knew that folding her arm back toward herself meant "This is me," so for extra emphasis, just to make sure, she folded it as tight as she could and stuck her index finger in her armpit, her elbow bobbing like a chicken wing: "Baby!" Now that she had a clear word for herself, and a percussive one at that, she wielded it like a baseball bat, asserting her will. If I handed her a cracker, she flapped her arms in desperate disapproval and rained *b*'s down on me, boxing my ears, "Baby! Baby!" — meaning that baby must get the cracker out of the bag herself. This demand was not merely to show me, and herself, that she was physically capable of reaching into the bag, but to exercise choice. Confronted constantly with her own powerlessness — carried wherever Pamela or I needed to go, eating what we gave her, unable to do this and forced to do that for unfathomable reasons — naturally she needed to exercise power in the tiny areas allowed her. At this age, alas, those were often areas in which her choice not only didn't matter, but *obviously* didn't matter, yet she had learned how to pretend, and make-believe is the toddler's therapy, so by God she would pretend, and believe, that the choice was crucial, that the world hung on it. Baby certainly did not want *that* cracker. What on earth did I take her for? Ahh, yes, *this* one (clouds parting, angel breasts descending, bliss)!

I doubted she had any understanding at this point of the difference between generic nouns and proper nouns. (She had not yet named any of her animals or dolls.) It didn't help that our personal names all sounded like family nouns, and the wrong ones at that. Madeleine often heard her own name and rendered it "Mama." When speaking to Mama (Madeleine), I referred to Pamela as Mama, but when calling upstairs to the study, I yelled "Pamela!" so when Mama called upstairs to her mama, she shrieked "Papa!" Fortunately, the double consonant at the beginning of my own name intimidated her into silence, or I would have been Baba, and the confusion would have been total.

But the confusion would have been ours, not hers. Madeleine made do with what she had, and she knew what she meant. She had not kicked her habit of doubling initial syllables — Theodore was Ti-ti, Kristen was Koo-koo, shower was sha-sha — so our comprehension depended on subtle vowel shifts or minute variations in stress. I wondered if this was good practice for learning Chinese, a tonal language similarly poor in consonantal variation. Consider Madeleine's *b* words: ball was ba, and balloon was boo, and blue was boo, too, so a blue balloon would be a boo boo, but boo-boo meant a scrape (or a knee), which was not to be confused with a bump, which I called a bonk and Madeleine rendered bok. That sounded pretty close to buk, for book, for which baby sat on my boo-boo, pointing first to any boo or ba that might be in the buk. Ba was also bath (unless it was a bubble bath, in which case it was bö-bö), for which we took off her ba-bö, and she played with the baba (shampoo bottles) or stirred a bo (bowl) and told us she was cooking papa (by which I assumed she meant pasta and not Pamela, or the post office, or the potty chair, or the piano). Madeleine grew familiar with my blank stares and learned to repeat herself slowly and clearly: "Bö-bö!" When I finally understood, I often said, "Ohh," a tendency I wasn't aware of until Madeleine started saying it herself:

I: Do you mean bubble bath?
M: Ohh!

Coming from her, it sounded sarcastic. But as its novelty wore off, she shortened it and dropped the tonal mimicry. Like many toddlers, she had an oiled and loaded "no" but no working "yes" (because "yes" was harder to pronounce? because it was so much less useful?), so eventually this simple, declarative "oh" became her affirmative:

I: Should we go to Ti-ti's house?
M: Oh.

"Dö" was door, another important word. Doors had once fascinated her because they swung like enormous board-book pages. Now she was more interested in what lay behind them. This had been our second-snowiest winter on record, and although we had at last reached April, we were still buried. For months the snow had lain too deep for walking, and anyway it was so blinding in the sunlight that Madeleine cried and asked to be taken inside. So the only home life she could remember was this stale hibernation in four small rooms, with her books, her chairs, her dolls, her crib. Doors represented the possibility of something new, or failing that, at least something else. (When I was little, I frequently had a dream in which I glanced into some well-known corner of my parents' house and saw a door I had never noticed before. I would open it and find, for example, a monumental staircase, glowing white, vaulting down into cavernous open spaces, halls, courts, new continents of the house that I had never imagined existed. These dreams always filled me with euphoria, a sense of enormous possibility, as though I had discovered I could live ten different lives.)

For Madeleine, the kitchen door no longer led outside, to grass or the clothesline or the warm porch steps, but to the car, whose doors closed and then reopened on a magically shifted scene, one of several stage sets in our repertory. She had little sense of the distance between these places, or their physical integrity. When she heard the doorbell at home, she expected Hounh-hunh (Susan) to appear, because this ten-year-old neighbor who sometimes came to help out didn't feel comfortable walking in unannounced, as most of our friends did. Consequently, when I took Madeleine to the Friendly's restaurant in town, she turned toward the door and said "Hounh-hunh" every time the deep fryer dinged. Her puzzlement was not that Susan would be coming to play with her among the plastic booths, but merely that I wasn't letting her in. Perhaps I could have rolled the restaurant up like a window shade, revealing the walls of our own house behind, and hurried toward the door, calling "Coming!"

Another of our scrims represented Ti-ti's house. The highlights there included little wooden race cars and a swing hanging from the ceiling. Then there was the bakery, where we could sit by the window and watch bigtucks and bans (vans) rumble by on the busy street outside. There was the food co-op, where she could ride in a cart and eat a hunk of cheese and keep an eye out for other babies in carts — or better, older children, who elicited a joyful shout of "Bigkid!" and arm-pumping demands that we put her down so she could go to them and beam up at them and (who knew?) perhaps be adopted by them and taken off to wherever bigkids went when they wished to carry on with their unimaginably rich and capable lives.

In these magnificent wide-open spaces, nondescript utility doors (the ones most like our doors at home) always elicited a yearning reach and a "Dö!" If our lowly kitchen door led *here*, what might this door reveal? Something beyond normal experience, perhaps, her version of my glowing marble staircase. One of Madeleine's favorite games during this period was to crawl into a cardboard box, pull shut the flaps, wait a moment, and then burst out, shouting and laughing, her own adorable self, received with delighted cries. Where was the door out of which would bound something as wonderful as herself? Where, indeed, was the door hiding the thing itself, *herself*, a life-size, live Bald Baby, the girl in the mirror with the display-window glass removed?

Back at the house she tried to amuse herself with her old, tired things. On the refrigerator were magnetic letters, which mostly she liked to sweep off, but back in February she had become interested in a particular letter, and if I had thought about it, I should have been able to guess which one: O. She knew its name was *oh*, and when she pronounced it herself, perhaps she thought, Yes. Faces, breasts, and eyes, yes! The second letter she learned was Y. She had often pointed to it in her alphabet book, and I had wondered if it looked like a person to her, with feet together and arms raised in welcome. (Even as adults, we're cheered by the icon of raised and open arms, which is why the time in watch advertisements is always ten past ten.) Perhaps, too, the name was made easier to learn because of the word "why," which she was beginning to hear more often, as in, "Why won't you go to sleep?" In town with Madeleine, I enjoyed the way O's and Y's called to her, bodies and faces planted here and there just to keep her happy, to help her along like crossing guards. Agway had a stunning white Y on a crimson wall, and the Tops supermarket's italic *O* was a roguish eye. Columns with struts and bifurcated trees had also become Y's. On the refrigerator at home, Madeleine and I spelled out her first two words: oy and yo-yo.

She had a duck push-toy that she maneuvered through the rooms, calling "Cack cack!," but the house was so small she was perpetually catching it in corners. She relieved her frustrations by smashing three wooden balls with a mallet through rubber-ringed holes in the top of a hollow box. The balls were blue, green, and red, or as Madeleine styled them, boo, gr, and ya. She had identified purple — "purpuh" — as long ago as Christmas, on wallpaper and in her stacking toy, and I suspect it was her first color word because it most resembled "appuh," for which she had been so much praised. Now she had boo, gr, ya, purpuh, pik, back, yaya, and aish. I had once used these balls she was vigorously whacking to test her color comprehension. She correctly identified them for me twice running, but when I held up the green ball for the third time, she paused and blinked. Didn't I have anything better to do? Why didn't I put the ball back down so she could whack some more crap out of it? "Boo," she said. "Blue?" I said. "Boo," she repeated firmly. Her first joke.

Her second occurred at dinner. Pasta was still her favorite food, and since it usually came to the table steaming, I would say "Hot!" and she would exhale the word, and I would say "Hhhh" to the pasta before handing it to her, and before eating it she would also say "Hhhh," holding it right to her lips, blowing a kiss to me (a gesture she had just learned) and kissing her food simultaneously. Perhaps all those *h*'s got her thinking about another *h* word. She reached up and plastered a wet flap of pasta to her crown and said "Hat? Hat?" Quite possibly she was just borrowing the word to mean "on the head" and intended no joke, but Pamela's and my laughter was not lost on her. She made it into a running gag, Madeleine's pasta-on-the-head routine, whereby she slew us night after night. I've mentioned power, and to make people laugh is a heady draft of it, since laughter is not only spectacular but involuntary. Not wanting to encourage her to play with food, I tried not to laugh, and Madeleine could tell I was trying, and time after time — at the sight of her big head completely filling the circle of her arms, her dainty fingers affixing the piece of pasta to its top like a well-licked postage stamp, "Hat? Hat?" — I failed, turning my face away, snorting, unmanned.

∿ 10 ∾

SPRING! In *Anno's Counting Book* it arrived in the third month of the year, and I pointed out to Madeleine the three tulips and three daffodils, the buds on the three trees. In our own March, we had three feet of snow in the yard.

Madeleine didn't know the months yet, or the seasons, or even, as far as we knew, the idea of yesterday or tomorrow, but she had discovered numbers some time ago. When she bathed, she liked having the shampoo bottles lined up next to her plastic tub, three upright columns like the six straight-up dials on the stove that so comforted us on our way out the door. Pamela would arrange the bottles for her, saying firmly, as though commanding them to stay in their places, "One! Two! Three!" Madeleine immediately picked up the idea of two, first with the bottles, then with the myriad paired items in our bilaterally symmetric lives: shoes, socks, gloves, eyeglasses, ears, nostrils, hands, legs, feet, arms, elbows, cheeks, knees, sleeves, pockets. Finally she had a word to capture the fascinating idea of one breast and another breast, of an earring on this side and the other on the other, of herself and the twin in the mirror. Subsequently, as one of her earliest word pairs, she learned "udder sigh" (other side), and with it she combined her love of symmetry with her growing need to exert her will. Pamela now never gave her the correct breast. "Udder sigh!" she would shout, Pamela obliging, and she would suck for a moment before realizing: she wasn't on the other side at all! "Udder sigh!" she would complain again (with postmodern self-referentiality, now that I think of it), and back and forth they'd go until the stomach juices started by those off-and-on sucks became too urgent, and her dominatrix's pride was drowned in need.

By sixteen months, Madeleine never pointed to three items and called them two, but when she counted, she said, "Wuh, two, two, two." Her counting was simple imitation of us, complete with bobbing finger, and she made no effort to "count" each object once. She may have stopped for a while at two merely because "three" was hard to pronounce. At nineteen months she began to count "Wuh, two, hee, hee, hee." But she gave no clear sign that she understood three yet as a cardinal number. When I pointed to the three March tulips in Anno's book and asked "How many?" I got no reply. Now we were in April, anyway, so I turned the page: four children fished, a woman fed four pigs. The meadow flowers were out. I wanted to live where Anno lived.

But at least we could walk outside now. The drifts had sunk to low mounds of Sno-Kone slush, and the brown grass wept lymph. With no memory of the previous autumn, Madeleine rediscovered the joy of space and air. "Saiee!" she pleaded, flinging her arms toward the windows. Outside! Tulips were another month away, but we found snowdrops, one, two, three, three. Madeleine pushed her stroller up and down the driveway, up and down. This outside was as big as the shopping mall.

I took her to the park, brushed rotten ice off a bucket swing. She had been on Theodore's indoor swing and had absorbed from me the lesson that it was fun, but dangerous. In truth, I thought the swing itself was safe, I was only worried, in that enclosed space, that the kid who wasn't swinging would wander into its path and get smashed in the head, losing consciousness or teeth or both, as in fact nearly happened several times. At the park I strained to exude ease, but the damage had been done. Madeleine clung to the bucket's rim at her chest and, wide-eyed, let me push her through an arc of about twenty degrees. Anything higher — anything approaching an actual swing, that is, as opposed to this Jell-O-like undulation — inspired whimpers and "No?!" I sat her on a seesaw and, still holding her firmly, raised her and the board off the ground. "No?!" She willingly trudged up the steps of the twisty slide, and I sat with her in my lap at the top, ready to push off. "No?!" We walked back down. She did like stomping in the puddles, though, and the next day in the car she suggested "Powk?"

Her first phrase came that April. At a friend's house she saw a cat go into a low cupboard: "Cat innair!" (This gave cats the triple crown: first word, first identifiable dream, and first phrase — remarkable considering we didn't own one.) When the cat vacated, Madeleine crawled in. "Baby innair!"

She plunged on. Only a few days later, she came back from a visit to Theodore's house and told me a whole story: "Ti-ti! Ti-ti hurt! Ti-ti hit head! No?! No?!" She repeated this several times before the day was over, accompanying it with slaps to her own head. The narrative always climaxed at those No?!s, her voice high and urgent, an emergency appeal for confirmation. Yes, Ti-ti was not supposed to hit her head. In the following days, Madeleine dropped the mention of Theodore and generalized her concern, turning to me and rapping her crown fairly hard with her fist: "No?! No?!" Three fears were here conflated: that Theodore might hit her, that she might hit me or Pamela, that she might hit herself. Would we protect her from Theodore, from herself? I could only keep assuring her of the rule, of the powerful, protective *no*, and the shake of the head that was a mime for shaking off the encumbering, obnoxious world. She often sat now in a booster chair, and would hit her fork against the table, which she knew she was not supposed to do: "No bang?!" Sometimes I was busy getting breakfast ready or sneaking a glance at a magazine, and didn't respond, and her "No?!" got louder, her face grew disconcerted. At last I would agree, no, and she would stop, relieved, free now to eat her breakfast in peace.

And yet Theodore did hit her head. How could this be? There was a rule, wasn't there? We taught her to say to him, "No hit, Ti-ti!" but he paid no attention and thus undermined the reassurance she looked for in *no*. She had to direct her appeal to us, who would intervene in the only language a barbarian understood: banishment.

Violence, transgression. Chaos was pressing against the tissue of our words and our rules, always probing. It might sneak out of the darkened rooms ("Dar?") or slither up, growling, through the bathtub drain, to which she now pointed fearfully after her bath, "No?!" At the end of April she latched on to words for aspects of chaos: first "dödö" (dirty), which she said grimacing, holding her hands out to me with fingers sprung apart, waiting for the towel, and then a more powerful word, pronounced with evident relish, the *s* overlong like the serpent's hiss: "Mess!"

Armed with her word and her index finger, she was vigilant. A smudge of oatmeal on her highchair tray: "Mess!" She figured out that she could increase the urgency of her warning by adding "Oh no!" At the supermarket checkout, she pointed to a droplet of water on the otherwise pristine black field of the food conveyor belt: "Oh no! Mess!" She would not stop sounding the alarm until I reached past the customer in front of me, apologizing, and wiped it up.

Spring came on, and her world continued to widen. She stood among the chickens, feeding them dead leaves they didn't want. She hadn't seen them since November, but their memory had been kept alive by the chickens in *Moo, Moo, Peekaboo!* and she called up the old word immediately: "Tik'n." She was comfortable, among friends.

She spread grass seed with me: "Gas." She learned a new phrase for chaos, suitable for the laundry basket, cups, her ridable car, the rake, the hoe, the wheelbarrow: "Oh no! Tip over!" Under her watchful eye, I bent down, straightened, squared away.

But chaos kept probing. Our neighbors' tractor was the "chacke," and its noise as cheekily aggressive as its name. Madeleine covered her ears. Then our grass grew, and I paid the neighbors' boy to cut it on their rider mower, and that was a chacke, too, she would recognize that violent growl anywhere. As the machine worked its way boustrophedonically toward the house, the volume growing, Madeleine sobbed "No?!" A night or two later we were privy to a second dream, when she bolted up, crying "Chacke noise!"

She could only keep testing the defense perimeter, pale by pale. "No chnai?" she said, standing in her chair or the bath. Yes, no standing. "No chnai buk?" she said, her feet planted squarely on a prostrate book, as though it were a pedestal and she an allegorical statue: Sin. Yes, don't stand on the books.

It was mid-May and our tulips were out, and Madeleine sat on her plastic car in the driveway and said, "Push you?! Push you?!" The kids next door, on the side opposite the tractor boy and his sister Hounh-hunh, could be seen from our dining room window, seventy yards away, playing behind their house. Matt, eight years old, was the first Madeleine knew, because he always dropped by when we were gardening to give advice, usually on the order of "You'll be sor-ryy!" "Matt!" she called from her booster chair whenever she saw him, and whenever she didn't, she said "Matt?!" and I said, "Matt's in school." Soon she could answer it herself, having no idea what it meant, but accepting, from the sentence's intonation, that it was adequate, settled: "Matt in shoo!" Then she met the girls: Amy, six, and Rachel, four. Matt was the all-powerful one, who talked like an adult, and Rachel the one who kept compulsively picking Madeleine up and squeezing her, so now when Madeleine saw movement in their yard (the tiniest twitch caught by her reptilian vision, a fly on a distant wall), she cried "Yichi'nmatt!" Amy, the quiet middle one, did not yet exist.

We hung a bucket swing from the apple tree by the garden, and changed the whole complexion of Madeleine's world. "Sing!" she cried at the window, and "Push you?!" in the swing, and she swung and swung, like a rocking chair, like the beat of her heart, gradually higher and higher. I'd give her a good push and hang five diapers on the line while she slowed down. I'd sneak in two more while she called "Daddy! Push!" and one more while she whined, and then I'd run to her. Or I'd pick peas in the garden, for which she was more patient because she knew I'd bring them to her. Rachel and Amy might come over and push her, too, or climb into the low fork of the apple tree, which then Madeleine wanted to do, and I had to lift her up and hold her there, telling myself not to be so neurotic, but clutching her anyway. Rachel and Amy pretended to be cooking something on the play stove in their shed, and brought a pot of it and a plate to Madeleine, who gazed at it, nonplused. It was grass. She knew about pretend, but it had not occurred to her that these bigkids, gods, would not be cooking something real, something ambrosial in fact, and she had been so excited to taste it.

Now she wanted to try other swings at the park. There were four swinging animals: a pig, a chicken, a ram, and a pelican. Madeleine's favorite was the chicken, perhaps because she knew chickens — she had fed them leaves, they had whirred and clucked around her feet. She was still afraid of the seesaws, but finally tried the twisty slide, and slid a dozen times, all by herself — "aw bai seff" — quietly ecstatic. The next time we came, however, she balked at the top and cried and had to be rescued.

Two steps forward, one back. One day one of the chickens pecked her foot. She ran from them, wailing, minutely injured and maximally betrayed. Foot-eating, after all, had formed the core of her reassurance that certain fears would reliably prove to be baseless. As it happened, the chickens were all over our yard that spring because their run needed repairing, and whenever we headed for the garden or the hammock they hurried toward us, hoping for feed, and to Madeleine they were the size of ostriches. She scrabbled at my legs, pleading to be picked up. We taught her to clap her hands and tell them to go away — "Go why, tik'n!" — and unlike Theodore they paid some attention: they actually scattered before her. She brimmed so with delight at this proof of her power that she danced in the driveway. But as soon as she turned away, the chickens crept closer again. Vigilance!

The things she knew now, the handles she had on her world! She could recognize our car in a parking lot from far away. She was comforted that it always waited for us, never moving as much as a space. She no longer merely gestured toward doors; she could sometimes open them herself, and insisted on trying: "Baby ope dö!" Hands over her head, she wrestled with the knobs, and had learned to step back as she pulled so as not to stub the door against her toes. Everywhere we went people were friendly, their O's smiling and their Y's waving, and she waved and smiled back, feeling at home, secure. When I carried her off, she called back "Küss?" and I had to explain that the cashier or the salesman or the mechanic did indeed think she was wonderful, but was perhaps too busy to give her a kiss.

At the parking garage was a bit of misrule, a fundamental law broken: the earth moved. Madeleine clutched Pamela in fright. They were in an elevator. But this was the sort of beast — wholly predictable, once she got to know it — that she could tame by bringing inside the pale. In *Carl Goes Shopping*, an elevator conveyed the dog and the baby to their adventures on the several floors of a department store, and I twice discovered Madeleine sitting with the book open to that golden-doored elevator, twirling her hair and sucking. The parking garage became one of the principal landmarks in town, identified from the back seat every time we drove down the block, and when we parked there she urged us toward the elevator, and had to push the buttons herself. When I was taking care of her I often had nothing in particular to do except take care of her, so we rode up and down elevators wherever we saw them, around town and up the hill at the university. The doors closed, then opened at a different place. Here were the scene shifts that Madeleine had always suspected were possible. Taking me into our bathroom at home, she closed the doors and pushed an invisible button next to the sink. When we opened the doors again, would we be at Theodore's house? The food co-op?

This beast had come over to her side, but the chickens were

still probing. They were now getting into our compost bin. Madeleine told us every day about her foot getting pecked. Weeks went by, it became June, then July, and she still talked about it. As far as I knew, this was her first long-term memory of an incident, and with memory comes the first inkling of time. "That was a week ago," I said. "That was a month ago."

We woke in the morning to the whirs and clucks of chickens in our driveway. Perhaps now she knew: they had been out there all her life. They would be out there tomorrow.

"Oh no! Huk — *aw!*" she said, pointing to the porch screen door. I obligingly put the dangling hook back in its eye.

∾ 11 ∾

MADELEINE'S widening sense of the world was a cause for pride, but perhaps it was disconcerting not to have yet run up against the world's limits. How big *was* this thing, anyway? Bigger than the house, even bigger than the mall. She quailed at the prospect of walking the forty yards from the garden to the house, and in the park the grass stretched on forever, the people dwindled to bugs, and beyond was the lake, and beyond that the hills, and somewhere up in those hills was our house, so inconceivably far away that she couldn't even see it. Sitting taller now in her car seat, she could look out the window and begin to form some sense of inhuman distances. She could watch the houses and fields pass by, get confused by the turns down one road and then another on our slow progress through the maze toward home. And at night, how much darkness there was! We forged through it in the car, streetlights sliding above, and then long minutes groping through the dark of the countryside, Pamela and I hushed in the front seat, perhaps awed, too, by this black sea.

Madeleine knew now that the coffee grinder and the food processor were not animals. She didn't mind them when they sat quietly on the counter, and knew they wouldn't erupt into life on their own. But the noise still frightened her, perhaps because of its earlier associations (in the same way that my clock alarm, accidentally going off in the middle of the day, will flood me with adrenaline, as my body tries almost comically to wake to some higher state). I would open the front door and return to the kitchen, warning, "I have to grind some coffee," and Madeleine would flee through the dining and living rooms and straight out onto the front porch, where the grinder was a distant drone, but where she would nonetheless cry pitifully, pacing up and down in consternation, until I called, "That's all!"

In a small park in town, Madeleine wanted to greet a couple of dogs, and as always she insisted I hold her safely above them. But as it turned out, not safely. The younger one, a puppy, jumped up and clawed her bare leg. It probably did hurt a bit, and she screamed, terrified. Pamela and I did not want her to be afraid of dogs. We always spoke brightly about the ones we saw. We inducted Wolf into service as the Friendly Dog, the photo-album icon of all that was friendly and doggy in dogs. Did she remember Wolf? we asked. (By now, she thought she did.) What a wonderful dog! And so *friendly*. How she had loved him! But Madeleine kept recycling the memory of the terror in the park. For weeks she said daily to us and all visitors, "Two daw — jup Maya!" ("Two dogs jumped up on Maya," her latest attempt at her own name.) "Only one dog jumped up," we quibbled.

In this cavernous world of tractor noise and chicken-raptors, of darkness and snarling appliances and attack dogs, nothing could be more natural or understandable than that Madeleine did not want to sleep alone. Many parents don't expect their children at this age to comfortably play alone in a room for long, but do want them to learn to fall asleep that way. This is ironic, since surely the child feels most vulnerable when slipping under in the darkened room. Madeleine knew now that the world continued to exist when her eyes closed, but that was exactly the problem. As soon as her vigilance relaxed, the chickens would turn as one from their flight and converge on her. The tractor would abandon its sneaky shuttling and head straight for the house.

Pamela and I had agreed from the start that we could not let Madeleine cry herself to sleep. It felt too wrong. When she had been an infant, we nursed or bottle-fed her into a trance, then substituted the pacifier and sang, and she usually dropped off easily enough. When she woke in the night, one of us always went to her (usually me, since Pamela had the more onerous nocturnal responsibilities) and either sang a little again, a hand on her back, or if it was around three A.M., we brought her into our bed for another nursing. After she fell asleep again, I carried her back to her crib.

By the time she was one year old, the process was somewhat trickier. For one thing, if she fell asleep in our arms, she often woke when we put her down. For another, she now knew a few things. She knew the crib was where she was supposed to sleep. She knew when bedtime was approaching. She dimly sensed that after she went to sleep, Pamela and I stayed awake. (*Doing what?*) Like many parents, we became pop Pavlovians, trying to induce sleepiness and a feeling of security by stage-managing props and atmosphere. The routine was always the same: the last diaper change, pajamas, three books in the rocking chair, the light out, a song in our lap and one or two while she lay in the crib. The coziness of the crib was laboriously maximized and much harped on. She had her Winnie-the-Pooh bumper, her flower fairies frieze, the mama cow and baby calf with the Velcro nose, her wolf mama and two pups. Each step in the process was supposed to nudge her to a deeper, quieter level, until the coup de grâce was delivered by the lowering into the cozy crib and onto the lambskin, on which she always slept, so that the simple touch of it against her cheek, as we lay her down, would call up all those other nights of soundless slumber and drag her merci-lessly under.

For a while it even worked. But on a Christmas stay with Pamela's parents when Madeleine was fifteen months old, she woke up one evening in the crib upstairs in a strange room and cried and cried, and in that big house, roaring with guests, we didn't hear her. When I came up for a routine check I found her face-down, awake, stunned, cried out. She didn't seem to blame either me or Pamela. She blamed the crib. Back at home, she no longer wanted to get into it.

Perhaps it would have happened sooner or later, anyway. She was getting older. She was a big girl now, who could walk, who could stand in the crib and hold on to the bars. She had never used a playpen. She had always had the run of the downstairs, which was everything except the study, so the crib was a unique confinement.

She could talk to us, and understand what we said, and use a fork and spoon, and sit in a booster chair, and pass the salt, and stir the spaghetti sauce. She wore my shoes and clunked around, she put on my right winter glove and offered to shake hands. She opened doors and folded diapers and picked peas and worked a broom. She was our helper. She was one of us, and all day long we encouraged her in that belief. She shopped with us, cooked with us, ate with us, cleaned with us. Then came eight-thirty, and we broke all the rules. It was her bedtime, not ours. She slept here alone, in this cage, while we got to sleep together in the other room, comforting each other.

On my nights with her I read, Pamela nursed, and then I sang, and when I put Madeleine in the crib she sat up. She stuck her legs and arms through the bars and pleaded to be taken out. She asked to have all her animals and dolls brought to her, and then she threw them out one by one, not petulantly, but having fun, wanting me to have fun with her. I cajoled, I soothed, I offered to rub her back. I sang whole recitals with my hand on her back, watching her twirling finger, waiting for it to stop. I often sang "The Demon Lover," which had an ungodly number of verses, and when I got to the end I would start all over again, and then I would start separating the verses with long bouts of humming. I have never practiced meditation — the mantra, the emptying of the mind — but I think I have an idea now what it's like. I gradually slowed the rubbing, and stopped, and I slowly, slowly lightened the weight of my palm, and with truly ridiculous slowness (I thought of it as performance, a parody) I edged toward the door, testing each step on the old floorboards with calibrated toe pressure before committing myself.

Didn't this prove what she had always feared? As soon as her vigilance ceased, we crept away, abandoned her. Our skulking betrayed our guilty consciences. "Daddy?" The quiet voice would come out of the four-watt gloom, freezing me on the threshold. "Yes, honey?" "Daddy, come back." "In a minute, honey." Standing outside the room, I would hope she might drift off, which did sometimes occur, but more often she would call for me again, and then I would try not answering, and she would call again, becoming tearful, and I would go back in.

She figured out quickly enough that her mistake was letting us put her in the crib in the first place. The crib drastically weakened her position. Pamela one night could only get her in by taking on the plaintive voice of the mama wolf, wondering "Where's Madeleine?" And when Madeleine reached, stricken, to get into the crib and comfort her, Pamela herself was stricken — with shame at playing so cynically on Madeleine's tender feelings.

Soon Madeleine was climbing out of our laps and leaving the room after the reading, just as we began the songs. She would wander the house in a daze. Often, whichever one of us was not putting her to bed would be up in the study, since both Pamela and I had pressing deadlines throughout this period. So the downstairs would be empty and quiet, and I would sit in the rocker in the darkened room, offering Madeleine a hug and a song as soon as she came back. Perhaps she was puzzled by this atmosphere. I wasn't going to sleep, but I didn't seem to be doing anything else, either. I sat motionless in the dark, like one of her dolls that stopped moving as soon as she let go of it. Perhaps this was frightening. Perhaps she was just exhausted. Whatever the reason, she often cried. But still, she did not want to come back to the rocker. I would wait for five or ten minutes, then get up, turn on the living room light, sit with my own book. She could stay up, but I wouldn't play with her. If she wanted my attention, it had to be for rocking and singing in the dark.

Our bedtime rituals were like labels for stigmatized social groups. We would inevitably have to change them as they became tainted by association. Madeleine started telling us not to sing lullabies. The worst of the lot was "Hush Little Baby," the one Pamela most often sang, but before long she would accept none of them, and proposed instead, night after night, "Somewhere over — *Rainbow?!*" This was a logical tactic, since that was our morning song. I would obligingly sing it, just the opening strain over and over (Madeleine objected to the second strain because the mobile didn't play it), and every now and then, despite its auroral connotations, it actually succeeded in lulling her to sleep.

Which I suppose is why she started telling us not to sing that song, either.

All right, no songs. I waited until she was quite tired, then read books with her on my lap until she was partly under, then got her into the crib by saying she could rest there — not sleep of course, oh no — while I briefly performed some chore. When I was done, the implication was, I would take her back out of the crib and we'd read twenty more books or build cardboard-block houses or blast some rock music and dance till dawn. She would consent to lie down, and I would move quietly around the room, tidying, or go into the bathroom and rinse diapers, butt rags, washcloths, whatever else I could get my hands on. If she called, I would say, "I'll be done in a minute."

This worked fairly well for a while. Then she twigged. Now the crib, under any circumstances, was unacceptable. The whole room was suspect. The kitchen was the best place, because it was the brightest room, patently uncozy, lacking even chairs. Pamela and I moved to meet this latest gambit. We started saving the dishes for Madeleine's bedtime. When she was tired enough, I would set to work. She would play on the floor by my feet. The lambskin would be there waiting. The linoleum would be cold on her cheek, so when she needed to rest, she would lie on the lambskin. I would wash on. The radio would play quietly. If I got done with the dishes too early, I had a magazine or book secreted by the drying rack, and would continue to stand at the sink, reading.

We would do anything, that is, except the obvious thing, which was to forget the crib and the separate bedroom and the whole rigmarole and take her into our bed, where she thought, quite reasonably, that she belonged. Pamela and I had little interest in night life, none in television. When Madeleine was asleep, I wrote or read, and I preferred doing both of those things in the morning to the evening, anyway. Moreover, Pamela and I had made a habit for years of my reading out loud to her for a few minutes in bed before turning out the light, as a way of ending the day together. So a perfect arrangement was staring us in the face. We could all get in bed, read a book for Madeleine, then read our own book aloud while she fell asleep, and at that point either get up or go to sleep ourselves, and get work done early the next morning, before Madeleine woke.

We didn't do it. Our parents hadn't done it; our friends didn't do it. Madeleine fell asleep on her lambskin on the kitchen floor, her toys scattered around her. At least she had grown out of the phase in which she woke up whenever we moved her. I picked her up in the lambskin and transported her to her crib. She would sleep there until the first nursing, around three A.M. When we checked on her before going to bed, she had always worked her way into a corner, her face pressed into the bumper. The language was clear. In her sleep, she was searching for us, and we weren't there.

∾ 12 ∾

"KOO-KOO?" Madeleine called, bending slightly at the knee. She stood up. "No-o," she said pensively. She took a few steps, turned, bent at the knee again. "Koo-koo?" She stood up. "No-o . . ."

She wasn't looking for her doll Kristen, who lay in plain sight on the floor. I had just found her and given her to Madeleine, after walking through the rooms and calling "Kristen?" and getting on my hands and knees to look under things, and standing up, saying "No" when I didn't see her. I don't think Madeleine was *pretending* to look for Kristen, either, if by that we mean she was pretending she didn't know where Kristen was. For her to do that, she would have to have realized that *I* hadn't, in fact, known where Kristen was. I don't think Madeleine as yet had any idea of that. (Her discovery, in a few months, that I or Pamela might not know something would be quite apparent.) I had known where Kristen was all along, because I knew everything. This was just one of the myriad things Pamela and I did, and Madeleine was doing her job, imitating it.

She had begun by echoing single gestures and single words: the wave, the Bronx cheer, hi and bye. Now she was producing groups of words, and although some were real phrases of her own design, many were single syntactical blocks, indivisible and inflexible: bigtruck, bigkid, diapercover, nohitTiti. (From here on, I will generally transcribe her utterances as though she were pronouncing them correctly.) Similarly, many of her gestures were sophisticated enough to give the illusion of social understanding, but then revealed themselves to be free-floating blocks of choreography, cued by a word or object. When she was learning how to use a fork several months ago, the first twenty or so times she managed to stab a piece of food with it, she would turn toward me (if I wasn't at the table) and say "See?" That routine became part of her programming, so that even when I *was* at the table, facing her, she would twist in her chair and address emptiness, "See?" On hearing the phoneme *bye* ("time to say goodbye"; "perhaps we should drop by"; "I think he might be bi"), she would start industriously blowing kisses — at a person, if she happened to be facing one, but if not, then into my shirt, into the closet. She knew she was supposed to pull out the tape measure, set it against something, and call out a number in a businesslike tone of voice. She performed the ritual perfectly, briskly stretching the tape measure along chair legs and stripes in the rug, announcing, "One year old!" On successfully completing some task, she had recently taken to bending to the right, closing her right fingers on air, and tucking her elbow into her ribs. I puzzled over this strange gesture until one day I caught myself performing its model: a facetious "All ri-ight!" complete with the crouch and the pulled-in fist. Madeleine would sometimes cycle through several gestural-verbal complexes in succession, usually when she had my attention and wasn't sure what to do with it. She might say "Pass!" and hold up an object as though it were a dish to be passed during a meal, then point up to the light and say "Hot," then pull an invisible object along her leg and say "Shoe." This was conversation, a riff from her repertory.

Madeleine's way of learning by means of adopting chunks of unexamined material was fascinating to watch, partly because it presented, in bald form, the chimplike imitative urge that all of us display throughout our lives. Children pick up set phrases, comments, or judgments and juggle them like Homeric formulae, rarely breaking them. Like adults' clichés, these linguistic containers are powerful because they precede thought, so the thought that eventually fills them seems God-given, inevitable. I can remember only the later stages of the off-the-rack mixing and matching that was my character formation. There were the preadolescent political arguments on the school bus, in which I parroted my parents while my conservative colleague, Bill Rising, parroted his, and whenever either one of us brought in a new and devastating point from home, the debate would freeze until the next day, when the opponent could come back with a crushing response. Adolescence is almost nothing but trying on different roles, each one coming to us complete with costume, posture, and prescribed lines, and we gradually play one role more than the others, then play it exclusively, and last of all adjust it here and there, but in relatively minor ways, so that, as professional clowns must do, we eventually have a costume and routine that is unique to us, but only barely. The "All ri-ight!" gesture that Madeleine had picked up from me was something I in turn had stolen, and so unconsciously that I had no idea, now that she had called my attention to it, where it came from. (Professional athletes? Kids imitating professional athletes? Professional athletes imitating kids imitating professional athletes?) Pamela and I, after a dozen years together, talked and gestured so similarly that we sometimes made people laugh, and for the same reason that Pamela and I laughed silently at our adorable daughter: the illusion of individual essence was shattered, the motley revealed.

This impulse toward thoughtless imitation is important for *Homo gregarius*, since social conventions are arbitrary across the species but, within each group, totalitarian. In fact, a case can be made that humans are *more* imitative than chimps, since we are born with far less hard-wiring in our brains and rely on mirroring others in order to become human. The first game Madeleine and Theodore actually collaborated on was a replica of a parent-child game, and a little absurd in the context. Out of the blue, Madeleine said "Chase!" and dropped to her knees (as we did when chasing her, in order to match her size and speed), and Theodore, instantly recognizing the reference, hid behind a chair, shrieking as custom demanded. But Madeleine's progress on her knees was very slow, so Theodore had to keep hyperventilating for quite some time as she inched across the floor. When she finally reached him, neither had any idea what to do next. They stared at each other, the excitement on their faces slowly fading. When in doubt . . . Madeleine retreated, spun around, and dropped to her knees again, and Theodore recommenced happily shrieking. He did it dutifully, but at the same time with real, delicious panic. The form of the game had brought its content along.

The urge to imitate seems even stronger between children — like liking like — and this is where our genetic programming for social lubrication proves to have bugs. Whenever Madeleine picked up her bottle Theodore ran to get his (or vice versa), and the two would stand, almost stomach to stomach, almost mirror images, drinking in each other along with the juice. This worked fine, but there is a betrayal lurking down the road from the child's early delight in our bilaterally symmetric lives. Many objects don't come in twos. The fighting over the unexpectedly singular toy that kids are so constantly drawn into starts off as form — the imitative urge — and fills with content: the belief that what another values is valuable. This belief, of course, lasts into adulthood, by which time we've learned to displace, suppress, or finesse it in a variety of ways, and even while impatiently arbitrating the tenth tearful dispute of the morning between Madeleine and Theodore, I could appreciate the purity of the honest grab and regret the hard-learned niceties that had prevented me, over the years, from simply pushing my smaller father-in-law down and taking away his Steinway grand.

Theodore pulled harder than Madeleine. Her instinct was not to fight for the object herself, but to appeal to authority for justice. Naturally, her idea of justice, like Theodore's, was that whatever she wanted, she got. Pamela and I had wrested objects away from her only while uttering certain protective spells, invoking the rules that shielded us all: hot, sharp, breakable, poisonous. Theodore took things Madeleine knew were safe, and without a word, either. Now she had to learn new rules. They were more complicated, and went more against the fundamental desire to possess, but they were rules, and she liked rules, and after the first few shocks of discovering that Theodore did not behave like us, and that we did not expect him to behave like us, she turned to these rules with relief. She quickly learned the words, thus internalizing the concepts more easily: "sharing," "taking turns." "Turn," in particular, was a great comfort. As words do, it created a thing, and now every object could be magically doubled, becoming "Theodore's turn" and "Madeleine's turn." (And here was another, vivid lesson in time: through turn-taking, Madeleine began to appreciate what a minute meant.)

With similar enthusiasm she mastered the corollary rules, the subrights, the conditional clauses. Turns lasted different amounts of time for different objects — a turn at the slide was a few seconds, a turn on the swing, a few minutes — but for each particular object, her turn and Theodore's turn were of equal length. (In practice, she usually took shorter turns than Theodore, not so much because he was hogging as because Madeleine had much more emotion invested in the rule than in the object. What she wanted was the turn itself, the turn reified, and she could get that instantaneously.) Whoever lit on a toy first got to have the first turn. To abandon the toy before the end of its turn-time-limit was to lose first-turn rights to it. Putting the toy down for two seconds while rearranging personal equipment did not count as abandonment. A soupçon of extra allowance was accorded whichever child was on home turf, since sharing under those circumstances was acknowledged to be tougher. There were certain so-called special toys that were not subject to standard turn-taking. Special toys could be so designated "for cause" — they were bed companions, recent presents, and the like — or peremptorily, but the latter designation could be applied only once or twice in each play session.

Theodore more or less ignored all of this. He took what he could and gave up what he was forced to. He was younger, but more important he still had little language with which to digest reality, to break it down into terms useful to him. He heard German at home, French in daycare, and English everywhere else. He would eventually be enviably multilingual, but for now he was literally a barbarian: incapable of speech. He could not be satisfied with taking a "turn" because, lacking the word for it, and not seeing it, he could not believe it existed. If Theodore did something Madeleine didn't like, she could shout "No, Ti-ti!" and feel within her the compensating power of that mighty word. Theodore could only bite. Unable to take "Madeleine" in his mouth, he took Madeleine.

Sometimes instead of hitting or biting he would grab her and shake her. She would make no attempt to get away or retaliate, and her face, in the seconds before I separated them, would take on a moribund, masklike cast, her eyelids at half-mast. She was playing dead, obeying a biological directive designed to make the predator leave her alone. But overlying biology was the superstructure of her awareness, this whole other reality in her head, and she would sometimes do what no nonhuman young-ling would do. She would deliberately place herself in harm's way, sitting a few extra seconds at the top of the slide, say, or standing provocatively in front of Theodore while holding something he wanted. Her face would automatically take on that deadened look, as her genes tried to protect her, but her brain was after a more sophisticated reassurance. She wanted to know that the rules would be enforced, just as when she once had threatened to hit us. That old test had been reassuring and up-setting at the same time. This one was more satisfactory. Theo-dore would attack her, yes, but what was a slap or a nip compared with the fact that *he* would be punished? Reassurance, revenge, and the sating of prurient interest, all at once! Theodore, the sucker, fell for it every time, but unfortunately I knew what

Madeleine was doing, and she discovered she risked getting both hit by Theodore and reprimanded by me.

Her more benign response to Theodore was to become parental. She would explain rules to him, while he tottered off, holding up his oversized shorts, a dazed and slightly crazed look on his face. While he sat immobile at the top of the slide, she would stand below and semaphore, sweeping her arms down the incline like a lion tamer coaxing her beast along, repeating, "Ti-ti! *Down* the slide!" He usually paid no attention, but once at a picnic when he stood up on a bench — danger! danger! — Madeleine yelled "Sit down, guy!" with such authority that he dropped immediately.

Her interest in social relationships grew beyond figuring out how to deal with Theodore. Joint enterprises suddenly became of great interest to her, and she would frequently stop an activity in order to comment on it in a tone of wonder: "Two — *people!* Eat!" or "Two — *people!* Walk!" One evening, while each one of us was hunched greedily over a bowl, she came out with "Daddy eat my ice cream, Maya eat your ice cream." She wasn't proposing a switch (she got her possessives, like her pronouns, backward) but was floating the idea that this was comforting, our eating together, this was "cozy," a word she also picked up at this time, wriggling under the covers of our bed in the morning and announcing "I'm cozy!" Activities she previously had not shared with me, such as rocking her horse, could be turned into joint efforts by having me observe her, and it was probably no coincidence that now she began the refrain that I could expect to hear for years to come: "Daddy! Watch!"

❧ 13 ❧

WHO was she?

She was Baby, she was I, she was You, she was Maya.

Babies asked for things, so when she made a request, she was Baby. "Baby hold Mama ring?" Babies got upset, indignant; babies had to claw for their scraps of power. She could say it like a one-two punch, a BB in your ear: "Baby!" Babies hurt themselves. When she hit her head, she said, "Poor baby!"

She knew there were other babies, at the food co-op, in strollers, in *Baby's World*. There was Big Baby. There was Bald Baby. This was a group she belonged to. Babies wore diapers. They pooped. You needed to be gentle. They liked to be tickled. When you tickled a baby, you said "Ticka-ticka-ticka." She took good care of Bald Baby.

There were babies in songs. She still liked songs, as long as they were sung before dinner. I sang "All the Pretty Little Horses": "Go to sleep, baby child, go to sleep, my little baby —"

"Baby?!" she said, interrupting. "Baby?!" She held out one hand, cupped upward, and placed the other over it, palm down.

"You want Bald Baby?"

"No?!"

"You want Big Baby?"

"No?!"

"Kristen?"

"No?!"

I went back to the song: "Go to sleep, baby child —"

"Baby?! Baby?!" She put her fingers in my mouth, opened my lips, looked in. "Baby?!" Her voice was urgent. She again held out her two cupped palms, hinged at the wrists, a nest for a robin's egg. "Hold?!"

"You want to hold the baby in the song?"

"Oh!"

I thought it was such a lovely idea, but it was painful for her, not being able to touch this little baby, formed and rocked in my mouth, made beautiful by the melody.

She was also I. I was the ego, resident behind the eye. In control, simply declarative, as in adult speech. "I did," she would confirm when we asked her if she had enjoyed such and such. I was for informing her parents, giving them information they might not have, bolstering her claim to maturity. "Last night I see big truck on road," she said, her longest sentence so far. We were amazed; she was nonchalant. I, big girl.

But I was only the actor, the doer. When acted upon, done to, she was You. "Should I carry you?" I would ask.

"Carry You."

Push you, swing you, hold you, feed you, pick up you, let go you, help you, nurse you, cuddle you, chase you. You was in need, like Baby, but You was not making a special request, You was not trying to change adult behavior. You was entitled. You was loved.

She was Maya. Things happened to Maya. Stories were told about Maya. Two dogs jumped up on Maya. A chicken bit Maya's foot. Theodore hit Maya's head. Maya had a history.

She was a toddler. She was one year old. She was almost two.

She had a Mama and a Daddy. Mama changed her with her feet pointing toward the bathroom. Daddy changed her with her head pointing toward the bathroom. Mama and Daddy went upstairs to work. Mama went straight up. Daddy hung around, heating coffee, dithering. "Daddy, work!" she said.

Mama always understood what she said. Daddy sometimes didn't.

"Fuh fies."

"What?"

"Fuh — fies!"

"What?"

"Call Mama!"

Mama shouted down the stairs, "French fries!"

She was a girl. Ti-ti was a boy. Ti-ti was her friend. But Ti-ti was in daycare. Matt, Amy, and Rachel were in school. She could play with Bald Baby, but Bald Baby was herself, as Baby, a pooper and nurser, in diapers. She could play with Kristen, but Kristen was herself, as Big Girl, walker, talker. She could look beyond the mirror now, to others, to friends, but she had no doll as other, as friend. As boy.

Then came Hans. He arrived that summer. He had been Grandma Peggy's doll when she was a girl, and she had called him Hansel, because of his south German clothes. He was in mint condition. He looked as though he had spent the fifty intervening years stored in argon. He had a blue felt hat, a yellow jacket, blue waistcoat, black knee breeches, black buckled shoes. He had skin of peach cloth, electric-blue eyes, a kiss-me cherry mouth, lemon yarn hair. Madeleine stripped him. Why don't you stay a while, Hans. The cardboard soles of his shoes popped out, the button on the back of the waistcoat disappeared. Hans swung naked in the apple-tree swing. He went down the slide face-first. (He was a fabulous turn taker.) He was a kite, tied with string to Madeleine's plastic push-car, and she threw him out the back and raced off to give him lift. He went around the circle of rooms and up and down the driveway, flying beautifully, though on the ground. Some turbulence, there. Grandma Peggy took it well. "If he's loved . . . ," she said. He was loved. Madeleine banged her head against the table and ran off, crying "I hug Hans!"

Hans watched Madeleine do things. She was almost two, and the things she could do! She expected objects to obey her will. The pulp of her juice clogged in the nipple, the mama bear's bloomers caught on Hans's knees (better not go out looking like that, Hans), the rubber insect wouldn't stick to the window. "Not working?!" she said, and her standard intonation here was exactly right: queenly, indignant.

If she stood on the bathroom stool to the side of the sink, she could reach the cold-water faucet. She was the water genie. I donned rubber gloves to rinse a diaper, and Madeleine, water genie and surgical assistant, put on Pamela's gloves. The empty fingers drooped. "Water, please," I said, and water flowed. "Enough," I said, and it stopped. Hans sat on the windowsill, lost in admiration. "You're such a good helper," I said.

But how can you really know you're a helper without testing the importance of your help? An experiment: see how everything grinds to a halt when Maya's help is withheld.

"Water. Water, please. Hello! Look, if you don't —"

All right. Maya only wanted a little begging. The way she often had to beg. It was only fair. She was one of us, after all. Come to think of it, sometimes she never got what she wanted, no matter how much she begged. Come to think of it, she cried futilely, in frustration.

"Madeleine, if you don't turn on the water *right now,* I'm going to do it myself."

Yes, she eventually got angry, too, she understood. The next step was —

But I cheated. I pried her helper's hand loose and turned on the water myself. I smashed her illusion of parity, of power. She cried. "I'm sorry, honey, but if you . . ." Blah, blah. Nothing meant anything except that I had cheated.

Later she could stand on the stool by herself, undisturbed, and wash her hands. Soap, faucet, water. On and off and on and off. Dry her hands on the towel, climb back up, wash them again. Then I came in. What did I want now? "Don't do that too long, hon, it wastes water."

She was strong enough now to open the refrigerator door. Dark, then the light coming on. Interesting. Open and closed. How strong she was! "You're letting all the cold air out . . ." Blah, blah. Every time was the same. I always won. Helper, ha!

She hugged Hans. His blue eyes began to flake off. Pamela repainted them. His yarn hair came loose on one side and hung down in a long skein. Did she want us to fix it? No. Madeleine and I drew with colored chalk on the driveway. "Who's that?" I asked, pointing to a peach figure with a streaming pendant of yellow hair, a balding man with a comb-over in a gale. "Hans!" Madeleine yelled, dancing.

She helped us do the dishes, rinsing the unbreakable things in a bowl on a chair, a bib around her waist like an apron. She helped hang the laundry, either handing up the items from the basket as I requested them or, more awkwardly, insisting on attaching them with the clothespin herself, a manual feat only barely within her competence. I held her up while she struggled, pinching thin air, until my arms gave out, then finished the clothes myself while she complained. I tried to make it up to her by stringing a clothesline just for her along the baseboard behind the door in her room. She hung Hans's clothes there, the felt cap and breeches and jacket that he never wore, and sometimes she hung Hans, too, by standing him against the baseboard and putting the line under his chin. I think she liked it because he couldn't stand up on his own, and he thus looked more alive to her, but when I first caught sight of him, with his head lolling forward, naked except for the bear's bloomers, it was a small shock, like something from *Jude the Obscure*, dear little Hans behind the door, hanged in his underwear.

The rest of the sewing on his scalp gave way, and now he was bald. She didn't want us to fix him. She seemed to regard his aging as natural — she was finally getting hair, he was losing his — while our interference was artificial. Or perhaps not artificial, but indubitably interference. She had us drag the car seat into the house, so she could buckle Hans in. Bald as he now was, he looked like a crash-test dummy. Dirt had turned his peach skin to dun. We were afraid that if we washed him, his face would come off, all his seams give way. Like a mummy, he'd been removed from his sealed tomb, and now he was crumbling.

With the car seat back in the car, Madeleine and Hans rode together. It had not taken her long to figure out the one chink in our armor. At home, whenever she refused to do what we wanted, we announced we would not play with her, not interact with her at all, until we got this first thing done. We never got angry, we merely told her what had to be done, and waited. We could always outwait her because, as freelance writers with quiet social lives, we almost never had to be anywhere at any particular time. In fact, we positively enjoyed these waiting contests, because they gave the parent on duty a chance to sneak in a few extra minutes of reading time.

This must have been infuriating for her. In the car, things were different. She loved to play in the car, climbing from seat to seat. The supermarket parking lot, or a cool rainy evening outside the Chinese buffet, was not as pleasant a place for us to wait as at home with our books. And we could not drive anywhere until she got into her car seat. Hmm. Interesting . . .

She worked out an impressive array of feints, diversionary tactics, disingenuous promises, deceptions. She had to climb in by herself. Fine, climb in. But first she wanted to look at this — No, climb on in. But this was really quite fascina — Climb in *now*, or get put in. She didn't see what the hurry — All right, up you go — No! No! (Wail.) She'll get in! She climbed in. Right past the seat. In the seat, Madeleine. She was getting something from the foot well that she wanted to hold. That's the last thing — All right. See how she could open the driver's door! In the seat, Madeleine. And roll down the window, too. What a big girl! This is your *last chance*. She stepped into the seat. Good girl. Sit down, now. She'd prefer to stand, thank you. Sit down! All right, she'll sit down. Sit down, then. Soon. Madeleine, if you don't sit down *right now*, I'm going to force you down.

She was in heaven, entirely in control. She could have written my lines for me, including the last warning when I really meant it. At that point she usually sat down, recognizing she had played it out as long as she could. But sometimes she had to go on. She had to test the full limits of her power, which was to force me to force her. I pushed her down and held her until I could get the straps over her head and clicked into place. She writhed, screaming and sobbing. "I get in self!"

"I'm sorry, honey. I told you it was the last time." At least I (finally!) was upset, too. I handed her Hans, and he hugged her.

❧ 14 ❧

"I HAVE to go upstairs to get Aunt Martha's curtains. Take good care of the baby, Carl."

These were the opening lines of *Carl Goes Shopping*. I had read them so many times, they had dug a deep trench through my cerebral cortex, and the words moved down that trench like a barge heavy with freight, freighted with heaviness, resonant with resonance. They didn't mean any more than they ever had, but they meant it with a vengeance. They had an effect on me similar to the words "Wonderful Counselor, Almighty God, the Everlasting Father, Prince of Peace," which I had probably heard, read, or sung about as many times.

It seems reasonable to suppose that the words had at least as powerful an effect on Madeleine. Like most children, she asked for the same few books over and over again, perhaps partly (and prosaically) because she required several readings to piece together a decent understanding of what was going on in each story. But even after she had understood as much as she would, the rereadings continued. Changes on my part, as I struggled to emerge from my stunned state, were not allowed. Getting stunned was the whole idea. To crib from Mircea Eliade, this was the sacred, eternal present, the charmed moment outside profane time, which Madeleine, only barely conscious of past and future, could enter readily, and I less so. Eliade's idea was that religious festivals were not reenactments of previous events but, in a way, doorways to the events themselves, which existed outside time. That abstruse idea finds concrete embodiment in books. The story exists on the shelf, end and beginning together, without duration until we supply it through reading. Every time we opened *Carl Goes Shopping*, we stepped through the doorway. There he was, as he always had been and would be: a good dog, ready to take care of the baby.

What mattered to Madeleine in this magic realm? Carl, for one. He was more now than simply a beast that turned out to be a protector, the external threat enlisted as internal defense. Now, as Madeleine began to realize that Pamela and I were not omniscient (or at least I wasn't, judging from my frequent stupid "What?"s), she could appreciate that Carl was subversive. He waited — O dependable dog! — until the parents were out of sight before taking the baby on adventures. Many of the high jinks themselves, such as freeing the animals in the pet department or rolling on the Persian rugs, didn't mean much to Madeleine, but she understood that the baby was having fun, and that the parents *didn't know.*

Angus was another dog Madeleine often requested. A Scottie in *Angus and the Ducks,* he wasn't the protector, but a stand-in for the child. He ventured beyond the pale — in this case the garden hedge, drawn appropriately as a world-encircling barrier, receding to the horizon — and on the OTHER SIDE, as it was styled in the text, he encountered the Beast, in the form of two ducks, who nipped his tail and chased him back. As an object lesson, the story had its delicious *frisson,* but wasn't close enough to Madeleine's personal experience to be positively frightening.

This wasn't the case with *Madeline's Rescue.* In the opening pages, Madeline tried to frighten Miss Clavel by walking on the parapet of one of Paris's bridges, fell into the water, and nearly drowned before she was saved by a dog. Obviously, the name alone was unsettling. Additionally, all summer long we had been warning Madeleine never to walk out alone on the dock at the neighbor's pond, and she had shown much reluctance to hold our hands. She was a big girl now, big enough to begin to doubt my rules. I expounded this one with as much emotion as I did the road rule, but in the latter case she could see the cars barreling by with her own eyes, whereas the pond was so quiet, and after all, I didn't even know what "fuh fies" meant, and Carl could probably fool me any day of the week. So in her mind she must have walked many times along the edge of the dock, hands out to show us how unattached to ours they were — and there was Madeline, walking the parapet, hands out; there she was, falling and screaming; there she was with her head under water and dragged like a limp doll to the water's edge. Because of its guardian-dog motif, Madeleine sometimes wanted to read the rest of the story, but these opening pages had to be skipped. Eventually they tainted the whole book, and it stayed on the shelf.

There were danger spots in other books. Madeleine developed a sharp eye for the warning signs. Tears in real life were streaks or splashes, but she quickly learned to recognize the illustrator's stylized teardrop and wanted nothing to do with it. She loved *Frog in Love,* because by the end the shy green frog had finally stammered out his devotion to the white duck, and on the last page, when they embraced, he wore such a dazed, happy smile. But there was that page along the way, the one that showed Frog sitting alone at his dinner table, his food untouched, the text saying "Poor Frog!" and below his eye one of those little pointy-headed globules. Passing that page was like leading Madeleine through a marshy stretch. I could feel her sinking as soon as we turned to the picture — "Why he crying?" — her finger beginning its helicopter whirl, and if I didn't hustle us fast enough to the dry ground beyond, I would lose her.

Far worse was the two-page "A Rainbow Story," a sketch in a saccharine collection by Joan Walsh Anglund. Here was a whole column of falling drops, plus a downturned mouth and eyebrows rising toward the center — the full blast of the iconic unhappy face, plastered on a rainbow. Moreover, the rainbow's complaint was far too close to the bone. It came out from the clouds on the first page, "a happy little rainbow," so proud, so naive, as it "waited, way up high, for someone to notice it." But no one came out of the houses, no one looked up. On the second page, crying, it "faded back up into the sky where no one could ever find it. Poor little rainbow." That word again, "poor." Like the teardrop, it was a sure sign of trouble. But worst of all — and this was truly shocking — the story ended here. Will of the new cap got his soda and a Band-Aid on his knee, and Frog won his duck, and Madeleine returned to these books precisely for the reassurance they offered that the worst she could imagine was not the end of the world. But the rainbow cried and died. "A Rainbow Story" was read to Madeleine just once, after which she banished it forever.

And then there was the book that went straight for the jugular. Angus getting nipped by the ducks, Madeline being swallowed by water, and Carl as the gentle beast were all glosses on the core theme of the predator that will eat the child, whereas *The Goat and Her Kids* was about a real wolf that really wanted to eat little kids. In the story, the mother goat, heading off to market, warned her three kids not to let anyone into the cottage while she was gone. When she returned, she would stick her white foot under the door, so they would know it was her. The wolf, however, went to the mill and coated his paw in flour. Fortunately, the flour rubbed off as he walked up the hill to the cottage, so when he put his paw beneath the door, even though he spoke in the mother's voice, the kids refused to open it. Enraged, he began to batter the door, but at that moment the mother returned. She charged the wolf and butted him into the river. He slunk off, bedraggled, while the mother cooked dinner.

This hit the big buttons: the parent abandoning the children at a time of danger; the literal beast coming literally to devour them; the parental figure, wheedling and promising, who, unmasked, proves to be the beast. Since the kids were saved, Madeleine did ask us to read it, but it was tough going. We had to punctuate the text with parenthetical asides: "Everything will be all right, though"; "You'll see, they'll be OK." Since the story, for her, was a magic re-creation à la Eliade, she also relived the initial suspense (she never seemed quite sure that any of her books would turn out the same as last time). Adding to her fascination, perhaps, was her confused response to the catharsis. One picture showed the wolf falling on his back into the water, and the next showed him skulking away, dripping, his ears and tail down. Perhaps Madeleine thought of herself falling in the pond, Madeline falling off the bridge, the good dog jumping in the water to save Madeline, Wolf in the photo album whom we always called "good dog," and Good Dog Carl. The water dripping from the wolf looked like tears. At the moment of triumph the avenging god banished evil, barricaded the stout door, and served the communion meal — and Madeleine cried. Poor wolf!

❧ 15 ❧

BY TWENTY-THREE MONTHS, Madeleine knew four letters: O, Y, M, and X. She had learned M because it was the first letter of her name, and X perhaps because it was an even more welcoming figure than Y, with both arms *and* legs open. If O's and Y's greeted her at various places around town, X was so ubiquitous — in crossed struts and aluminum panels stamped for tensile strength — it seemed to move along with us. M, on the other hand, was important mainly in its yellow-arch manifestation; Madeleine knew this device signaled "Old McDonald's," as she called it, and that meant french fries, her favorite food. At home, I arranged O, Y, M, and X with her on the refrigerator and pointed out that she could now spell "ox" and "mom" and the first half of "oxymoron." She still preferred sweeping all the letters onto the floor.

She had learned to count to ten in the course of trying to master her fear of the basement steps, a campaign that would continue for months, with many setbacks. This fear was both associational, since the basement itself frightened her, with its moaning washer and dryer, its cobwebs and gloom, and more direct, because the stairs had no balusters, and the yawning space beneath the railing was an invitation to any kid who wasn't obsessionally vigilant to fall through and crack her head open on the cement floor below. There were ten of these steps, and therefore "ten" had to be conquered. Madeleine managed — sometimes — to cut her fear into edible slices by confronting and labeling the steps one by one.

Thereafter, she referred to the act of counting as "one-two-seven-eight-nine-ten," and eventually this shorthand reference corrupted her real counting, so that she would reach ten only halfway down the steps and, her scabbard now empty, would need to be carried from there. Her idea of cardinal numbers still lagged behind her ordinals, so she had no idea of "five apples" or "seven buttons." She did, however, now know what "three" was, because we always read her three books before bedtime. She also knew that one plus two equaled three, because if I was holding one book in the rocking chair, she would bring two more.

She had made remarkable progress in her spatial sense of the world. Early in the summer, she and I had been out with the stroller on our road, and when I suggested we head home, she agreed, but wanted to do it by continuing in the same direction. My explanation that "that way isn't home" seemed to fascinate her. She climbed out of the stroller and took a few steps in the direction of our house (which was not visible), pointing ahead and nodding vigorously, and exclaimed, "This way — home!" Then she walked the other way, shaking her head and waggling her index finger. "This way — *not* home!" For fully fifteen minutes, she went back and forth between these two options, appealing to me for confirmation, but at the same time *telling* me, teaching me, in a mood of mounting joy.

Partly, her excitement stemmed from her old fascination with dualism, with this thrilling awareness that her mind could split the tangled world like a Gordian knot, but she was also, I think, enjoying her first inkling that the stage sets of her life were *places,* and that I could not produce home around any corner the way I seemed always able to pull a pacifier out of a pocket or a drawer. This new theory — that there was a way toward home and a way away from it — perhaps resonated with her interest in the protective barrier between inside and outside, between the garden and the wilderness. Home was security, and I was teaching her how to find it, how to get inside the wall. She wouldn't have to wait for me to conjure safety out of thin air but could turn on her heel at any time, shouting "Back!," and run straight for it.

Once she had the basic idea that places stayed put and you made your way to them, she learned the details quickly. Clearly, she considered it important to know. She began to monitor my driving. I first began to appreciate how good her spatial memory had become in midsummer, when for two days in a row she fell asleep as I drove with her toward town to do errands. On both days, deciding to let her sleep, I started a loop back toward home at the same intersection, and both times she opened her eyes as she felt the right-hand turn and cast a stunned glance around for no more than a second before falling back asleep. On the third day she stayed awake, and as we sailed straight through the intersection, at last errand bound, she spoke urgently from her car seat, pointing down the right-hand road: "No go this way?"

Even at night she usually knew where we were. Pamela and I had been in the habit, if Madeleine was drifting off as we neared home, of driving around the block, which in this rigidly sectioned landscape was one square mile. But now as soon as we took that first turn off the main road, west instead of south, she would pop out of her stupor — we couldn't figure out how she did it, since for the past three or four miles her eyes had been closed — and say, "Where we going?" "It's all right, honey," I would mutter, "we're just taking a slightly different way home." She would fall silent, and I would drive gently down the dark country roads, turning south, then east, and finally north again. Not a sound from the back seat as we trundled the last half mile. As I passed the house before ours (both it and ours invisible in the blackness) and just as I began to brake for our driveway, she would come alert again and announce, "Home!"

But she was capable of more than that. One night Theodore was over late and Madeleine's sleeping schedule was all messed up, so for the first time in her life I took her out in the car specifically to get her to fall asleep. I drove all over the pitch-black countryside, down roads I'd never been on before. It took her a long time to grow quiet. When at last she did, I spent another fifteen minutes trying to find my way back. Eventually, I emerged at a place I recognized. It was the main road from town, about two miles past our usual turnoff. I turned toward home. Madeleine immediately piped up from the back seat, protesting: "No go home!"

It was astonishing. I thought of a legend concerning, I think, Genghis Khan — that he had a swiveling rod mounted on a cart that always pointed back toward Karakorum. I wondered if young children had a homing sense, as many animals do, and if it peaked during this period of early mobility, when they were physically capable of wandering off but still lacked any conscious skills for finding their way back. (Madeleine's sense of distance would be fooled by the car, but not her sense of direction.)

Home was by no means the only landmark on her internal map. One day, in the parking lot of the food co-op, she stared, thrilled, as the coal train slowly passed on the abutting tracks. When the engineer in his classic cap returned her wave, the experience was complete. After that, if we were anywhere down-town, I could turn her around five times and stand her on her head, and she'd still be able to point toward the train line. She also knew where both parks were, and our trips to do errands increasingly became running arguments about whether, or when, we would stop putzing around and head for the merry-go-round and the chicken swing. Those were both in the main park, the good park. The other park was really no more than a lousy little playground, with a single rusty slide and a few cracked swings and never any other kids, but it had the one great advantage, as far as Madeleine was concerned, of lying just off the route we took toward home, down a side road that intersected with ours at a light that was usually red. So with my errands done, and Madeleine knowing they were done, I would try to race for home and lunch and Madeleine's nap, but I'd get stuck at that light. "Powk?" she would suggest during the long seconds of red.

I would wearily try to fight it. "Oh hon, let's just get home and —"

"Powk! Powk!" I nearly always succumbed, which I suppose was the problem.

Madeleine also knew where the doctor's office was, and since it wasn't in town, she could always tell when we were headed for it. Fortunately, she liked it. There was a Sesame Street pop-up toy in the waiting room and a receptionist who always seemed delighted to see her.

For her two-year checkup we all went, and Madeleine wondered, as we waited, why a little boy was bawling his head off. We casually surmised that perhaps he felt sick. Madeleine hadn't cried much at her own vaccination shots at three, six, and eighteen months, and didn't seem now to remember them. But something potentially upsetting loomed on this visit. The nurse was going to prick her finger to take a blood sample.

I would have blown it, as the nurse nearly did. I would have talked, like the nurse, in a falsely cheery voice that would have put Madeleine instantly on her guard. I would have cringed inwardly as the blow was struck, and Madeleine, feeling me tense, would know she had been murdered. Luckily, Pamela took over as we went into the examination room and did a simple, wise thing. She told Madeleine, in a tone of wonder, that there was this thing called blood, a red water, which was everywhere inside our bodies — wasn't that amazing? — and Madeleine would get to see it in a moment because the nurse was going to take some blood from her finger. When the prick came, Pamela breathed "Look! There it is!" and Madeleine didn't even notice the pain; she was too busy being fascinated by this red water coming out of her finger.

I was lost in admiration for my wife.

Then it came time to weigh Madeleine. She had never before stood on the adult scale, so Pamela stood on it first, to reassure her. See? Easy! The nurse, still beaming cheerily, balanced the weights.

Pamela glanced at the result and shrieked, "Oh no!"

Madeleine was stricken. "Mama said 'Oh no!'"

"It's all right, hon, she's just — "

"Mama said 'Oh no!'" What *was* that diabolical thing?

We tried to get her on the scale, but like the boy in the waiting room, she bawled.

∾ 16 ∾

MADELEINE did not yet understand September. She did not understand the twelfth. She didn't know what a month was, or a season, or a year. I talked about autumn coming, and snow, but she didn't remember autumn or snow. I told her to enjoy her apple-tree swing because soon it would be too cold, but of the many pointless things I've said in my life, telling an under-two-year-old to live in the present must rank pretty high. She knew a week was seven days, but she didn't really grasp what seven was. She was intrigued by the idea that days had names — Monday, Tuesday — but showed no interest in the order. "Tomorrow is your birthday," we said, and faced with our transparent expectations she made excited noises. But by morning she had forgotten it.

She understood "two." Two meant two shampoo bottles by the bathtub, two books on my lap, two eyes, two ears, two candles on her cake, two friends coming for her birthday party. Weeks ago she had learned to say "I'm almost two." Dropping the "almost" was easy.

"Birthday" meant the song, which she could sing, and had proudly sung almost daily for the past month, alternating with "Barbara Allen" (humming) and "Old MacDonald" ("On this farmer had a pig, ee-ai-ee-ai-ohh!") and an old Southern ditty that began "Shoo-fly pie and apple pan dowdy," which she rendered, "Shoo-fly pie and apple daddy pie." When she sang "Happy Birthday," it was always her birthday. She knew what "happy" meant, so she probably figured it was desirable to have a birthday, but beyond that, things got hazy. Even presents were unclear, because new things floated into her ken all the time. A movie tie-in toy from a McDonald's Happy Meal was as exciting to her as the bigger items that came at birthdays and Christmas.

We had asked her what she wanted for her birthday dinner, and she had stared at our waiting faces, thrilled to be asked, but panicking at the pristine blank in her mind. We had never asked before. "Umm . . ."

Distress was approaching fast. "Well, you like spaghetti," Pamela gently suggested.

"Spaghetti!"

"And carrots."

"Carrots!"

"So . . . should we have spaghetti and carrots?"

"Oh!" The relief on her face was so strong, my heart went out to her. I could remember, from when I was four or five, my own feelings of intense pride and gratitude when my parents asked for a suggestion, any suggestion, from me. I could remember my iron conviction that the least I could do to show my gratitude, the least I *should* do to demonstrate I had earned this sacred trust, was to pick something that pleased them, and I could remember my fear that I would pick wrong and see the awful disappointment march across their faces (they were kind, so they would try to hide it, but I would not be fooled).

Late that afternoon, Theodore came, and Katha, a girl Madeleine had met during the summer. The adults cut out cardboard birthday crowns on the porch, and the kids did some action painting on them with Elmer's glue, sequins, and glass gems. Like the year before, the opening of the presents was a ritual the adults observed with glad cries of anticipation and fulfillment while the children looked on unimpressed. From Katha, a dress-up pillbox hat with a veil; from Theodore, a cotton suit with a painted giraffe; from us, a felt board Pamela had made, with letters, numbers, geometrical shapes, animals, and people for arranging into scenes. Theodore and Katha correctly ignored Pamela's and my thanks, since they clearly had never seen their gifts before. Madeleine was placid and polite. All three found jumping on the couch more fun.

After the spaghetti and carrots came madeleines (rimshot, please) and an ice cream cake, and here the ritual did seem to awe Madeleine. The dimming of the lights, the parental entry with cake ablaze, the singing of the Song, for her, as always, but now with a whole choir singing it, all for her. Unison singing is so evidently a communion and a rapture, it must be powerful before familiarity dulls it, and we almost lost her. I could see it in the widening and flattening of her eyes. But she was saved by the two candles — one, two; two fingers and two friends; she was two! — and the invitation to blow them out. She knew now how to blow, but she blew high, inching closer with each attempt until the flame was at her chin, barely flickering in the backwash of the overhead gale, and Pamela, cheek to cheek with her, surreptitiously helped. At her first birthday, the winking out of the flame had disconcerted her. Now, more aware of her agency, she was abashed. Had she broken them, killed them? A photograph has caught her with fingers in her mouth, worried and guilty, wisps rising from the candlewicks like souls departing. But we cheered.

After Theodore and Katha went home, we realized that no one had cried. And Madeleine, for whom the day had not meant much, felt no great letdown now that it was over. She lay down on her lambskin on the kitchen floor and fell asleep while we cleaned up. Her finger lay caught behind her head, tangled in a knot of hair. While I finished the dishes, I contemplated a mystery. It had taken her two years to grow enough hair to explain the circles she drew on the back of her head. All that time, like an amputee with an itch on a phantom limb, she had been twirling hair that did not yet exist.

2

✤ 1 ✤

RAINY AUTUMN; upstate weather.

We had a set of cardboard blocks in a garbage bag at the back of the toy closet. I would haul them out and, boylike, want to build towers. I especially wanted to see if I could make a tower reach the ceiling, but Madeleine never let me. For one thing, she loved to knock the towers down, and simply couldn't wait, but there was something else. "That's too high, Daddy," she would say, and require me to remove the top layer. "Imworried-about . . ." It was one word, adopted from me. She was worried about the tower falling on her, or on me. If she knocked it down, a piece might hit her on the head. I proposed we build a tall one and leave it standing, but she never agreed. I think she disapproved of having such a hazard in the house. I think, too, that as a tower grew taller than her it began to resemble a figure, and this silent stranger in the middle of the room made her uneasy.

As I said, the towers were my idea. She wanted to build houses. They were modest post-and-lintel jobs, usually without any interior space. But they always had garages: two blocks side by side, fanning out, with a sliding-block gate at the end. Madeleine owned a couple of Matchbox cars that had been mine when I was a kid — a Cougar and a Mercedes — and she liked them, but she didn't spend much time rolling them around, saying

"Brrm," and she certainly didn't drive them off cliffs to the accompaniment of explosion noises. She far preferred to get them into that garage and close the gate. Home! She drove them up into the narrow space at the far end of the fan, where they looked cozy.

She also liked me to build an identical house next to hers. Home's friend! Mine had the Cougar and hers had the Mercedes, and she took great delight in the contemplation of these twins that yet had one distinguishing mark. She knew "one" and she knew "two," and here was one and two together, unity and duality, the synthesis of opposition!

Some time ago, we had bought a box of smaller, wooden blocks, called "architect" blocks, which included flat panels that could be wedged into corner posts so that you could construct two- and three-story buildings. Clearly, the set would be great for making houses. But Madeleine had already been doing that with the larger blocks, and had perhaps established in her mind what she considered the appropriate scale, so she firmly resisted all my attempts at house construction. Instead, she insisted on making something smaller, and without any suggestion from me she immediately hit on another icon of domesticity. If I had thought about it ahead of time, I might have been able to guess: a table. On her own, she saw that by using the corner posts horizontally we could create a table, with two panels for legs. She also saw that we could make chairs. So day after day she instructed me to build the same thing, a table and two chairs, with a blue block on the seat of each chair to represent a booster (hers was blue). Bald Baby sat in one chair and a small Raggedy Ann doll in the other, and they faced each other all day over a meal of block food. The first time we set this up, Pamela and I asked Madeleine what food the two dolls were eating, and after pointing to a yellow block and saying "Corn," and a blue block and saying "Juice," she got stuck, and the same near-panic came into her eyes that we had seen when Pamela asked her what she wanted for her birthday dinner. She was standing at the threshold of an almost inconceivable power, the ability to tell us stories, to *hold our attention* with words, to create something in her own head and plant it in ours, like feeding us, mouth to mouth. But her repertory was so small, and even smaller when she panicked. Would she lose us? Her eyes flitted from Pamela to me and back.

We rescued her. Carrots, perhaps?

Oh!

Naming things represented another power and another challenge, and here, too, Madeleine stood on a threshold. By the month before her second birthday, her awareness of names had coalesced around songs. When we sang to her, she had started to ask, "What that song called?," probably because we sang a lot of different songs, and she realized she needed to know the name if she was going to request one in particular. But she had not yet named anything herself, except by highjacking the generic, as in Baby. As far as she could tell, names came out of nowhere — as I suppose most do, at least in American culture — and it is in the arbitrariness, the sheer creativity, of naming that the power and challenge lie. Kristen could have been called Blond Girl or Braid Girl, and it would have sufficed for our in-house purposes, but there were other blond girl dolls, other dolls with braids. Any descriptive name had that problem. What made this doll *this* doll? Her ineffable individuality had in fact been made effable, and precisely by choosing a name that had nothing visibly to do with her: she was Kristen. But how on earth had Pamela and I known she was Kristen? (Answer: we looked at the label. Madeleine surely couldn't know that naming is difficult for adults, too.)

At the end of September, we visited my parents in Boston,

where my mother gave Madeleine a new doll. Now she had several, picked up here and there: Hans, Kristen, Big Baby, Bald Baby, Lemon Girl (so named by Pamela or me because of the lemon on her apron), Raggedy Ann, Brown Baby. The new doll was big and brown, but "Big Baby" and "Brown Baby" were taken. If nothing else had come up, Pamela or I, I'm sure, would have started calling her Big Brown Baby. But after a day of carrying her around, Madeleine announced that her name was Barbara Allen.

We happily noted the milestone, and within the next few days, back at home, Madeleine named several other things. The plastic car that she scooted up and down the driveway became Baby-bye. Another castoff doll that had never been important enough even to acquire the name Castoff Doll was suddenly Holly. And a stuffed raccoon, which in one of those mysterious developments became an essential bed companion for three nights running, was dubbed Somewhere over the Rainbow (later shortened to Rainbow).

It had been my turn to wonder: where was she getting these names from? But with Rainbow, it belatedly dawned. She was taking names from songs. Barbara Allen and Rainbow were obvious. Baby-bye was from the song that began "Baby bye, here's a fly." And Holly was from the Christmas carol "The Holly and the Ivy." She had already begun to associate names with songs, as a purely practical matter, but there was a more intrinsic reason for the link. Names powerfully meant *something,* but they only meant themselves. Madeleine had discovered that she did have a store of words at her fingertips that were both resonant and meaningless. She had heard the key words of certain songs many times, and the melodies made them glow, but they largely floated free of meaning because the texts of the songs were too compli-cated for her to understand. She had never asked what "holly" meant, nor ever seen a holly tree, but she knew the word well, and it was as lovable as that tuneful baby she had once tried to get out of my mouth.

∾ 2 ∾

IN GOOD WEATHER, we often went to the park, to store up on space and fresh air for the long confinement ahead. The merry-go-round only ran on weekends in September and was going to close for the winter at the end of the month, so I made sure we got in a last few rides. Madeleine had just graduated to riding a horse by herself, with me on the horse next to her, but the horses themselves didn't interest her as much as the old woman who opened the gate and took the tickets and who, during the ride, sat in the motionless middle and worked crossword puzzles.

As I had done as a child, Madeleine focused on adults. She wanted them to smile at her and notice what a big girl she was, what a good girl. Adults who didn't come and croon at her of their own accord were challenges, objects to be won over. (For several months around her first birthday, she had captured strangers' attention by leaning out of my arms and flopping her head sideways. It was a brilliantly effective maneuver, since it looked as if I were about to drop her.) At the gate she would hand her ticket to this stooped, sour-visaged, preoccupied woman and hop around with glee when she was rewarded with a brief smile and a gravelly "Thanks, dear," and when she told me she wanted a second ride, as she always did, I think she was mainly dreaming of the ticket and the smile.

She was still frightened by the seesaw, even when I held her firmly on it and lifted her and the board together, and on many days she would not go down the twisty slide, either with or without me, though I reminded her that she had done it before and everything had been all right. She preferred to throw down pebbles, because she loved the skittering sound they made, and sometimes after a few handfuls she got inured enough to the idea of the descent — the pebbles seemed to survive — that she consented to follow them. Always, when she did, she then had to slide down a dozen more times, crowing at herself and the slide for this fear once again conquered.

Cautious girl! The leaves were now falling, and at home I raked together a big pile. I told Madeleine how much fun it was to jump into a pile of leaves, and demonstrated, collapsing backward into it. When Madeleine took her turn, she waded into the pile and carefully sat down. She had accepted on faith that this was exciting, and having settled herself and determined that she was unhurt, she properly emitted a thrilled squeal. I suggested we try a running start. She walked all the way to the compost bin, about forty feet away, and came trotting up the slope, stopped halfway to walk for a stretch, then broke again into a "run" that carried her into the pile at a speed about ten percent greater than her usual sidling walk. She paused for a moment to take a quick look around for sharp sticks or thorns, then gently sat down again. Then squealed.

Oh, well. As long as she was enjoying herself. I lay with her and enjoyed myself, too, looking up at the maple branches and the blue sky and wondering how many years it had been since I had done this. Certainly not since childhood. When I had demonstrated to Madeleine by falling backward into the leaves, I had been surprised how little they broke an adult's fall. It was a good thing Madeleine got her prudence from me. If I had run and jumped, legs out, I might have broken my back.

In mid-October we went on a weekend camping trip with Theodore and his parents. Theodore refused to be carried anywhere, while Madeleine refused to walk. Theodore was still a cautionary example to her, as he tripped over tree roots. A person could get hurt that way! Pamela and I had recently started telling Madeleine that exercise was good for her, but to no effect. Our own sedentary, bookish childhoods were staring us in the face. In the evening, she showed us what tree roots were really for. She straddled a big one, called out "Ding ding ding!" (in imitation of the bell announcing the start of the merry-go-round, which the old woman always rang three times), and began bouncing up and down. It looked wildly incongruous, like a small animal humping the tree.

Inexorably the weather worsened, and the house became our world again. Madeleine would take my hand and draw me through the arch separating the dining room from the living room and explain that we were now at the playground. Back there (the dining room) was the house. Since this was her idea, I waited for instructions, but nothing came. "Playground!" she repeated. "Yes," I agreed. A good time was to be had by all, I was sure, but doing what, exactly? There was no slide, no swing. We stared at each other. Then Madeleine straddled a pillow, yelled "Ding ding ding!" and bounced.

I cut out more figures for her felt board. Halloween was coming, so I made a witch on a broom and a ghost. I explained them to Madeleine — a warty herbalist who could fly, a dead person who could float through walls — leaving out any mention that they were supposed to be scary. I also said they didn't really exist. (I'm sure parents disagree on this. I think children have no trouble populating their world with frightening phantoms, and need no help from adults.) Madeleine still pointed to the flies on the flypaper and said they were sleeping, so the ghost made little impression, but she liked the witch, because as a proud sweeper's helper she liked brooms, and as a proud cook's helper she liked herbs (which she called germs, confusing the small good things that you deliberately put on food with the small bad things that accidentally get on it, and that other small good thing we deliberately put in bread, wheat germ). The connection with sweeping probably explained why, when she was being a witch, she rode the broom around the house with the brush forward. As for the felt board itself, Madeleine showed little interest in seasonal themes. Her tastes were simple: mothers and fathers wearing Snuglis or holding babies on the hip, and people sitting at the table eating . . . what was that stuff, anyway?

Madeleine had relearned how to count to ten correctly, and did so several times a day while I went to hide. Later, hide-and-seek becomes a competitive game, as you hide with cunning, wait for the right moment, dash past obstacles, and touch the prize. But for Madeleine at this age it was a whole-body version of peekaboo having nothing to do with resourcefulness and everything with reassurance: the reassurance that when she hid, I would come looking for her, and when I hid, I would hide in the bathroom and not in Canada. For long stretches, Madeleine would hide in the same place, both because original ideas still came with great difficulty and because being found was a delight, and why not re-create the delight in every particular? Her under-the-crib period was followed by an under-the-middle-couch-cushion period. The advantage of the latter was that her head stuck out, so she could watch me wander around the room, looking under the piano or in the pockets of the felt board (a joke I'd picked up from Pamela, which Madeleine found richly amusing). This would go on for about ten seconds until, unable to delay gratification any longer, Madeleine would yell "I'm here!"

and I would turn with dumb amazement and descend on her, now a writhing mass of hilarity.

There were few places big enough for me to hide in, but that presented no problem. Madeleine would always look in the place I had hid last and then be at a loss. She would not move anything, but would simply go around the circle of rooms calling "Daddy?" For me, the game was a lesson in how a child's talent at mimicry makes it easy to overestimate her understanding and competence. The first time I had gone to hide, I'd intended to get under the piano, but saw there wasn't room. Since Madeleine could count to ten in about six seconds, I had no time to go anywhere else, and crouched in the corner. When she came in and looked right at me, I started to get up, but her gaze shifted away. "Daddy?" She looked under the center couch cushion. Did she think this was just a rule of the game, like counting to ten and saying "Here I come," or was she joking as I had done, or did she really imagine I might be there? Her expression suggested the last, which surprised me. She looked around, and her eyes passed over me a second time. "Daddy?" Perhaps she was looking for something tall. Perhaps she expected to find not just me physically, but the whole complex of me: me doing dishes, me picking her up, me reading to her. Me crouching in the corner was not one of the options. "Daddy?" Now her tone was uncertain. She was beginning to fear that I had, in fact, absconded. So I spoke, and she came running.

On many long afternoons, hide-and-seek would pall, and so would the cardboard blocks, and everything else would be dull, and life would stretch away, flat and gray and hopeless. "I need something new," Madeleine would announce. She no longer ever wanted anything; she needed it. She had figured out that "need" was a stronger word, and besides it had that resonant *n* (nursing, nana), as did "new," which she pronounced *nnnew*, so that it sounded like a lamb's bleat of deprivation and desire. The toy closet in the playroom, Madeleine was convinced, was where new things resided, and she would lead me there and stand looking in, twirling her hair.

"I don't think we have anything nnnew," I would say. "How about this? You haven't played with this in a long time."

"No, something nnnew!"

I sometimes felt it myself on the fifth or sixth gray day. Unease, emptiness. What did I want? Another life, another planet? As a kid I had read reams of science fiction, and only later realized that all the years I was growing up I had believed, too deeply to acknowledge or question it, that in my life I would see other worlds, other stars, other intelligent life forms. Infinite possibility! Experience as wide and wild as my imagination. Where now was the darkened closet I could stand in front of and demand that something entirely new, something I had never imagined, burst on me, drench me?

My attempts to lower Madeleine's expectations in the closet were undermined when, three or four times running, after assuring her there was nothing new in there, I waded in and found something new. Not hidden future presents, but some ancient game or toy we had taken months ago from my parents' attic, stored away, and forgotten. One was The Visible Man, a plastic model with transparent skin and a glistening pile of removable internal organs. Madeleine liked the bright enamel colors, painstakingly applied by my mother thirty years ago, and the jigsaw-puzzlish way I could disembowel and reconstruct the guy. She liked the skull, which struck her as quite a friendly thing, with big open eyes and that unbeatable grin. She liked to hold the pig-pink stomach and ask me once again where her stomach was.

On a different day, I came out with a puzzle map of the United States, fifty colored plastic pieces that fit in a sea-blue frame

(Canada and Mexico having apparently gone the way of Atlantis). Like The Visible Man, this map dated back to the sixties, and I enjoyed its earnest, somewhat hokey didacticism. Each state had two holes for posts, one with a bas-relief dome to identify the capital city (the state flag went on the back) and the other for listing state products — you know, "corn and hogs." The accompanying sheet encouraged us to hold contests to see who could name all fifty capitals, who could construct the puzzle the fastest, and so on. Even as an earnest and somewhat hokey kid I had never gotten around to cutting out all the capitals and products from the printed sheet and sticking them to the posts, so Madeleine and I, over several afternoons, set about finishing the job. Madeleine adored stickers, the smaller the better, so I would hand her a Montpelier or a Jackson smaller than my pinkie nail — "little tiny" she called them, with the appropriate adult simper — and she would daintily remove the backing and plant them on the posts. I would look up the state on the capital-city chart and find the flag on the other sheet and cut it out, and Madeleine would stick that on the back and we'd pop the post into the starred hole in the right state: Jackson

She loved this ordering process, snipping apart randomness and binding it to its proper place. For my part, I enjoyed the game because the thought of it waiting for decades in my parents' attic and then finding this second life appealed to my own orderliness, my love of efficiency and conservation. So there we were, father and daughter, enjoying ourselves in our separate anal ways, accumulating a whole grove of little anarchists tied to stakes.

But these diversions were stopgaps. What we needed was spring — the swing, the hammock, the driveway, the park — and that was at least five months away. Cats will look for the door leading to good weather, but Madeleine had progressed beyond that. Doors had lost much of their cachet as soon as she had learned to open them easily, and in any case, now that she better understood the nature of place, she knew that when she opened a familiar door she would find behind it what she had always found, and if she opened an unfamiliar door at, say, the food co-op, it might lead to more co-op but it would not lead to the park, let alone another world where the moon floated down to her arms and furniture danced.

So doors were no longer her transporters to a better life. Buses were. Every morning a yellow bus picked up Matt, Amy, and Rachel on one side of us, Brian and Susan on the other, and churned out of sight, carrying them for the day to that unimaginable land where bigkids dwelled. Unimaginable, yes, but Madeleine had a book that gave a hint of its wonders. In *The Wheels on the Bus* the trees were purple and the houses orange, puddles in the street swirled with rainbow colors, and everything sang.

Madeleine's illusions had been preserved because she had not actually been on a bus, at least not in her memory. When we were in town, she was perpetually pleading with us to hop on every bus she saw. Finally there came a day when we were all together doing errands and I had to stay longer with the car, so Pamela took Madeleine to catch a bus for the six-mile trip home. We didn't exactly want the experience to be a letdown for her, but we hoped it might calm the subject down a little.

The bus doors opened, just as they did when she pulled the tab in the book. The driver didn't sing "Move on back!" but he smiled when she handed him the money. Madeleine hopped and trilled, "We're on a bus!" She and Pamela agreed that one of the great things about buses was that you could see so well out the big windows. Another was that Madeleine didn't have to sit strapped in a car seat. Freedom! She watched the people on the bus go out and in, out and in.

A man Pamela had never seen before was sitting across from them. He reached into a paper bag at his feet and pulled out a furry purple rhinoceros with a golden horn. "This is for you," he said to Madeleine, reaching across the aisle. Speechless, wondering, she took it. His hand went into the bag again and came out with a bright orange fox. "This is for you, too."

Something nnnew. Orange and purple. Buses! They were everything she had dreamed.

∾ 3 ∾

ONE NIGHT in October, when Madeleine was playing with Pamela on our bed, she suddenly stopped and said, "What's that?"

"What?" Pamela asked.

"In the closet."

"Is there something in the closet?"

"A blue dog."

"A blue dog?"

"A blue dog that goes 'Ha!'"

Frightened, she reached up. Pamela lifted her off the bed.

Later, when we were trying to get her to lie down in her crib, it came up again. "Imworriedabout the blue dog." We assured her there was no blue dog in any of the closets. Pamela told her she could make herself feel protected by hugging her two fluffy rabbits, which were favorites at the moment. She obediently did so, mouthing a few cozy noises, but naturally what she really wanted was real protectors, namely us, and it was some time before she fell asleep.

Up until now, Madeleine's fearful scenarios had been either

recapitulations of real events or, if imaginary, very vague: the dark, the unknown. Perhaps she hadn't had enough words to express more concrete fantasies, but I tended to suspect she hadn't had enough words to think them, either. Here, then, was perhaps the first real creation of her fearful mind, and I mulled it over.

The dog part was clear. Barking had always frightened her, and she still occasionally mentioned the two dogs that jumped up on her in the park. ("One dog," we corrected.) But blue? She had been mentioning colors a lot lately. In the summer we had hung a multicolored quilt next to the changing pad, and recently, while getting changed, Madeleine had enjoyed pointing to a color and announcing that she was dark blue, or I was green, or Pamela was pink. She was practicing her color vocabulary, of course, and perhaps she had also realized that colors were pretty good all-purpose adjectives for extending sentences. Earlier, she could match the music of her speech — cadence, phrasing — to ours by babbling nonsense, but now she knew she had to use real words, and getting the rhythm right required study. Naming body parts was an easy, well-trodden path, so she might start with "I have ears." Then she would conjugate it: "Daddy has ears." Now came the nifty color-extender trick: "Ti-ti has yellow ears." Then she'd add an adverb and get a statement not only of adult length but with an adult's judicious hedging: "Mama has partly blue ears."

While she was on the changing pad there was still the mobile, with its red bear, yellow tuna, green turtle, etc. Off and on, she had enjoyed a game where I held her up to the mobile and asked, "Do you want the orange rabbit?"

"No!"

"The black seal?"

"No!"

We would go through them until she picked the red bear. (It was always the red bear. Perhaps she had initially picked it at random — which is to say, I couldn't figure out the reason — and then repeated it according to the previously established principle, that if the fun ain't broke, don't fix it.) Sometimes I would say something like, "Do you want the orange turtle?" and she would laugh — oh, you card! — and say, "The turtle isn't orange!"

So a significant number of her synapses were devoted to color-animal combinations. Why a blue dog instead of a green dog? The blue animal on her mobile, a shark, was theoretically the scariest one, but this particular shark happened to be very friendly. Perhaps she had hit on blue because it sounded like "two," and "two" had been her principal epithet for dogs ever since the park incident. But as I thought more about it, I remembered that blue did have a frightening connotation for her. She was afraid of the blue water you sometimes find in public toilets. (When I was a kid, the most innocuous novelty could seem sinister to me. In a curious coincidence, I can vividly remember the blue milk we were given without explanation one day in elementary school as part of some half-baked Great Society social experiment. That milk terrified me. It was a warning that all bets were off. As far as I knew, my beloved teacher might now have forty-two teeth and be a cannibal.)

As for the closet, kids are always scared of closets. It's not just that they're dark but that they're fake rooms. My humid four-year-old imagination, in which a lingering adualism allowed me to confuse my own breathing with that of the world, sensed some living thing lurking behind every closed door or just beyond the jamb of an open one, but with doors into real rooms there was always the chance that the creature was one of my parents. I knew damn well my parents weren't in the closet, so that only left monsters. (Allowing myself to imagine my parents in the closet was, if anything, scarier.)

So, fine. We had a blue dog in the closet. But why wasn't it barking, which was the first thing Madeleine had feared about dogs? I puzzled over this "ha!" There was nothing like that in any of her books. It occurred to me that a panting dog was saying ha-ha-ha, and one of Pamela's myriad tickling games with Madeleine was to announce she was going to give her a doggy kiss and descend on her neck, chuffing. But the connection seemed farfetched.

A few nights later, Madeleine told Pamela that she was worried about the pigs that would come into the house and bite her toes and say "Ha!" in the closets.

Now I had more to chew on. The toe-biting didn't surprise me: Madeleine still occasionally said, "A long time ago, a chicken bit my foot." ("Pecked," we cavilled.) As that incident was now more than six months old, I had begun to wonder if it might remain with her always as her earliest memory, and perhaps would be the last thing she would think of, in 2080, as she died. The memory had recently been reinforced because Madeleine and I had been throwing wild grapes through the wire to the chickens in their newly fixed run. Madeleine had been thrilled but a little alarmed, and she betrayed her unease by calling up the formula related to her fear of dogs, although she said it in a happy tone: "Chickens jump up!" In fact, they were not jumping up, but they *were* rushing madly at the grapes and pecking, and wasn't it really all the same?

I spent a minute or two wondering why it was pigs that might bite her toes. We had no books on pigs, and she had never seen a pig. Then I realized: pigs and toes! Pamela and I played This Little Piggy with her toes all the time. She loved the game, but it had its dark side for her, in this case not so much the sublimated fear that we might actually wrench off one of her toes as we tweaked it, but her pity for three of the five pigs: the one that couldn't go to market, the one that didn't get any roast beef, and the one that cried "Wee wee wee" all the way home. She had burst into tears the first couple of times, and afterward directed that no toe or pig could be sad. Since then, my text had run something like: "This little piggy went to market. This little piggy stayed home, but that was OK, because she wanted to stay home. This little piggy had roast beef. This little piggy had none, but that was all right, too, because he doesn't like roast beef and is perfectly happy with a cheese sandwich. And this little piggy laughed and skipped and jumped and generally had a great time all the way home." So perhaps her sense of something dangerous in the little-piggy game (the slough of sadness around which we tiptoed) had lingered inside her, mated with chickens and vacuum cleaners, and reemerged as the danger of pigs biting her toes.

This brought me back to the "ha!," which Pamela and I still couldn't figure out. Most puzzling was our impression that Madeleine genuinely thought she was hearing something, because she would mention these fears after suddenly breaking off what she was doing.

One night, when Madeleine was asleep and I was upstairs in the study, Pamela was reading in the silent house. The heat came on, as it had been doing for the past couple of weeks in these cool fall evenings. Through one of the hot-air registers Pamela caught the low growl of the gas jets lighting down in the furnace: "Wwwha!"

When she told me, I thought of Madeleine's ability to hear an airplane in the middle of town, or to follow a fly with her eyes as it caromed around a room. This, perhaps, was what it was like to have no foreground and background. Nothing yet had been judged insignificant and banished from her awareness. Her world was bright and flat, like a stained-glass window in which the line around a fly was as thick and black as the one around an angel.

We explained the heating system to Madeleine, and she stopped worrying about the "ha." But animals continued to haunt her.

"Imthinkingabout a donkey bothering me in bed," she said next. Pamela discovered the source of this one, too. We had been reading a Christmas book called *The Carolers*, and in the illustration for "Away in a Manger," Joseph had dark hair and a beard like me, and Mary, crouching, looked quite short, like Pamela. Madeleine knew that the baby in the hay was named Jesus, but surely he was just a prefigurement of the Baby, herself. (Just as, for me and my sister, Fred and Wilma Flintstone had manifestly been rough sketches for our portly, large-headed father and slim, pointy-nosed mother.) In the illustration in *The Carolers*, Pamela and I faced forward, seemingly oblivious of the three donkeys behind us, who with ambiguous intent craned their heads over a rough balustrade very much like Madeleine's crib railing. And in fact, the song even mentioned a crib, one of the few words Madeleine would have understood.

On another night, it was goats. I think the scenario kept changing because, although her fear was real and urgent, she was getting no information from us, or from her books, about its object. Nothing we had read to her so far alluded to this problem. Working in a vacuum, all she knew was that *something* was out there, planning to do *something* to her.

During this period, purely by coincidence, we found an old copy of *Bedtime for Frances* in Pamela's parents' basement, and brought it home. It burst on Madeleine like a revelation. Frances, a badger, did not want to go to bed, but her parents forced her to. She didn't want them to leave her alone in her room, but they did. She started to think about tigers. She thought she saw a tiger in the corner of her room, and went out to tell her parents. They didn't take her fears seriously, and sent her back. Then she saw a giant, and went out again. Her parents sent her back again. A few other things occurred, and a more or less happy ending was achieved, but for Madeleine these were all secondary. She had immediately grasped the core text: tiger, giant, corner.

Closets promptly disappeared from Madeleine's scenarios. She decided the most likely corner for the spawning of tigers and giants was underneath the stereo table in the living room, a shadowy space largely obscured by the end of the couch. Feeling as though I were enacting a scene from *Night of the Living Dead*, I barricaded the corner by pushing her dollhouse under the front of the table. "There! That should hold!" I said, resisting the temptation to mime nailing it into place. But of course it didn't hold. After a couple of days' respite, the dollhouse had shrunk enough in Madeleine's estimation that she barely took it into account.

"To the tiger in the zoo, Madeline just said, 'Pooh pooh,' " I tried quoting, but she didn't much like *Madeline* (in which, instead of almost drowning, her doppelgänger almost dies of appendicitis), and anyway that tiger was safely in the zoo, in a cage, not prowling around at night in the old house covered with vines.

In our thrice-daily readings of *Bedtime for Frances,* I chirped through the sighting of the tiger, then slowed down, deepening my voice for hypnotic effect, when I reached this passage:

"Did he bite you?" said Father.
"No," said Frances.
"Did he scratch you?" said Mother.
"No," said Frances.
"Then he is a friendly tiger," said Father. "He will not hurt you."

I reaccelerated to 78 rpm until I was past the giant, then slowed again, honeying these words: "There was no giant. It was just the chair and her dressing gown."

Madeleine found both these ideas reassuring and often asked me to repeat them, or solemnly stated them herself. But her worries would reemerge. Since she still felt suspense on the twentieth reading of a book, then Frances's giant, after many times being a bathrobe, could always *this* time turn out to be a real giant. How much more possible, then, was the giant in Madeleine's room, which she hadn't yet seen and determined to be a bathrobe even once?

I tried pointing out that the word "giant" didn't necessarily mean something scary, anyway; it just meant something big. You could talk about a giant tomato, for example. Since I was taller than average, you could even, in a way, call me a giant. Madeleine was somewhat taken with this idea, and deduced that she must then be "a daughter giant." She stomped around in boots for a while to get a feeling for gianthood.

All of Pamela's and my clever ideas worked fine as games, but none of them really touched on her fear, because none of them took it seriously. It was fatuous to think I could dispel the million-year-old fear of the predator by talking about the literal definition of the word "giant." And it couldn't have been comforting to her to think that when the tiger did appear and came slinking toward her, Pamela and I would be saying, "It's all in your imagination, dear," or as it dragged her away I'd call after, "Perhaps it's a friendly tiger!" For this primal fear, we had a primal responsibility, which was to protect her.

"Look," I said one day, when for some reason the ratiocinative blinkers were briefly off my eyes, "if a tiger came in here, I'd give it a karate chop." I mimed the blow, then the animal running stricken from the house.

Madeleine danced. "Do it again!"

"If a tiger came in here," I growled, getting a little carried away, "I'd do this —" I grabbed it by the throat and squeezed. My arms trembled from the effort of crushing its windpipe. I slowly leaned over as the beast's knees gave way, then straightened to gaze down at it on the floor. One sorry-assed tiger.

"Do it again!"

❧ 4 ❧

AT THE liquor store, Madeleine had been holding up her two index fingers and beaming "I'm two!" and the charmed cashier had been laughing and chirping "She's so cute" when Madeleine decided to change the subject and sang out, "Daddy has a penis!" The cashier continued to smile, saying nothing. Either she assumed she had misheard or she was quietly memorizing my face. I paid and left.

It had been some months since Madeleine had learned the words "boy," "girl," "man," and "woman," and now she was in the process of tackling the next level of classification: male and female. She had recently mastered urinating in the potty, and Pamela's and my ritualized ecstasy over this event had raised the status of pee. This, in turn, may have provoked new interest in penises, both because their name made them practically synonymous with pee and because they, unlike Madeleine's apparatus, visibly produced the stuff. Theodore was so enraptured by the sight of his little pecker peeing that, whenever his diaper came off, he ran a few feet away from his mother and tried to spritz a few drops on the floor, his whole torso vibrating with the effort. After witnessing this performance a few times, Madeleine pointed out that Theodore and I both had a penis, whereas she and Pamela did not.

She seemed to understand my explanation that boys grew into men and girls grew into women, and that what distinguished the sexes was the possession of a penis or a vagina. When I quizzed her, she correctly inferred the genitalia of various people we knew. But she didn't seem much interested in "ginas," while penises gradually took on a comic and mildly scandalous coloration. Occasionally now as I stepped out of the shower she would murmur "Daddy's penis" and turn away, snickering. Since neither Pamela nor I had ever showed embarrassment on the subject, I briefly wondered if there might be something inherently silly about penises, but took refuge in the theory that the taboo derived from pee, which Madeleine had long known was "dirty."

My confidence that she understood gender was rattled as she began saying, whenever she needed me to lift something heavy for her, "When I a big man [I'll be able to do it]!" This seemed to be her only instance of confusion, however, and I wondered if the word "big" was throwing her off. "Big," she well knew from our daily exclamations, was what she was getting, but as an epithet she often heard it yoked with "man" (on the theme of Daddy-as-giant) and never with "woman." (As it happened, none of our female friends or relatives were large.) "Big man" might have been a syntactical unit to her, bigman, the thing that bigkids of either gender grew into.

In any case, the phrase "when I a big man" did clearly suggest another dawning awareness: that of change. One day she would be able to carry the milk jug to the table. One day she would be allowed to use the sharp knife. The future! This was the first indication that she had some conscious image of it beyond the next few hours.

For me, the most intriguing mystery about Madeleine was her sense of time. She said "last night" when referring to things she remembered, and "tomorrow" when referring to things she expected, so she did have some sense of time stretching in two different directions away from her, but the relative distances were vague. "Last night," on rare occasions, meant last night, but usually it meant five minutes or an hour ago. "A long time ago" had initially been reserved for the twin cornerstones of her consciousness, laid when time began: the chicken that bit her foot ("Pecked!") and the two dogs that jumped up ("One!"). But now she also used the phrase to indicate things that had happened one or more days previously, apparently having decided that "last night" didn't stretch back that far: "A long time ago, I said, 'Aahh! I don't want my diapers on!' "

Actually, yesterday. The original "aahh!" had been prolonged and earsplitting, while this knowing reference to it was brief and earsplitting. Madeleine began frequently to refer back to crying episodes, and the time lag shortened to a few minutes. She had discovered that she could use time and memory to step away from her emotions and examine them. She called up her previous self — screaming her head off, unable to listen to any appeal — and standing next to this inconsolable dervish, became her interpreter, her liaison to the world of adult reason. "Why I crying?" she would ask with genuine curiosity, and I might say, "You didn't want to leave Katha's house." "Why we go?" "We had to go because . . ." Her mood during these post-trauma sessions was always one of intense relief, as the storm was taken out of the hands of malignant and unfathomable gods and shown to be the natural consequence of two colliding fronts: her understandable desire, my reasonable inability to satisfy said desire.

She began to take the same approach to happy moments. In

the first instance I remember, I was holding her in one arm while breaking ice on the kitchen counter with a heavy metal spoon. The ice sometimes shot off the counter and streaked away across the floor, and the sight of this inanimate object being disobedient, running away like a girl whose diapers needed changing, made Madeleine shout with laughter. A minute later she informed me, "I yaff! 'Ha ha ha!' " and the tinkling, jokey sound of her imitation laughter made me laugh as well. The technique allowed her not only to view her amusement from outside (why had she laughed?) but also to extend it a little into the long, flat stretches of non-laughter, non-ice-breaking, that her developing sense of time enabled her to glimpse all around the isolated, ecstatic peaks of her life. Here were the beginnings of both self-consciousness (she was a girl who laughed) and nostalgia (remember when we broke ice and laughed?). Here were two more layers, like refractive filters, over her perceptions; two more steps toward sophistication, away from freshness. (Years into the future she cannot see, one of the layers she will probably add will be regret at the loss of this freshness, even though, after all, it's the freshness of idiocy.)

A long time ago, she was a little baby. She looked at old pictures of herself and handled old clothes that she remembered wearing but that were now too small. We measured her against the door frame, and two months later did it again, and she was more than an inch taller. "Look how big I'm are!"

A long time ago, Wolf licked her in the face and she cried. She didn't remember that, but she remembered looking at the photographs of it.

A long time ago, she had no hair. Now she twirled it until a knot came off on her finger, and she handed it to me, laughing, "That's not hair. That's fuzz!" (I had asked the grandmothers if any of my or Pamela's siblings had ever twirled their hair, and they had said no, none.)

A long time ago, a chicken bit her foot.

A long time ago, two dogs jumped up on her.

Last night Ti-ti hit her, and she cried "Aahh!" Why did Ti-ti hit her?

A long time ago, she rode a bus and a man gave her John the Rhino.

A long time ago, she rode the merry-go-round.

Last night we ate at the Chinese buffet.

Last night we had breakfast.

A long time ago, we measured her against the door frame.

Now she would hold up one of her shoes and ask me where it came from. "From Woolworth's," I would say. "And before that" — I would look at the label — "from China." And her sock? "Since it's cotton, perhaps from the Carolinas." We would find China and the Carolinas on our globe. Places where the past dwelled.

Inevitably, one day she asked, "Where Maya from?"

In other words, what had happened before the chicken pecked her foot? Going backward, how small did she get? Why, since she could remember the chicken, the dogs, the merry-go-round, the buffet, why couldn't she remember anything before the chicken?

"You came from Mama's tummy," I said. I couldn't discern anything in her face. What did she understand? That all of our pretend Madeleine-eating referred back to a real swallowing of her?

Not understanding it myself, I had unthinkingly coughed up the clichéd response, but it wasn't the answer to her question. In a way, she came from the Carolinas, too, since my father had been born there. She also came from Alabama, New York, and California. Or she came from England, Russia, France, Hungary, and Scotland. Or she precipitated out of blind luck, the winner of a spermatozoan lottery, designed by a DNA Virginia reel. Or "she" arose, shimmering and insubstantial, from a trillion neural connections, a mirage of mathematics. "Where did you come from, baby dear?" as the George MacDonald poem asks. *"Out of the everywhere into the here."*

And as though I had answered that question, Madeleine went on. She threw out her arms and asked, "Where all this from?" She said it, I thought, with a tinge of exasperation. What unreasonable place was this that demanded such a question?

"Do you mean the house? The world?"

"The world."

I had a load of diapers to wash, so I only said, "That's a big question."

Madeleine spoke much less of the future. She knew it existed, but could hardly visualize it. The only concrete images she could fit into that expectant void involved the things that she as a big girl (or a big man) would be able to do, since these were simple extrapolations from the things she saw Pamela and me doing. When she was a big man, she would wash her own diapers.

That was where Maya was going: toward largeness and competence. But she didn't ask where other things were going. She knew that socks and shoes wore out and were thrown away, or grew too small and disappeared. (Did they shrink to nothing in the future, as she shrank to nothing in the past?) And the world? And her parents? As I said, she didn't ask.

One morning in midwinter, I was with her in the kitchen when she happened to glance up at the Arcimboldo print high on the wall. I could see it happen in her face: the breaking off of thought, the brief incredulity, the flood of excitement. "Mister —!" she began.

I held her up to the portrait, as I hadn't done for more than a year. "Zucchini-Nose," I said.

"Zucchini-Nose!" she repeated, remembering. The last time

we had done it, she couldn't talk. We named all four faces, and she remembered them all. Did she have any idea that this memory was earlier than the chicken and the dogs? By the time her foot was pecked, she was speaking, and her memory of the incident was continually renewed in her retelling of it. She said it was "a long time ago," but that was just an adopted phrase. She had kept the memories close by her, bringing them forward. In her excitement over the vegetable men that day, she didn't cheerfully tell me it was "a long time ago," but I thought I saw in her face the scalp-prickling discovery of the deep well, the first abashed inkling of the real stretch of time: that was a *long, long time ago.*

∾ 5 ∾

TO BACKTRACK a little: since Madeleine still had virtually no concrete expectations of the future, holidays were not anticipated. They swept over her, appearing on her horizon the morning she woke to them and sailing off the edge of the world as she fell asleep that night. To her, "next year" was not even terra incognita. Her map didn't extend that far.

So Halloween, for a week or two, was the felt board with its witch and ghost and a jack-o'-lantern that she drew the face for and I carved. With mismatched eyes on the same side of a nose that looked like an ax wound, it was suitably unsettling, but we didn't tell her that. The only impressions left by the day itself were the exciting sight of Matt, Amy, and Rachel in costume on our front porch and the red lollipop Madeleine got from a neighboring house, her first experience of pure, worthless sugar, which she at once recognized as the plug that precisely fit the hole in her life.

Thanksgiving arrived and decamped with even less fanfare: a bunch of people came over, and Madeleine, Katha, and Theodore bounced on the couch.

Christmas, in the weeks running up to it, took on a much greater importance, but here, too, it wouldn't be accurate to say that Madeleine anticipated it. I don't think she quite realized that an actual day called Christmas was approaching. Instead, she loved the Christmas books and Advent activities for their own sakes.

Since she didn't yet care much about presents per se, or understand either the Christian or the pagan consolations of the winter solstice, the attraction was largely based on two coincidences. The first arose out of her increasing delight at the daily proofs that Pamela and I were not masters of the universe. Her ears were evidently tuned to the sound of me dropping something or stubbing my toe (both frequent occurrences), because even if she was two rooms away she would immediately call out, "What Daddy did?" She wasn't concerned for me, but fascinated by the spectacle of a parent screwing up. Her oppressive sense of dualism, Madeleine on one side and the rest of the universe ganged up on the other, was yielding to a more pleasing vision of multilateralism. My will, like hers, could be in conflict with the world's. If I was that hapless, perhaps she really could grow into someone like me.

And it wasn't just fuh fies I didn't know, in case she had any lingering doubt that that problem might have had something to do with her pronunciation. No, on any given day, I might think that the rubber dish gloves were hanging up, when in fact they were on the kitchen counter; that the juice she already had in her bottle was orange, when in fact it was apple. We held many merry colloquies that went like this:

M: What did you think?

I: I thought it was the right shoe, but it turned out to be the left shoe.

M (*thrilled*): And what did you think?

I: I thought it was the right shoe, but no, by gum, it was the left shoe.

M (*thrilled*): And what did you think?

I: I thought it was the right shoe, but darned if I wasn't one hundred percent incorrect on that one; it was the left shoe.

M (*thrilled*): And what did you think?

Et cetera.

A favorite book during this period was *The Carrot Seed*, in which a little boy planted the eponymous item and was told, first by his mother, then by his father, then by his big brother, and finally, for good measure, by all three together, that nothing would come up. The little boy ignored them all, and after a few weeks of watering and weeding he pulled up a carrot the size of a bazooka. I read out the parents' warnings ("I'm afraid it won't come up") in a voice of calm condescension, and the big brother's terser comment with an open sneer. The rumbling of the ground that preceded the upspurting fountain of carrot top was perhaps also the sound of those insufferably smug convictions collapsing into rubble. The Carl stories had already hinted that parents didn't know everything, but this was the first book to make them look positively foolish, and Madeleine was requesting it a dozen times a day.

Here, perhaps, was her first lesson in dramatic irony. After the initial reading, she knew the carrot would come up, but the parents and the brother did not. Here came the father again, like a clock cuckoo, popping his head into the frame, his patriarchal pipe stuck between his teeth, and saying the same assured, dumb-ass thing. Madeleine would snicker, the way she did at my penis. Daddy's penis, Daddy's pomposities. Wrong again!

But why wait for chance to provide such pleasures in real life? By making a slight adjustment to one of her conversational templates — the one setting up an opposition between true and not true — Madeleine could savor whole strings of clueless comments from me. "Ask me," she would command, climbing onto her kitty car, " 'Are you getting off Baby-bye?' "

"Are you getting off Baby-bye?"

"No, I'm getting *on* Baby-bye. Now ask me, 'Are you getting on Baby-bye?' "

"Are you getting on Baby-bye?"

"No, I'm getting *off* Baby-bye."

Et cetera.

To return to Christmas: as it happened, a book Pamela bought for Advent dovetailed with Madeleine's Jacobin interest in kid rule. *The Carolers* opened on five small, outlandishly dressed children walking through a forest, led by the smallest child of all, a girl, who was holding up a long staff with a star affixed to the top. Entering a hamlet and calling the villagers to worship with "O Come, All Ye Faithful," they made the rounds of the houses. For each house, the book first showed the carolers out in the snow, singing to the lighted windows, and then moved inside, where the families were pictured turning toward the sound in excitement, rising from their chairs to answer the call. Eventually the entire village was out in the snow singing together, and on the endpapers the five carolers were heading off again, through the starlit forest toward another hamlet.

The shamanistic quality of the strange children as they brought joy and wonder to closeted adults was only one of the book's attractions. The songs were another. Madeleine deeply loved singing, as nearly all children do (for reasons I've already touched on), but the songs Pamela and I usually sang had been tainted by her dislike of going to bed. Here was a whole fresh batch that was not bed-related but book-related, and with a speed that took me aback, Madeleine learned them all. Then, as if more encouragement were needed, one day when Madeleine and I were singing "We Wish You a Merry Christmas," I forgot one of the lines, and as I paused, vacantly mumbling "um um," Madeleine supplied the words. *"Thank* you!" I hymned, and sent her into a transport of dancing, jumping ecstasy. The real, unscripted thing! For weeks afterward we replayed this scene (now scripted, but shining with reflected light) scores of times.

A third attraction, obviously, was the story that the carols collectively told. This was Madeleine's first exposure to the tale of a kid hailed by angelic hosts and lit by his own personal star, a kid before whom shepherds kneeled and kings kowtowed. Personally an unbeliever, but believing belief to be personal, I explained to Madeleine that some people thought this child was very important, that his birth was extremely good news. But we had often told her similar things about herself. Didn't the moon follow her in the car as loyally as the star shined on Jesus? Didn't I sometimes sing "Who's That Girl?" to her while she lay on the changing pad, as the villagers sang "What Child Is This?" to the baby in the crèche? Another indication that she identified with baby Jesus was that she asked where he came from, as she had done for herself but for no other child in any book.

For the entire winter, then, *The Carolers* took up residence at the center of Madeleine's world, and Christmas became important to her because of the book, rather than vice versa. She wanted a staff like the one the little girl held, so we taped a paper star to the end of a yardstick and sang the carols as she led us around and around our circle of rooms. She kept looking up. Now she, too, had her personal star.

Several paragraphs back, I mentioned *two* coincidences that made Christmas attractive to Madeleine. The second arose out of her persistent fear of intruders. Imagining herself a daughter giant, or me the bane of a tiger's existence, helped for the moment, but the anxiety always returned. Even when she wasn't voicing them, her fears were there, just below the surface. Every time I paused while carrying her or talking to her, to look off in some direction — say, to check if a light in the next room had been turned off — she would ask, "What Daddy looking?" with an unmistakable edge, her hand going up to twirl her hair. Did I see a tiger? (You can tell me, Doc . . .) And in a way, she was reading me correctly. I was tensing at the thought of my own "intruder," the sneaky light itself, which might switch on behind my back if I didn't fix it hard enough with my gaze.

The one thing Madeleine knew for certain was that something was getting into the house. *Bedtime for Frances* tried to argue that it was really bathrobes, and I was obviously seeing something in the corner and lying about it. Nobody was being honest with her. The single exception was Clement Clarke Moore, who in *The Night Before Christmas* openly conceded the point. Yes, at night, while you slept, a stranger entered the house. But — surprise! He was friendly! He left gifts!

The story about the visit from Saint Nicholas did not supplant Madeleine's fear of tigers, but as an attractive alternate scenario, she dwelled on it. Now when she built her cardboard-block houses she always placed a cylinder on top, which was the chimney for Santa to come down. The post-and-lintel structure below then became, as is possible in dreams, both the whole house and an immense fireplace. In the latter incarnation, it was the magic doorway at last, the one she had been searching for at the food co-op and the bakery, through which would arrive unimaginable wonder. Not presents but pure approval, infinite newness, endless and unsurfeiting fulfillment.

Christmas became a continent on her mental map that she

explored daily. All evergreen trees became Christmas trees. She and Pamela made ornaments and baked gingerbread cookies, just like the family on the page illustrating "O Little Town of Bethlehem." Pamela drew and cut out a cardboard Santa that Madeleine could drop into the chimneys of her block houses. A special Christmas stocking arrived from Grandma Graydon, and in the absence of a real fireplace, she hung it on drawer knobs and rocking-horse ears.

In Madeleine's view all of this *was* Christmas, as repeatable as our readings of *The Carolers* and *The Night Before Christmas*. Pamela's and my efforts to help in the joint make-believe grew more strenuous. We went out and cut a tree — a real tree! — and brought it into the house and decorated it. Then we apparently decided to mount an elaborate reenactment of *The Carolers*. We and Madeleine and some friends would *pretend to be carolers ourselves!* The friends came over, I got out a trumpet, which was much like the one in the book that one of the daddies played, Madeleine gripped her yardstick with the paper star on top, and out we trooped. And although this could have been an early lesson to Madeleine that things in real life aren't as ideal as they are in children's books — there was a freezing rain, and no snow on the ground, and many of the houses were dark, and no one came out and joined us — I don't think she saw it that way. This was make-believe, after all. She could imagine the snow and the hearty welcome of the homeowners perfectly well.

If this was indeed her understanding, it helps explain the lack of extra excitement she brought to Christmas Eve. She hung her stocking on a rocking-horse ear, as she had done many times before. We suggested a new variation: she could leave out a cookie and glass of sherry for Santa, and a carrot for his reindeer. "He's coming tonight!" we said, and she nodded. Of course he was.

When she woke in the morning, we asked, "Do you remember what day it is?"

A blank look. Tuesday? September?

"It's Christmas!"

OK . . .

"Look!"

She looked first at us, then followed our pointing fingers. She gaped. The stockings were full. Presents lay under the tree. This Christmas game was getting to be *very* elaborate.

~ 6 ~

MADELEINE got an easel for Christmas, and tempera paints in white, blue, yellow, and red. We made a solution of each color and set them out for her, but she happened to begin with yellow, and after that she only wanted to use yellow. I made suns and bananas while she brushed out a brilliant blotch, passing and repassing until the paper was soaked and yellow dripped on the floor. How about red? I suggested. Or we could make a blue —

But she only wanted yellow. For days it was only yellow, and when I finally got her to try red, it was only red. She had also been given Play-Doh, and these colors were not to be trifled with, either. Katha's mother knew how to make a Play-Doh face by forming a lump and arranging on it tiny balls (for eye whites, pupils, nostrils, surprised mouth) and then flattening it face-down against the table. Madeleine was impressed but refused to try it herself, and later asked me to separate the colors again. She wanted me to make babies, all pink. This monochrome rule was partly my fault, I recognized. When she had first opened the

Play-Doh I had thoughtlessly blabbed something about trying not to mix the colors too much because otherwise they would all turn brown. But clearly there was a facet of Madeleine's personality that caused her to take these comments so much to heart, and to clutch them in the face of my subsequent backpedaling. Which I suppose only shifted the blame from my comments to my genes, since I had been that way as a kid, too (as Pamela had not been).

Madeleine's and my restraint, our hanging back, came out of our wariness. Anything new automatically triggered caution, so Madeleine went slowly, testing the ice inch by inch. But there was also a savoring quality to this mincing of experience. Thirty years ago, I had always watched my brother and sister open their stocking presents before touching mine, not because I wanted to trick them into envying me (although I think they did just that, when, surrounded by torn paper and the toys that couldn't quite live up to their expectations, they saw me whip out my pristine stash, still all promise), but because I enjoyed seeing what they got and I enjoyed even more seeing what I got, and I wanted my delight to build. I also wanted to stave off the letdown at the end. For days Madeleine and I had worked in glistening lemon yellow, basking in its anti-winter warmth. When it grew dull, the first swath of cherry red felt like a second Christmas morning.

Parceling out her pleasures wasn't Madeleine's only technique for surviving this impoverished season. "I never seen this before!" she would sing out happily as she handled something she had in fact seen several times before. She had heard us use the phrase and had taken a shine to it because of her fascination with our admissions of ignorance. Now she discovered what we all do sooner or later — that saying something, anything, about yourself makes it at least partly true. The vessel is formed, and emotion slops into it. For the period during which she daily announced, on her changing pad, that she had never before seen the Chinese quilt hanging next to her, the words made the green lizards or the red squiggly beasts come into focus, and she fingered them with a real air of surprise, as though she had never properly appreciated them, as perhaps she had not.

More momentous than novelty in her surroundings was novelty in herself — the future Madeleine, the emerging big girl — which she seemed to greet with a similar mixture of excitement and caution. Her growth had become a frequent theme. "Look how long my legs are!" she would shout, pointing down to her toes, as the penciled lines on the door frame crept up and the age at which Pamela and I estimated she would shoot past her mother went down. "You're *strong*," she would enthuse whenever I lifted something large, an echo of all the times we said it to her. In a campus parking lot she strode away from me, out onto the pavement, torso plumped like a courting quail (big girl!) when someone nearby started a motorcycle and she spun on her heel and dove for my pant leg. She had reliably peed in the potty for some weeks, and now she insisted on moving up to a child's seat on the regular toilet. One evening she announced that she didn't want to wear a diaper at night. "As soon as you wake up with a dry diaper," we said. The following morning, it was dry. Madeleine did a victory lap.

But like so many children who find themselves on the brink of abandoning this most conspicuous sign of infanthood, she hesitated. Since pee had never seemed quite real to her, it was easy to give up to the toilet's silencing maw. But poop was another thing. I've already touched on its importance to her ego, both as the object of Pamela's and my laborious devotions and as a stand-in for musk, an attention-getting stink that made every room Madeleine's own. Now as she sensed the approaching end, this importance was magnified, a development I would not have thought possible.

Fecal production among Madeleine's dolls was already virtually round-the-clock, so there was little room for improvement there. But what about underexploited areas such as, say, Christmas carols? Madeleine started singing, "O Come, All Ye Poop" and "Jingle Poop." What about Valentines? Madeleine's preferred salutation that year was "Happy Valentine! Poop and pee!" What about dinner table gossip? "Ti-ti poops," she would toss out as an opener. And just in case there were any aspects of the subject she had not yet thought of, her grandmother sent her a book entitled *Everyone Poops*. Now we could talk about pellety rabbit poop and cream-pie cow poop, semi-liquid hippopotamus poop, sand-grain insect poop, and cyclopean elephant poop.

A sure-fire way for Madeleine to get us onto the subject was to announce, "I need to poop!" and watch us scramble to set her on the toilet. She could perch there while we asked eagerly how it was going, and she could reply that she was working on it, and in the meantime would we read her a magazine? This was a ruse from heaven, getting us to drop whatever we were doing in favor of reading from her latest issue of *Ladybug* and conducting probing chats about shit. Best of all, no matter how many times she tricked us (she never actually produced anything during these sessions), we seemed determined not to wise up.

By contrast, we always knew she was serious when instead of heading for the toilet she demanded a diaper. "Wouldn't you like to try —?"

No. A minute after the diaper was on, she was done. But that was only the beginning, because, in another development, she no longer submitted peacefully to a diaper change. Lacking a temporal sense of sufficient scope, she could express her long-term anxiety about giving up poop only in the short term. This poop, this time: she would not be moved. And incidentally, she discovered that when she really fought it we could not change her, at least not with any of that dignity which signaled our superiority. Red-faced and shit-smeared at the end, we were on her level. At home, we returned to the infuriating tactic of ignoring her until her desire for company overcame her Will to Power, but at friends' houses she had us where she wanted us. We couldn't let it go too long because it was stinking up someone else's house, and if she pooped shortly before we had to leave (which, not coincidentally, she began to do regularly), we were faced with the prospect of her falling asleep in the car and getting a rash, not to mention making the car unbearable. Evenings at friends' houses, then, became the setting for our fights, as Madeleine poured all of her justifiable need for self-assertion and self-possession into holding on to the damn shit in her diaper. "No!" she would run away, cackling, and we'd call after her, "Five minutes!" "One more minute!" "We mean it!" Unlike the confrontations over her car seat, which had involved only power and not personal integrity, these fights Madeleine usually took all the way, until Pamela was holding her down at one end and I the other, and she was howling like a cat being declawed.

There were large issues here that had to be mulled over, accommodated. She had always done this best with the aid of a story in a book, whose existence in sacred time — Will was always falling, always being comforted — served to remove the dilemma from the personal realm and elevate it into a principle: *this is how life is.* We had no book about fighting over a diaper change, but now that she was scribbling with markers and paintbrushes and asking us to join her, she knew that Pamela and I could draw recognizable figures. Thus began a five-month period during which she asked each of us to draw dozens of pictures showing various stages of the götterdämmerung of Madeleine's world: the child with diaper and sneaky smile, as yet undiscovered, stink lines rising (a pictorial convention Madeleine appreciated immediately, perhaps because it seemed to enhance the child's presence, like solar rays); the child again, still stinking, and the parent leaning down with an admonitory forefinger, saying "You *have* to have your diaper changed!"; and the child *in medias res*, held down, wailing, the parent scowling, the inner sanctum with its awful secret laid open to view.

Madeleine's emotions in contemplating Will's fall and redemption were simple: sympathy, fear, reassurance. But the diaper pictures called up something more complicated. Here, parents were involved, and Madeleine had a strong urge to adopt the parental point of view. Far from feeling sorry for the poopy kid, she *wanted* her to be forced, and she laughed ungenerously as we drew her wailing. The rule of law! That's all those toddlers understand! This was the wretched condition to which she wanted to see Theodore reduced after he hit her. But beneath the rejoicing was hesitancy, a persistent confusion. This sinner was herself, after all. She was both law and chaos, the one chastising the other. Stop me before I poop again.

Although poop, with its associated taboos, was a special case, Madeleine expressed ambivalence about all aspects of growing up. The attractive part was obvious. Entirely on her own she invented a game she called Savior Wolf in which, sitting with me (or Pamela) on the bed, she would push me over onto my back. I would lie there waving my arms pitifully and mewling "Help! Help!" until she bent down to cup my shoulder, cooing that she was my savior wolf, and help me back up, all the while applying consoling hugs and kisses. Then she would knock me over again. As a delicious dream of empowerment, the game was a logical elaboration of her pretense that I didn't know something she knew, or had a wrong idea and needed correction. (The curious name derived, I think, partly from *Madeline's Rescue*, in which the rescuer is a dog — because of "Wolf dog," the words were confused in Madeleine's mind — and partly from all those "Christ the Savior"'s in her beloved Christmas carols. Also, her favorite stuffed animal at the time was the mama wolf with the birthable cubs, because we had recently told Madeleine that another baby was growing inside Pamela.)

Savior Wolf soon gave way to other parent-servicing games of the sort many young children play. Madeleine thought up a scenario in which I needed eggs, and she had them. The bathroom was the chicken coop, and she was the chicken. I would knock on the door and ask for eggs, and she would count some out for me, informing me as she handed them over whether they were black eggs (coffee eggs) or blue eggs (blueberry) or green eggs (the accompaniment to green ham). She thus in a single game could pretend to help me, play with numbers and colors, and embody, yet again, a creature that she slightly feared.

While the allure of these set pieces was clear, they also provoked a dim anxiety. "Don't take my eggs all gone!" she tremblingly warned in the latter game. Why was it so important? Well, if she had no more eggs, I wouldn't need her anymore, and these scenarios implied that she didn't need me. She thrilled to the idea of her growing independence, but where, after all, did independence lead?

"Look how long my legs are!" Yes, and look how far it was — on our globe, in our atlas, in the plastic puzzle United States, in our annual car trips — to Boston and Washington, D.C., where her two sets of grandparents lived. Madeleine's slowly deepening acceptance that the bald baby in all those album photos really was her brought with it, like a shadow, the haunting hazy idea that those other babies in old black-and-white shots really were me and Pamela, that we really had been children, that we had grown up and — yes, apparently, one was forced to conclude — moved far away from our parents, whom we hardly ever saw.

So in between her helper fantasies, Madeleine played another sort of game. She was a little frog (derived from leapfrog, which she had seen in *Aunt Nina and Her Nephews and Nieces*) crouched on the forest floor. I was supposed to saunter by and say, "Look, Mama, a little frog! Can I keep it?" and Pamela was supposed to reply, "Only if you take good care of it." "I will, I will!" And we would bundle the amphibian home, exclaiming all the way how lucky for us that we had found it because we had no children of our own, and now we could devote all our etc., etc. Or she would hide in a collapsed cardboard box (the very same, now pummeled into submission, through whose flaps months ago she had burst out, to the sound of our delight) with the toes of one foot sticking out. Again I was supposed to amble by and cry, "What's this? A horse? A jeep? A little kid?" and on "kid" she would leap out and I'd shout ecstatically, "I've always wanted a little kid! Can I bring you home?" etc., etc.

It was interesting to see how she could take old play patterns and, by means of a slight adjustment, significantly change their emotional import. The original bursting-through-the-flap game (itself an elaboration of peekaboo) was a reassurance about her: she was wonderful and we loved her. By combining it with the oblivious-parent game (I ambled by ignorantly, even somewhat fatuously, not knowing, as she did, that she was there), it became a reassurance about *me:* though neither all-powerful nor all-knowing, my instincts were right, and I would care for her if given half a chance. This new version also introduced the elements of time and change. I was transformed from a stranger into a parent, a far more comforting progression than the one hovering at the edge of her awareness, the real one, which went the other way.

All these thoughts and feelings on the ramifications of the passage of time required a better concrete sense of time itself and a bigger vocabulary. She was working on that. "I want to hold this for a few whiles," she would say, or "I want to hold this for a few hours." When she counted, I would point out that those were seconds going by. Minutes were defined in terms of eggs: four minutes was a soft-boiled egg, ten a hard-boiled egg. Fifteen minutes was a trip into town. Half an hour was one bath. Four hours was the time between lunch and dinner, and a day was the time between darknesses.

Madeleine and I would look together at a calendar. We were here, I would point. Tomorrow was here. A week from today was here. The whole page was a month. Did she remember what month it was? No? February. And next month would be . . .

"Mowch."

"Exactly."

Madeleine's great incentive for learning these longer time units was so that she could look forward in more detail, with greater discernment, to the reopening of the park merry-go-round. All winter she had been arranging her stuffed animals around the edge of the oval rug in the living room and ordering me to sit on one critter while she straddled another. "Ding ding ding!" she would shout, at which point I was supposed to start singing what she called "the runky a-dunky tune," which was in fact "American Post," one of the melodies frequently heard on the real merry-go-round's wheezy calliope recording. While I sang, we would hop around the oval, holding furry animals to our crotches. Every time I went down on all fours — to pick up crumbs under the table, say, or rinse out the bathtub — she would climb on top of me and shout "Ding ding ding!" and I was supposed to sing "American Post" while undulating my lower back. When I sat on the couch she would cling to my knee and shout "Ding ding ding!" whereupon I had to sing "American Post" while lifting her repeatedly with my leg, a practice that had resulted in a more or less constant ache in the tendons of my groin.

She hadn't been able to anticipate Christmas because she had no way of picturing it, not having remembered it from the previous year. But she could vividly recall the merry-go-round, and I think true, breathless anticipation, the first paling of the present in the bright light of future promise, was born here, in this winter, while she hopped around the oval rug and sat with me looking at the calendar. By the middle of March she had learned the months and the milestones in each that were steps toward the blessed day. At the end of March came Pamela's birthday. At the beginning of April was Easter. Then came May Day. By mid-May we would have tulips. And toward the end of May was the Memorial Day weekend ("Here," I pointed), and on the Friday before that weekend was — ding ding ding! — the opening of the park merry-go-round.

Once she had that nailed down, we could venture further. After May came June, toward the end of which Conor or Cora would be born. In July was America's birthday. In August was my birthday. And in September, Madeleine would turn . . . ?

"Three!"

Exactly.

From counting seconds to counting years, we were laying down the rudiments of the grid, the net, with which Madeleine could catch time. One day (she could see it right on the calendar) she would be three years old . . .

Unimaginable, really. Out there somewhere hung the merry-go-round, and spring, and adulthood. It was hard just to remember tomorrow, when we would go to Theodore's house.

At least now, at night, contemplating aging, twirling her hair, she didn't have to sleep alone. On a December trip to California we had all had to share a bed, and it had been so comfortable and easy that when we returned home we couldn't bear to force Madeleine back into the crib. Finally, we simply did what felt right. I read to Madeleine as she lay happily between us, and when I switched to the adult reading she slipped quietly away. She would not have remembered it, but this was a return to her first weeks and months, when she fell asleep in my arms as I talked and talked. The future could wait.

∾ 7 ∾

THEODORE still couldn't talk much, so his occasional hitting and biting continued. Madeleine would cry and get back at him later, verbally. "Ti-ti eats his diapers!" she might tell us. She spread these rumors with the snicker I was familiar with from our readings of *The Carrot Seed.* Daddy's pomposities, Ti-ti's perversions.

She still said Theodore was her best friend, along with Katha, but as is the case with most young children, Madeleine was poignantly powerless when it came to the selection of her friends. She saw Theodore and Katha frequently because Pamela and I were friends with their parents. While we exercised choice, relaxing with people who made us feel comfortable, the children warily coexisted, bartering like members of neighboring tribes that spoke different dialects and were only barely at peace with each other. It was no wonder that superordinate rules of conduct were a continual necessity.

Katha was a very bright, verbal girl, three months older than Madeleine, odd and notably unhappy. She always spoke in a drawling whine, as though on the verge of tears. She referred to herself in the third person. Her most frequent utterances were "She doesn't want to!" and "She doesn't want that!" She often ended her visits draped over the back of our couch, bawling, not wanting to stay, not wanting to go, not wanting anything, not wanting nothing.

It wasn't a question of being spoiled. Pamela and I wondered if Katha might have a mild form of autism. Whatever the cause, life seemed to be genuinely, deeply difficult for her. During one period of several weeks she would wail a protest if anyone called her Katha. Her name wasn't Katha, it was Skadiddlehoffer. Then it wasn't Skadiddlehoffer, but Abelard. Then it wasn't Abelard, but Liverwurst. Finally she decided it wasn't any of these, but some other name which, unfortunately for all of us, she refused to divulge. When she felt like it, she could vehemently contradict everything you said, from "Let's go this way" to "The sky is blue," for hours at a time.

Whenever she got hold of a marker she immediately started drawing on her face. In another child I might have found this merely interesting (lots of kids love face paint), but in Katha it seemed disturbing, as though she were trying to disfigure herself or cross herself out, like a mistake. She never spoke directly to other children when, say, they had something she wanted, but appealed to her mother to deal with them. Other children were machines whose buttons and dials she couldn't be expected to understand. If a child spoke to her, she would again turn to her mother, not to reply, nor to comment on the substance of the child's remark, but to ask, "Why does she say that?" or "Why is she speaking to her [i.e., Katha]?"

For some reason, Madeleine was an exception, and when Katha was in a good enough mood the two girls could play together better than Madeleine ever could with Theodore. But often she wasn't in a good enough mood, and at those times, if Madeleine proposed that they do something together, Katha would say "She doesn't want to" and retreat to a different room.

Madeleine, for her part, was fascinated by Katha. For one thing, she had to mull over this phenomenon of rejection. Too young to analyze it, she could only replay it, striving through brute familiarity to make it acceptable. Among her dolls, Kristen had the name closest to Katha's, and Hans was Madeleine's alter ego, so now it was not unusual to find Kristen enjoying in regal solitude the cardboard bucket-swing we had made and hung from the ceiling, while Hans lay sprawled on the floor. "Hans wants to ride with Kristen in the swing, but she won't let him," Madeleine would explain, cheerfully enough. "He's crying." If Hans tried to climb in, Kristen would push him out. With the arrival of the first spring weather, I set up Madeleine's apple-tree swing, and she would ride in it with both dolls, holding Kristen to her chest with her right hand and Hans by his neck with the left. But she kept her left arm straight out to the side, so Hans wasn't actually in the swing. If this were an airplane, he'd be out on the wing. Thus did Madeleine try to bridge, within her own body, the conflict that Katha had raised. Kristen got her solitude, and Hans got his ride.

But there was a more fundamental reason for Madeleine's fascination with Katha. Adults were incapable of making Katha do what she didn't want to do. She was a magnificent boulder in the muttering stream of adult efficiency and complacency. Generally obedient herself, with a tender conscience, Madeleine got a huge vicarious thrill out of witnessing disobedience and remorselessness. Here was the road not taken, the kind of child she daily chose, perhaps ineluctably but surely with some regret, not to be. Her favorite poem, by a wide margin, was A. A. Milne's "Rice Pudding," in which a little girl named Mary Jane brought an entire household to a standstill with her tantrum over being served one rice pudding too many. Katha was Mary Jane come gloriously to life.

Madeleine started telling us stories about Ka-ka, an invisible girl of her own age, who put her feet on the table, climbed on the bed with her shoes on, and committed various other crimes inspired by current issues at home. Ka-ka had a black diaper bag (as opposed to Madeleine's green one) and black dancing shoes. She had purple hair (Katha's was red) and wore a purple cape. It's easy to discern here the psychological origins of the widespread folk belief in a doppelgänger, or an evil twin. (By contrast, I have no idea where Madeleine picked up such conventional signs of evil as black accouterments and a cape.) Surely we all, on some level, mourn our stillborn alternate selves, as with every personal decision we increasingly define who we are. These are the real ghosts that haunt us. Theodore was somewhat interesting as a barbarian, as chaos. But Katha, articulate and aware yet deeply disruptive, was entrancing, a Mephistophelean character. She was anti-order, anti-Madeleine.

With the coming of spring, Madeleine's casual contacts widened. She had by now more or less mastered the pronunciation of her own difficult name, and would approach groups of kids at the playground and announce, "My name is Madeyinn!" Usually they ignored her, or stared at her blankly. Aware of her difficulty with *l*'s, she assumed this blankness came from incomprehension, and she would repeat as clearly as she could, "Ma-duh-*yinn!*"

Since she had never been in daycare, her social being had been formed almost entirely by adults, and the first thing adults asked her was "What's your name?" She had thus come to consider the revelation of her name as a crucial part of establishing her existence, her claim on attention. Just as Kristen shared characteristics with other dolls but was uniquely Kristen, "Madeleine" was the only word that could express the totality of Madeleine, all the many things she knew about herself: she was two, she was a girl, she was getting bigger, she was getting hair, she was blond, she was blue-eyed, she was good, she feared giants, she was a daughter giant, she was going to be a big sister.

So at the playground she announced herself, not just to the children but, in a way, to the cosmos, and all she got was silence. The lack of response was baffling. "What's your name?" she would finally ask one of the kids, and even then she would only occasionally get an answer. The children would return to what they were doing, and Madeleine would wander back to me. She had not had the opportunity to learn the proper child-to-child technique, which as far as I could tell was to hang back and observe the game in progress, then join it by submitting to its conventions. Names only came later, when or if the joint activity made them necessary.

Still largely powerless in the practical world of errands and schedules, Madeleine had always been absolute dictator of games and make-believe. She would tell me what to say, and I would say it. She would spend several minutes at the park fussily arranging Pamela, me, and Hans on a four-seat bouncing contraption, speaking to us in a nurse's tone of jocose cajolery and with a characteristic gesture, her hand patting the air down, patting us into place. She would climb up on the last seat only after she was confident we could no longer screw up her exquisite arrangements.

Theodore didn't obey her because he didn't understand, and Katha because she was Disobedience, but most children, Madeleine had assumed, would behave like her parents and do whatever she wanted. I tried to explain why her peers were different, but it only sank in with the experience of a few rebuffs. Her response was to turn whenever possible toward bigger kids, who in addition to being sources of that heavenly manna, mature approval, tended, at least temporarily, to be more indulgent of her.

I had once assumed that the world of make-believe would be a freer place than the real world. I had thought its attraction lay in its possibilities, its lack of rules. Perhaps that would be true later, but for now, for Madeleine, its appeal was the opposite. In her make-believe the rules might be fanciful, but once formulated, they were enforced with far more consistency than were those of the real, inattentive world. It seemed to me a common need at this age. The children I saw were just beginning to play together, rather than merely next to each other, but they were not so much collaborating as struggling for imaginative dominance. The constant question was, Whose rules would rule?

Perhaps I should say "girls" here, rather than "children." When Madeleine played with Katha, or with a girl named Sarah whom she occasionally saw in a play group, I might hear them arguing, "No, that doesn't go there!" and the like, but if they fought over the rules, at least they all believed in rules. They spoke the same language. Boys, on the other hand, even when they could speak, gabbled in some outlandish tongue. A typical scene occurred one day in play group among Madeleine, Sarah, and a boy named Chris. The three of them were eating together at a table, and Sarah said to Madeleine, with the slightly desperate edge I was familiar with, the fear that the sky was about to fall, "Madeleine, you have to sit closer!" (Otherwise food might drop on the floor! or in your lap!!) Sarah didn't know that Madeleine had already voiced this concern to Pamela, who had pointed out that her chair couldn't be moved closer because a table leg was in the way. So Madeleine answered, with equal passion, "I can't, see?" and gestured toward the leg. Sarah craned her neck to look, and saw. Ah. She and Madeleine traded a glance of complete understanding.

Chair Placement Rule #1: All personnel shall sit close enough to the table so that food will not drop to the lap or the floor.

First Corollary to Chair Placement Rule #1: If a table leg intrudes, personnel shall not be deemed accountable for food dropping to the lap or the floor, so long as said personnel have positioned themselves as close to the table as humanly possible.

CHRIS: Madeleine, sit closer!

SARAH: It's all right, she doesn't have to, her chair won't go in!

CHRIS (*smiling*): Madeleine, sit closer!
Chris doesn't care about the rule, and probably hasn't even been listening. He has merely divined, for the twentieth time today, a way to bother Sarah.

SARAH (*aggrieved*): She can't. Her chair can't go in!
Note how Sarah continues to treat Chris as a rational human being. This is a mistake.

CHRIS (*gleeful*): Madeleine, sit closer!
Chris seems to understand Sarah better than Sarah understands Chris.

SARAH (*frantic*): The table leg is in the way!

CHRIS (*ecstatic*): Madeleine, sit closer!
Curtain.

∾ 8 ∾

MADELEINE'S WORDS had lost much of their sympathetic magic. She had pulled them out of the muck of the material and hollowed them out for lightness, because she needed them for a language, and a language is a flying machine, a workaday contraption for transporting loads of meaning wherever necessary. The magic remained, but it was becoming airy, a mix of music and sinuous meaning.

"I would have been," Madeleine sometimes said. "I might have been." "He could be going." "Maybe he could have been there." She wasn't discriminating between these moods and tenses, but trying to get the rhythm right, coaxing the machine off the ground.

I'm are. As in, "Look how big I'm are!" The rhythm here was right. And while she was strutting, why not declare her existence twice?

Eventually. A great word, a sentence-filler that really filled the sentence. "We're eventually going to get there." "Are we eventually there now?"

Positively. Another long-legged beauty. "I'm not positively sure."

Very, really, major. Likable no-brainers, these could be safely added almost anywhere. "Major big." "Very very big." "Really really really big."

Actually. A good word for setting up the oppositions she loved and sounding wisely discriminating at the same time: "I want grape juice. Actually, I don't want grape juice, I want apple juice."

Chopped liver. That's what I was, now that the new baby was only a few weeks away and Madeleine was clinging presciently to Pamela.

Right now. Or, more precisely, RIGHT NOW. As a spondee, it was a brilliant intensifier, two feet dug in at the end of every demand. It was particularly helpful in stressing the new status of chopped liver, as in:

"I like Mama so much! I want she come back."
"She will come back."
"I want she come back RIGHT NOW!"

Whole wide world. The music here was magical: "whole" with its full, round sound, "wide" opening her mouth wide, and "world" bringing it back to roundness, back toward the first word, so that the phrase went round and round. "This is the best apple crisp in the whole wide world!"

How about this. As Madeleine's adoptions grew to three words and beyond, Pamela and I started to hear our own voices echoing back at us. I tended (apparently) to say "How about this" as a way of introducing a new proposal when Madeleine and I were disagreeing about where to go or what she could eat. She began to use the phrase for the same reason, and adopted a hurried tone, dripping reasonableness, that I could only assume was mine.

Here's a compromise. Pamela's version of *How about this.* It wasn't long before Madeleine was cutting us off with both phrases, end to end, separated by a slight pause and a gulp, which gave her time to think. Generally, her compromise consisted of a proposal that we do what she wanted to do, while whatever it was we were talking about could be done at some later, unspecified date.

The whole point is. In the sense that. There are two reasons. That was me, the pedant, perfectly. When Madeleine wanted me to get out her color markers and I, with my lazy butt deep in the couch, said "Where are they?" she replied tartly, "You have to look. That's the whole point of finding something."

Tops never stops. I had the annoying habit of absent-mindedly singing jingles off and on for hours at a stretch. Chirpily piped into the ozone-enriched air of our local Tops supermarket was one that went, "Tops never stops / Saving you more." Madeleine, mothlike, was attracted to the rhyme, and she came to misconstrue the name of the store: "Are we going to Tops never stops?"

A fair amountain. This was her own invention. The mistake was unintentional, but perhaps on some level she had made the inspired connection. At the end of a meal she would contentedly say, "I ate a fair amountain of that."

Prettiful. Another graceful coinage. "Look! A prettiful butterfly!"

Compiano. As in, the large musical instrument in our living room. It was obviously related to the computer, since I played on both, and both had keys, and spilling juice on either one was a disaster.

Attempted. How we all, deep down, would prefer to deal with our temptations: "I'm attempted to eat ice cream."

The only trouble is. The only problem is. The two phrases Madeleine least wanted to hear, and heard often. Naturally, she adopted them with a vengeance.

M: Say "I want to go to the park."
I: I want to go to the park.
M: Theonlytroubleis, people are coming over.
I: Well then, of course, I understand that we can't go.
M: No, say "I want to go to the park RIGHT NOW."
I: I want to go to the park RIGHT NOW.
M: Theonlytroubleis, we don't have time.
I: OK, I'll just amuse myself here.
M: No, you cry.
I: Waah.
M: Say "I want to go to the park."

This could go on for quite some time. Occasionally, Madeleine would allow me to go to the park (or play with the blocks, or get french fries), and I loved her expression at these times: her eyebrows arched, her eyes wide, her mouth drawn down into a flat wide smile full of lower teeth. She seemed so thrilled to be able to tell me that yes, this time I could do what I wanted, and she wallowed in my hammy gratitude.

That's amazing! Self-sufficient phrases like this one had a special appeal, offering a moment of rest amid the hard work of grappling with new words and constructions. They popped out so easily, with the correct rhythm built right in. (Again I think of the formulae of oral epics, with which the singer could vamp while trying to remember if his hero died here or two hundred lines later.)

That's not an option. That's the best I can do. That's what makes it so good! This time, for sure! The last was an echo of an echo, reverberating across decades, since I had picked the phrase up as a kid from Bullwinkle, who says it to Rocky just before trying yet again to pull a rabbit out of his hat.

Then there were the set stimuli that provoked set responses. If I lifted Madeleine to my shoulders she would shout, "We'll touch the sky!," a quote from a book we had bought her about big-sisterhood, *Big Like Me* (leading us to hope that the bald-faced propaganda in the book might similarly sink deep). After being allowed a spoonful of honey, she would channel Pamela: "Put it away so I don't think about it." Whenever she helped me load the new washing machine she would point out, "The other washer lid lifted up this way, but this new lid lifts the other way." These were the current, sophisticated versions of an infant's imitation of parental facial expressions. Or to look at it from the other side, they were the crude precursors of an adult's musty collection of observational tics and bedrock attitudes. They provided not only a moment of rest, but also the comfort of their repetition. By commenting on the washer lid in precisely the same words time after time, Madeleine invoked all the times at once and thus made each instance of our joint machine-loading feel more significant, her words more true.

Now that she was growing comfortable with words, she could indulge in wordplay. "I want poos-juice!" she would call out. Or she might helpfully explain to us, "I say 'bot.' It's really bottle, but I say 'bot.'" Pamela sometimes called her Maya Papaya, so she began calling me Daddy pa-Daddy. Then this bled into other *d* words, so that, for example, she started asking me, "What are you doing pa-doing?" A game she invented in which I put down a little scrap of paper and then she squashed it with her own scrap was called Tick Tock, then Dick Dock, then Tick Tock pa-Dick Dock, and lastly Micky Dicky Dock. (Clearly, in her mind, Mickey Mouse was running up that clock.)

She was becoming interested in the relationship between letters and their corresponding sounds, and would pound out random strings on the computer and ask me to pronounce them. "What begins with 'truck'?" she would ask. "What begins with 'ball'?" When Pamela and I didn't want her to know we were talking about her pacifier (which she still called her ta-ta), we referred to it as the tee-ay-tee-ay. It wasn't long, naturally, before Madeleine started asking, "Where's my tee-ay-tee-ay?" Similarly, she knew that Aich-ay-enn-ess was another name for Hans. One night she happened to glance at the bottom of a teacup and excitedly asked, "Does that say 'Madeleine'?" It said "Made in China."

Wordplay's practical use was naming. Madeleine's lifting of names from songs had lasted only a week or so, to be followed by a less original period during which the name of, say, a rabbit in a book would be assigned to all her own rabbits. But now she could truly strike out on her own. The chubby ursine fellow at the end of her toothbrush, she announced one evening, was Koombie the Bear, a name perhaps modeled on her bathtub Gumby but with those all-important authorial adjustments. She had a "voice," favoring names that ended in the classic diminutive long *e*, even though neither she nor any of her friends were addressed that way. One of her rabbits became Kiki, and another, Funky. A new doll from her grandmother was Pooie. Over a period of weeks, she named several of her letter-string files on the computer, coming up with Boobee, then Koobee, then Googee-Pookee, then Kookee-Boobee-Googee-Boobee-Poobee. Madeleine told us one morning that her tummy was named "Bow-wa," and when we asked her what my tummy's name was, she said "Trashcan." Our impressed laughter pleased her, but also raised the stakes, so that when we asked her to name Pamela's tummy, she darted her eyes here and there, abashed into blankness, and fell back at last on an old standby: "Poopy one." "Poopy," of course, had been the hidden theme, the missing counterpoint, of many of her enigmatic variations.

Now that she could express herself reasonably well, she could disrupt my too tidy observations of her with imponderables, those thoughts that I would never have inferred because I didn't understand them. She came to me holding a toothbrush in each ear, with the brush ends sticking out horizontally, and said, "I'll be a girl."

"Putting toothbrushes in your ears makes you a girl?" I asked.

"If I don't have toothbrushes in my ears, I look like a boy."

When she drew or painted squiggles, she could tell me, after the fact, what they made her think of. A black lump embedded in a storm of black swirls was Noah's Ark. A tall orange squiggle caught in roomy loops of blue was an orange kangaroo in a blue cage (and once she had pointed it out, I could see the kangaroo quite clearly: the sloped head with ears set high and back, the two long springer feet and balancing tail). Various gray-blue and aqua splotches of watercolor paint were "a rooster and a seal under the covers, dreaming of a dinosaur on a leash." (I had less success visualizing this one.)

She could describe to us, for the first time, a dream: "There was a dark blue car driving in the grass, and it tipped over. It was kind of scary." She was relieved by the color, since our car was red.

She could hold up her end of fairly sophisticated conversations:

I (*holding a spatula*): Dinner's ready.
M: I want a pretend one of these.
I: You want a spatula?
M: I want a pretend spatula.
I: You can have a real spatula.
M: But I want a *pretend* spatula.
I: Do you have a pretend spatula somewhere?
M: Yes.
  We search through her play spoons, cups, and plates, but find no spatula.
I: Why don't I give you a real spatula, and you can pretend it's a pretend spatula? It'll be a pretend pretend spatula.
M: But I want a *real* pretend spatula.

She could make up her own songs, like the one she crooned from the back seat of our car at the end of a morning of errands:

> Where are you going, cars?
> Where are you going, cars?
> We're going to Washington!
> We're going on a long trip!
>
> Where are you going?
> I'm going home.
> I'm going home.
> I'm going home.
> But first I'm going to Matt's house,
> To swing on the swing.
>
> Where are you going cars, cars, cars?
> Are you going to Tops never stops?

And she could occasionally create toddler poetry, the lovely images that resulted, like Dadaist creations, from the yoking together of bits floating randomly and democratically around in her head, as when, deep into summer and the merry-go-round season, Pamela was pretending to eat Madeleine in our yard, and Madeleine kept saying "I'm back!" and Pamela kept responding "You can't be, I just ate you." Finally, Pamela challenged her: "How do you know you're Madeleine?"

Madeleine answered, "I know I'm Madeleine, because I have music inside me that makes me go around, and I always come back to you."

∾ 9 ∾

BACK IN late winter, Madeleine had been in the bathtub, telling Pamela a story:

She (Madeleine) went to the park and swam. Then she went to another park and swam. She didn't sink ("go *blblblbl*") because something was helping her float. Then she got out of the water, and a bug helped her dry off. Then she went to Old McDonald's, and there was a pool there, too. So she was in the pool. It wasn't very deep. She was eating oranges. The juice was getting in the water, but the juice didn't mind. The oranges would have minded, but they weren't getting in the water.

Madeleine loved her baths, but with an undercurrent of anxiety. Her toys had to be out before the plug was pulled, because otherwise the drain would swallow them. The fictional Madeline had gone *blblblbl* in the river Seine. In another book Madeleine had been reading lately, *The Sorcerer's Apprentice*, water rose out of a tub and almost drowned everybody, so she now whimpered and pleaded with us to stop when we added more hot water: "Imworriedabout it overflowing!" In her own story, she had to assure herself (via Pamela) that she wasn't sinking, that the pool at McDonald's wasn't deep, that the oranges were safely out of the water.

Why oranges? She had been eating them that evening. Why a bug? That was less obvious, and more interesting. "Something" had kept Madeleine afloat, and in the next instant she thought of the bug, and the bug helped her dry off. The bug was saving her from the water, from sinking, from — well, what? What was the word?

She knew the word, but not from any of her books. Will fell down, the wolf was butted into the water, Angus was nipped, a variety of characters fell asleep, and everyone pooped. But no one died. The rainbow that disappeared, crying, came the closest, but Madeleine had banished that story.

She knew the word, in fact, from bugs. They lay in the window casements and in corners, not moving, dried to husks. She used to say that the flies on the flypaper were sleeping, but that was back at the very beginning of her speech, and who knew what she had meant by "sleeping"? Now she knew that sleeping things woke up, and the bugs on their backs in the corners did not. She knew they did not because we assured her they did not, as we showed her the body of a yellow jacket or a roll-up bug and asked her if she wanted to hold it, and she worried it might spring to life in her hand. It can't, hon, we said. It's dead.

Dead.

She would hold the dead thing in the palm of her hand. It was "little tiny," too. The bugs inspired affection and awe. She wanted to help them, but they were beyond her, beyond everything. They knew something she didn't know. They couldn't be hurt, we said when we vacuumed them up. In a way, they were safe. So instead, the bug in the bathtub story helped Madeleine. From its position of safety and knowledge, it knew how to save her. In a way, it was her guardian spirit. After all, Pamela called Madeleine Love Bug.

Insect companions began to appear in other stories. She told me one day she was a soldier from China: "I came by car. First I went to China and stayed for five minutes, then I came back, and then I went to the North Pole and came back."

"You went all that way by car?" I said, impressed.

"Yes! I was holding a bumblebee in one hand."

While Pamela one evening cut my hair, Madeleine hacked away with a dull pair of scissors at Big Baby's glistening blond strands. There were bumblebees in Big Baby's hair, she informed us, "but they're dead, so they don't mind getting stepped on."

Love, death, bugs. In *Best Friends for Frances,* Frances's little sister Gloria said, in my best pathetic voice, "I wish I had a friend."

"Is she sad?" Madeleine asked, perturbed.

She had apparently mulled this over, seeking a solution. She came up to me one afternoon and brightly demanded, "Daddy, say 'I wish I had a friend.'"

"I wish I had a friend."

Madeleine hopped, brimming over. "I'll give you a friend! I'll give you a ladybug! It can't crawl away because it's dead! It's a *real* dead ladybug!"

In fact, it was a pretend dead ladybug. Madeleine led me to the place on the wall of her room where its tiny invisible corpse was stuck. Gently removing it, she placed it in my palm.

I sobbed in gratitude. A friend!

But as spring came, our relationship with these mortal familiars grew more complicated. Whenever I found a spider in the house I caught it in a glass, and Madeleine, following me outside, would ask, as I pitched it into the grass, "Does the spider like that?" and I would say, "Yes, her food is outside." I didn't save flies, however. I swatted them. Moreover, Madeleine helped me. She pointed them out, or ran after them herself, ineffectually waving the swatter and giggling. When they woke her, like us, early in the morning, she would urge, "Whack it, Daddy," while I traipsed up and down the bed in my underwear. But when, yelping in triumph, I did whack it, she would venture, "The fly doesn't like that?" and I would reply, picking it piecemeal off the swatter netting, "No, honey, the fly doesn't like that."

Her giggle, when she chased the fly, showed her ambivalence. "Don't hit" was one of the fundamental rules, but I hit them, so it must be all right. And yet, they didn't like it. I was putting them beyond hurting, but it certainly looked like I was hurting them.

She had to work on this. That spring, Kaia, the white cat at Theodore's house, disappeared. It went into the woods and never came back, like a toy going down the drain.

"Did Kaia die?" Madeleine asked.

"We don't know," I said. "Maybe."

"Maybe she's living with someone else."

"Maybe."

Madeleine vaguely knew now that first you grew up and then you got old. Grandpas Al and Larry had white hair because they were old. Grandpa Al walked with a cane because his body didn't work so well anymore.

"Do people die?" she asked.

"Yes."

"Will you and Mama die?"

Well. There it was. She had zeroed in on it faster than I had expected. "Everybody eventually dies," I said, reflexively holding off the *d* word with one of those long-legged beauties.

"You and Mama, too?"

"Ye-es. But that would be a long time from now. Very long."

"How long?"

"Longer than you can imagine."

That, of course, was part of the problem. She *couldn't* imagine. The milestones of her future now read: Birth of Conor or Cora, Daddy's Birthday, Madeleine's Birthday, Christmas, Death of Parents.

"Many years away," I said.

She reached as high as she could. "By the time you're twenty?"

"I'm already older than twenty."

This seemed only to alarm her. How old was I, anyway?

I said, "You will be all grown up and you'll have kids before I die. Even when you have kids, I'll still live for many years, many times longer than your whole life so far. Believe me, it's a long, long time away. Way, way far away."

Thus for the first time did I deliberately lie to her, promising certainty where there was none.

I wondered how she pictured our deaths. Would we just stop moving, like the bugs? But the bugs had not inspired her to ask about our own deaths, whereas the disappearance of Kaia had. She had feared, from before she knew what fear was, that we might go away and not come back.

One night when we were ending a visit to some friends, Madeleine turned to their nine-year-old daughter and, perhaps on the subject of leave-taking, said to her in a matter-of-fact tone, "You're ebenchewie going to die."

"What?" the girl asked.

"Eventually," I clarified. "Dead. You."

Throughout that spring and summer, every few days Madeleine would ask me out of the blue, "Who died?"

"Eleanor Roosevelt, she's dead," I usually said.

"Who else?" She wore a cautious smile. This was the way to deal with the subject, to turn it into a game.

"Winston Churchill is dead, too."

"Who else?"

After three or four more names, I often drew a blank for a moment. Like Madeleine when asked to imagine a food for her dolls, I was flooded by my choices, and my neurons shorted. "Oh, yes," I'd say at last. "Plato. He died a *long* time ago."

∾ 10 ∾

MADELEINE became a big sister on July 2.

Pamela's and my propaganda blitz had been three-pronged. *Big Like Me* presented the older sibling as wise mentor, lucky to have a disciple: "Hello Baby, little tiny baby. This is me. I'm going to show you everything." *A Baby Just Like Me* hammered away at the need for patience, as the big sister wondered, month after month, when this useless bundle demanding all her parents' attention would turn into a playmate. *Mom and Dad and I Are Having a Baby!* had assigned itself a more modest task: to prepare the kid for the sight of her mother in pain, yowling, spouting blood, and pushing out a misshapen, glistening creature of uncertain species.

The books probably prepared Madeleine for sisterhood about as well as my pinching Pamela's arm in our birth class had prepared her for her first labor. I always emphasized, as we read them, that the time covered in the first two books was more than a year, which put that future sibling-as-playmate off somewhere between next Christmas and my death. And as for the third book,

Madeleine always asked us to skip the drawing that showed the mother's face in a grimace, the blood pooling out from the place where the Gorgon's head sprouted like a purple cabbage.

Pamela's labor began at around four A.M. and by seven the two midwives were at the house. Knowing that cows, or at least the idea of them, had long been familiar to Madeleine, we told her that Mama would be mooing, and she seemed less upset than intrigued by the long, low moans. As Pamela rocked, Madeleine occasionally sat near her and made a histrionic gesture of stroking her foot sympathetically. As one would expect at this age, the action seemed less a real offering of solace than an expression of Madeleine's need, at this disturbing moment, to be noticed and appreciated for her grown-up solicitude.

My parents had arrived a few days previously to help out, and when the midwives suggested some exercise to urge the labor onward, Pamela and I proposed to Madeleine that she stay with Grandma Peggy and Grandpa Al at the sandbox while we went for a walk. "Sure!" she said, running to Grandma Peggy while we turned toward the road, saying to each other, "So mature! So independent!" As we reached the end of the driveway we heard a cry, and here came Madeleine, bawling, running with that endearing toddler hop, back on her heels, her arms bouncing with the effort of maintaining speed. We decided to cut the husband-and-wife-as-a-team crap and have Pamela walk with one of the midwives while I stayed back with Madeleine. Pamela would be able to focus better on the labor if she was sure Madeleine was happy, and although I was still very much a bowl of faintly steaming chopped liver, the sandbox was pretty new and enthralling, and we patted and dug and made sand cones while Pamela walked two miles.

By noon we were all back in the house, and it was time to push. Grandma Peggy, as planned, unveiled a big new floor puzzle for

Madeleine in the playroom while Pamela kneeled by the living room couch with her elbows in my lap. She gave a couple of trial grunts at the sound of which Madeleine promptly appeared, twirling her hair and chomping on her pacifier with that deadpan heavy-lidded expression I recognized as fright. I smiled at her over Pamela's head, but she didn't see me. With a loud grinding shout, Pamela gave the first big push, and either the shout or the sight of the baby's head popping into view — that page she had never wanted to see — was too much, and Madeleine turned and ran back into the playroom. I expected to hear a siren wail come sailing out, but instead she returned with her grandmother in tow, just in time for the second shout and push. My mother gestured to me a question about leading Madeleine away, but the baby was already born, having shot out so fast that the midwives had been caught by surprise and were now jointly grappling with the greasy body and struggling to shake open towels. Madeleine's fright seemed to be giving way to a glimmer of interest.

In the confusion, one of the midwives had mistaken the other's pinkie for a penis, and for thirty seconds Madeleine had a little brother. But by the time the baby latched on to the breast we knew it was a girl. She sucked avidly and Pamela laughed and the midwives hymned midwiferal praise. I took Madeleine on my lap and we leaned toward the spotlight, penumbral, like the Bethlehem shepherds. Subdued, Madeleine stared. Useless bundle, cynosure, tiny baby, animate doll, pink stork-bitten sucker, future playmate, little sister, interloper, rival. It all had a name now: Cora.

MADELEINE, three months out of diapers, stood on the toy chest and supervised Cora's diaper changes. She would undo the Velcro on the diaper cover and shout the news, to whichever parent was absent, regarding the amount, color, and consistency of Cora's poop. She wanted to hold Cora in her lap on the couch, and we took pictures, praising her big-sisterly gentleness. In those first photos, Madeleine is smiling for the camera, but her eyes have a haunted cast. What has happened? she seems to be thinking. What now?

"Mama!" she would announce toward the end of Cora's nap, striding importantly into the room. "Cora is going 'Aanh!' " She would throw open the bathroom door and pull aside the shower curtain to inform a rapidly cooling Pamela, "Just so you know — Cora's looking for the breast." She assumed Cora wanted a pacifier and kept trying to plug one in her mouth until a cup of sour milk shot out and she leaped back, asking, "What happened?" People came by and wisely brought presents for both girls, and told Madeleine what a good big sister she was, and how lucky, and wasn't she happy?

"Yes," Madeleine said, smiling.

She hugged Cora in the mornings, beaming down on her. Sometimes she hugged too hard. She wanted to carry Cora around like a doll, and our argument that she might drop her little sister didn't seem to impress her as a significant objection. She bounced a red field ball in the room where Cora was sleeping, and wouldn't stop until we took it away. She jiggled Cora gently in her cloth bouncy seat, garnering praise, and every now and then pulled the frame down so hard before releasing it that perhaps I wasn't the only one to imagine the seat acting like a catapult and tossing Cora out the nearest window. She clapped her hands in Cora's face, making her cry, and when we asked her why she was doing it, she smiled and said, "Because I want to!"

Those smiles were all the same. Appeasement gestures ("Take this cup away from me") rather than signals of pleasure, they were wide and almost flat, a hairsbreadth away from the grimace that precedes crying. Before I had had children of my own, I had witnessed parents from time to time gently reasoning with some obnoxious brat, and had inwardly seethed, "What that kid really needs is . . ." Now I saw it differently. Madeleine had lost her place as the sole center of the universe. When I saw her harass Cora, I moved to protect the baby but felt in myself a warm surge of love and sympathy for the aggressor. She needed us. She needed reassurance. The cool observer in me, the clinician, was impressed by the easy power of parental love.

Pamela and I had arranged our work so that she had no commitments for several months, and I none for six weeks. We had agreed ahead of time that I would mainly take care of Cora, so that Madeleine could receive as much attention and reassurance as possible from the parent she had most feared losing. By the end of the first month Madeleine had noticed that Cora, except when she wanted to nurse, didn't seem to prefer Pamela to me. "Cora doesn't call you chopped liver" was how she put it. It took her a day or two to mull over this, after which, on the occasion of a request for me to help her do some leaf rubbings, she made my rehabilitation official: "You're not chopped liver anymore, Daddy." I mock sobbed that I would try to savor this fleeting moment of favor. But of course I was pleased, and not just for myself. Now Madeleine's mixed feelings could be spread between both parents, making it easier for all of us to handle. The interloper liked me, so I couldn't be all bad, so my attention was a better comforter when Cora stole Pamela away for a nursing. (Madeleine herself had stopped nursing when Pamela's pregnancy ruined the taste of her milk, a neat trick nature has for reducing the physical demands on the mother.)

During Pamela's pregnancy, Madeleine had increasingly assumed the role of big sister or parent in her play with her dolls. She had had me construct a cardboard cradle to match the one we had borrowed for the coming baby, and she rocked Hans in it, bringing him a bedtime bottle of water and explaining to me, "Hans is saying, 'I want juice!' but I'm saying, 'No, you can only have water, because you've already brushed your teeth.'" She was, as usual, being so obedient that her wishes and ours were virtually indistinguishable. Through the books we had read with her, we had signaled our desire that she act like a big sister, and she was acting up a storm.

However, as soon as Cora was born, Madeleine's interest in Hans, and all her dolls, declined precipitously. The role of big sister had become too pressing, too charged with ambivalent feelings, to be an attractive game. In real life she soldiered on, instinctive obedience struggling with rational rebelliousness. She had me commemorate her vigilance over the diaper changing in a series of drawings. I've kept one that shows Cora on the changing pad, I engrossed in her rear end, and Madeleine supervising from the toy chest, smiling benignantly and saying (so accepting! so generous!) "I want to hold the baby." But I also remember that Madeleine, even as she continued to insist on witnessing the unveiling of the poop, developed the habit of gagging down into it. It was ritualized, but it was from the heart. She was gagging at the shit, which was becoming more solid and smellier, but also, I think, at the sight of Cora, at the whole thought of her, and at the thought of her own big-sisterhood. Next to the picture I've saved of Cora getting her diaper changed is another that Madeleine demanded: *Madeleine* getting her diaper changed.

That was the core of it, wasn't it? All of Madeleine's ambivalence about growing up had rushed back at the sight of this little creature who so completely and inarguably needed us, who still lived in wholeness, before Cora and not-Cora, before want (Good) and not-want (Evil), before knowledge and responsibility and disobedience and time. Pamela and I really were infallible gods in our relationship with Cora, it was no illusion, we were the breast and the hands to carry her there, we were everything she needed, right on the premises, walking in the garden. Shut outside, looking in, Madeleine felt the yearning at the core of the world's religions: the desire to be a child in the hands of an all-powerful god, a brainless sheep protected by its shepherd, a drop dissolved into the oversoul. Freud named this urge "the oceanic feeling," which in turn calls to mind Xenophon's nostalgic Greeks mounting the last hill of land-locked enemy Armenia and crying in ecstasy, "The sea! The sea!" Madeleine ached to return home, where she would fit so well into not-Madeleine you wouldn't be able to see the cracks.

Shit worship returned. Madeleine sat on a towel, placed a cork or a pacifier at her crotch, pulled the front of the towel up to her stomach, and commanded, "Say 'Did you poop in your diapers?'" Pooping was the ongoing, unignorable process of separating not-Madeleine from Madeleine. By hoarding it in the diaper, one retained an ersatz wholeness. At night she wanted to wear a real diaper, and our reminders of how proud she had been, just four months ago, to sleep without one were to no avail. She told us she would poop in the diaper, and we blanched and cajoled and appealed to some vestige of pride in her age, and she assured us she would only pretend to poop. A day or two later she said she wanted to really do it, and we said, No, pretend, and she said, No, really, and we said, No, pretend, and she said, What she had meant all along was, she would pretend to really do it, and we said, Fine. We discussed it again the next night, and the next, and the string of reallys was getting longer, the admission of pretense more uncertain. Please, we were saying, with what must have been pleasingly frank fear, please don't. Please don't.

She didn't. But her price was another long wallow in coprocentric daydreams and play-acting. Her favorite reenactment, for weeks and weeks, was of the old, nasty scenario: we at the house of friends, and she with shit in her diaper. She would be in costume, with the diaper on. She wanted the game strung out in excruciating detail, beginning with my speech about the fact that we had to go soon, and she had *ten minutes* more, and after ten minutes she would have to get her diaper changed. "Why?" she would ask, and the first time we had played she had fed me my answer, word for word: "Because you'll fall asleep in the car and get a rash."

Did she promise?

"I promise!" she would say, and play at playing for a few seconds. Then: "Say 'You have *five minutes!*'"

I had to go through three minutes and one minute, and she kept promising, and ultimately of course refused. "Then what did you do?" she breathed.

"We held you down."

"Did I like that?"

"No, you didn't."

"What did I say?"

"You cried."

She would want me to really hold her down. And would she really cry? I asked. No.

But it was close.

"I didn't like this the first time around," I complained.

But I submitted, because the game so evidently served needs beyond her mania, reminding her of a blessed time before Cora and displacing the conflict she felt *now* about wanting to shit in her diaper and us not wanting her to. At least this time around I only got pretend shit on my fingers.

One night Madeleine was lying on the living room floor, tired, having had no nap that day, and Pamela was holding Cora in her arms and singing "I Wonder as I Wander." By the end of the song Cora was asleep, and Pamela and I sat wordlessly for a minute, contemplating our two beautiful daughters, the quiet evening, the startling passage of time. Then we sang the song again, together, to Madeleine, and at the end asked, "Do you remember when we used to sing that for you?" Madeleine twirled her hair and said nothing.

We began "I Gave My Love a Cherry," but stopped.

"Are you a little bit sad?" I asked. (This was the phrase she herself used when upset: "I'm alittlebitsad.") She clearly was, but she shook her head and turned over, pushed my hand away, sucked on her pacifier, and twirled on, her eyes distant and half closed.

"Why are you sad, honey?" Pamela asked.

"I don't know," she quavered.

Pamela and I traded a glance. We had not forgotten her dislike of lullabies, back when she had slept in the crib. But that arrangement had ended six months ago. Bedding down now with us, she fell asleep to the sound of reading. She had heard so little singing in the past half year that her sense of pitch had slipped dramatically. And anyway, our singing to Cora didn't seem to bother her.

Pamela tried to put Cora down, but she woke up, so I held her and sang another song until she fell asleep again. Now I was in the armchair with Cora asleep on my shoulder, and Pamela and Madeleine were on the couch looking at a book of poems. One of them was "Hush, Little Baby," and Pamela, endeavoring to figure out where we stood, started singing it. She got about two lines in before Madeleine fell apart.

"Why?" she howled, tears spilling. "Why?" It was a voice of such bleak pain and confusion that I felt tears crowding into my own eyes.

"Do you mean why does it make you sad?" Pamela asked.

"Yes."

"I don't know, honey. Do you know?"

"No."

The next day, I asked Madeleine if she remembered sleeping in the crib, and she said yes.

"What do you remember?"

"I called Mama and Daddy. I stuck my legs out."

That was true. She used to put her legs through the bars as a game and a delaying tactic. "Did you not like sleeping in the crib?"

"No."

"Why not?"

"I was afraid you'd go away."

"Go away?"

"I was afraid you'd get in the car and go away somewhere and leave me alone."

Since she had been much less articulate when she was in the crib, this was the first I'd heard of it. I wondered if it came from *Carl's Masquerade*, in which the parents went off to a party, leaving the baby in her crib for the dog to watch over. Or perhaps it was a reasonable extrapolation from our sneaking out of the room.

"Is that why you don't like us to sing, because it reminds you of when you slept in the crib?"

Madeleine pulled out her pacifier and glanced away from me, squinting. This was the expression she used when she was about to say something she considered mature (and it was interesting how much the flourish of the pacifier-removal looked like similar adult flourishes with pipes or glasses, before similarly self-important pronouncements). "I don't think so," she said.

Neither did I. Perhaps memory of the crib was part of it, but her attitude toward lullabies back then had been impatient and resistant, not sad.

Music, like odors, can unlock not just memories but buried moods, whole past states of being. Pamela and I had sung lullabies to Madeleine every day of her life, and then had stopped — when? — oh, long ago, it must have seemed to her, back when she was what she termed "a little tiny baby." But last night she had been lying down, twirling her hair, and suddenly we were standing over her again and singing one of those old songs, and she had been transported back. It hardly mattered whether her associations of that past existence were good (pre-Cora) or bad (crib), whether she felt nostalgia or trauma or a stew of both. Simply, it was *past,* and it is painful to feel, deep and sharp in your body, the passing of time, the irrecoverability of the past, the death of your past self, and, by implication, the future death of your present self, the treacherous changing and slipping away of bugs and parents and all things.

The "Why?" that Madeleine had demanded of an unanswering world the night before had affected me so strongly because it sounded so bereft, so — I would have said — adult. But the word I had been groping for was, perhaps, human. In front of my eyes, Madeleine was shedding present-tense toddlerhood and becoming a person: ducked in the river, swept onward, clutching reeds that had failed to hold her.

∾ 12 ∾

ZACHARY AND DARIUS were identical twin boys, twelve years old. Madeleine saw them bounce on a trampoline. They became a fixture of our days.

I wasn't allowed to say "Darius and Zachary." That sounded funny. The correct term was "Zachary and Darius." Pamela sometimes referred to them as Daiquiri and Zarius, and that was all right, because it was obviously a joke, an invitation for Madeleine, the guardian of their memory, to laugh and say, "No, it's Zachary and Darius."

They both had long hair tied in ponytails, long faces, prominent front teeth. The only way you could tell them apart was that Zachary wore a headband. Or was it Darius? I never could remember. I would ask Madeleine for the tenth time, and she would tell me it was Zachary (or Darius?) as you might say, wondering a bit at your interlocutor, "This way is up, that way is down." For days Madeleine struggled to attach little plastic barrettes to her short hair, eventually achieving quarter-inch ponytails that looked more like the fuzzy sprigs that stick out of paper curlers. To better approximate the ideal, she proposed to us that we tie each of her hairs to a strand of uncooked spaghetti.

At Madeleine's request, I drew pictures of Zachary and Darius bouncing on the trampoline, one with the regulation headband, one without. I drew pictures of them looking at Madeleine's new swing set and saying in balloons, "Let's play on Madeleine's swing set." I drew them getting on the swings, and I drew them swinging. I drew pictures of our house, and the playroom within the house, and Madeleine's dollhouse in the playroom, and Zachary and Darius playing with the dollhouse, and Madeleine sitting between them. As I markered in that last detail, Madeleine would giggle and start jumping around in overflowing joy. Up in the study, at the computer, she would ask me to write "Zachary" and "Darius" and "Madeleine," and we would print out the sheet and she would carry the three names around with her, talismans of their togetherness.

At first she pretended she was Darius, but then her cousin Andrew came for a visit and she assigned him the role of Darius, and she became Zachary. The spaghetti plan having been vetoed by us, she and Andrew achieved ponytails by wearing tights on their heads with the legs dangling behind. Andrew, six months younger than Madeleine, was thrilled to follow her directions. They bounced on the couch, doing daring Zachary-and-Darius-style seat drops. They shouted their complementary identities at two-minute intervals. After Andrew left, Madeleine dictated a thank-you note to him: "Nice for visiting me. Come next time and play with me more! Next time you'll be three years old. After two is three. After three he's going to be four! After that, he's going to be five. Six. Then seven. Then eight. Then nine. Then ten. Then eleven. Then twelve. That's how old Zachary and Darius are! Thanks for visiting Zachary and Darius."

Yes, sometimes she was the two of them together. I could always tell when the amalgamation had occurred, because she would start saying things like, "We both don't want toast." But most of the time, post-Andrew, she remained Zachary and reassigned the Darius role to her doll Dolphin, who was not a dolphin but a chocolate-colored girl with beads in her hair that perhaps reminded Madeleine of barrettes.

Zachary and Darius helped Madeleine away from the slippery slope of diaper love. She hazarded the opinion that Zachary did not poop in his diapers, and we clamorously backed her up. She would command, "Say 'Did you poop in your diapers?' "

"Did you poop in your diapers?"

"No, I'm much too big. I'm twelve years old. I never, never poop in my diapers!"

In fact, I suspected she imagined that Zachary and Darius, in their perfection, did not defecate at all, since she invariably returned briefly to her own identity when she perched on the toilet. It seemed, in any case, that to be Zachary (or Darius, or both) was the culmination of existence, an idea that Madeleine framed implicitly when she began refusing to count past twelve. She subsequently made the point clear by counting up to that magic number and announcing, "And then you die!"

Madeleine had seen the real Zachary and Darius only once, for perhaps an hour, in the back yard of a friend's house. She had been fascinated but also frightened by the big trampoline they were bouncing on, and probably that had been part of their appeal: they were the geniuses of this strange, dangerous novelty. I held Madeleine up along the edge, and they made the earth move under her feet. They were amiable boys, but she didn't say a word to them, and they barely noticed her. When they disappeared into the house in search of other amusements, she ventured out to the center of the now-still tympanum, glanced around for an audience, and finding none (I didn't count), released to the air the winged words that must have been in her mind for some time: "I'm Madeleine." Her voice was tremulous, wistful. Zachary and Darius were not there, but this was their locus, and surely, on the plane that matters, they heard and welcomed her.

For her their appeal was magnified by their being identical twins, a phenomenon Madeleine had never before encountered in humans. Here was the mirror image that had liked its likeness so much it had stepped through the glass to meet it, making a pair of boys as startlingly symmetric as earrings, as breasts. Zachary bounced while Darius flipped, so you could place them in opposition ("Zachary — bounce! Darius — *not* bounce; Darius — flip!"), and yet they were the resolution of that opposition: they were the *same person*. When Zachary chose not to flip but to bounce, he left behind a stillborn flipping Zachary, and the ghost was right there, flipping, under the name of Darius.

Finally, it was probably no coincidence that Zachary and Darius rose to such high prominence in Madeleine's world only days after Cora was born. Big and brave, at the far edge of allowable age, and repeatedly pictured on either side of her — weren't they substitute parents during these weeks when Madeleine could only wonder where she stood with us?

For months now, I had periodically been the daddy giant and she the daughter giant, a formulation (you will recall) to protect her from the monsters in the dark. Being giants, we would eat those monsters. After Cora's birth, Madeleine altered the scenario. I was still the daddy giant and she was the daughter giant, but now she feared I would eat *her*. She asked it seriously, her voice edgy: "Will you eat me up?" (She was our love bug, and I killed bugs.) This took us back to fundamentals. In the first weeks of her life she had learned laughter by coming to trust that, pretend as I might, I would never *really* eat her. But that had been because she was my baby, and now, evidently, someone else was my baby. Her trust hadn't dissolved, exactly, but it had gotten porous.

Months ago, her dim anxieties about growing up had been expressed through the game in which she pretended to be a little frog that we found outside and took home. Now she aired her worries more openly by dropping the frog stuff and playing it as a little girl.

"Say 'Is that a little girl?' "

"Say 'Are you cold, little girl?' "

"Say 'Can I take you home with me?' "

Significantly, there were now two homes in the game, the one we wanted to bring her to and her own. "First you turn this way, and then that way, and then you go straight for a couple of miles, and that's where I live. It has a long driveway. You might have to walk for a while at the end. It's number 101." That other home had a baby, too, but it was a boy named Conor. In other words, that other home had the baby Madeleine had once looked forward to (worshiper, playmate) rather than the one she actually got (interloper, rival). She had logically decided that this missing, better baby must have been the other one we had frequently mentioned during Pamela's pregnancy.

We were to understand that it was not likely she would want to move in with us. "I used to live here, but I moved out because it was too crowded."

"Too crowded with . . . toys?"

"Yes. I used to play with these toys."

We were to understand that she had other parents now. But those other parents were really no more trustworthy or necessary than we were. "My parents live in that other house, but I'm not going back there."

"Not ever?"

"No. I want to live by myself."

"Won't you go visit your parents?"

"No."

"That will make them sad."

At the thought of this, Madeleine's eyes grew large and misty. "Why?"

"Because they love you."

"Yes, but I don't want to live there." After thinking about this for a moment, she seemed close to crying, and she edged away from the idea. "If you want to play with me, just call me up over there. Dial 101."

"But I thought you weren't going to live over there."

"I might be visiting."

Sometimes the fragility of her independent pose was considerably more obvious, as on the occasion when she was pretending to arrive at our house for a visit. Pamela answered her knock at the playroom door with "Come in!," not understanding that she was supposed to fling open the door and emote extreme joy. After a pause, we heard Madeleine's ragged voice through the panel: "I don't want to come in!" When we opened the door, she told us she was all alone in that other house and would have to go back there and eat her solitary dinner, and the more she said it the more she believed it, until she was hanging melodramatically from the doorknob and wailing over and over, "I have no parents!"

As I've mentioned, she had lost interest in her dolls, even Hans, and it seemed suggestive that she turned her attention instead to masks. What was she, anyway? Did she need human company at all? She became a pig, a dog, a raccoon. One morning she told us she was Matt, and spelled M-A on the refrigerator. Pamela and I helpfully stuttered "T-t-t," and when she added the T, we applauded. She flopped her head and arms around in what seemed to be her usual victory dance, then ran out of the room, buried her face in the couch, and quietly cried. For some time after that, she stood just outside the kitchen door, peering with one eye past the jamb at the MAT on the refrigerator, as though it were something malevolent. We offered to remove it, or to replace it with her name, but she shook her head. She was still upset, and frightened.

When we had applauded, as we often did when she got something right, had we signaled that she really was Matt? Had she accidentally trapped herself outside Madeleine? Or had our applause suggested that, although she was in fact still Madeleine, we *wished* she were Matt, and had momentarily betrayed our feeling that it would be very nice if she just moved out of the house so we could enjoy our baby in peace?

At last, when I suggested leaving MAT up but putting MADE-LEINE underneath, the cloud lifted. Relieved and beaming, she stared at the two names. Perhaps she was simply ready to come out of it. Or perhaps having the two names on the refrigerator at the same time allowed her to make the transfer back into her own identity. "My name is longer," she happily pointed out, as though relieved to be able to stretch her legs again.

She continued to be drawn to tests and games involving her power and its relation to ours, in moods compounded variously of pride, fear, and defiance. Her helper games, like the found-little-girl scenario, had all picked up the element of another house in which she lived in calm and capable independence. She was no longer a chicken selling eggs from our own back yard, but the proprietor of Madeleine's Corner Store, where she lived upstairs in rooms she was happy to describe in detail. While ringing up my purchases she would ask, with a polite show of interest, how things were going at my house.

Since she felt obscurely that Zachary and Darius were exactly the rescuers she needed, they tended to appear in games where *I* desperately wanted help. There were a number of these, and Madeleine would patiently feed me the narrative elements bit by bit ("Say . . .") until, after half a dozen run-throughs, and still elaborating, we would have something like this:

> *I am lying on the couch, under the mistaken impression that I am alone, talking out loud to myself.*
> I: Here I am, lying on the couch, and I need to feed Bob the Rat [a neighbor's pet we once took care of], and it really would be great if I had somebody to help me. Let's see . . .

Maybe a pair of twins. Yes, twins who are twelve years old. That's the ticket! Now, it would be just *perfect* if it was twins named, ohh, I don't know, perhaps Zachary and Darius, and if one had a headband and the other didn't, but they both had ponytails.

I begin to look around.

M: Look out the window first!

I look out the window.

M: Look at the ceiling!

I look at the ceiling.

M: Now look here!

I look and do a triple take. I vibrate my palms in front of my face to suggest my eyeballs popping out: "Boi-oi-oi-oi-oing!!" The catechism begins:

I: Are you twins?

M: Yes!

I: Are you twelve years old?

M: Yes!

I: Are you named Zachary and Darius?

M: Yes!

I: Does one of you wear a headband while the other doesn't, and do you both have ponytails?

M: Yes!!

I: Well, *you're exactly what I wanted!!!*

If her experiments in power were arranged along a spectrum from Helper to Hellion, then standing at about the midpoint was a new version of a game we had played for the past year or so in which Madeleine would say in mock warning, "If you kiss me, I'll kiss you," and Pamela and I would reply in mock horror, "Oh no, not a kiss!" It had always been an uncomplicated game whose fun resided in the absurd proposition that anyone would not want those kisses. But now Madeleine didn't want mock horror from us. She didn't quite want real horror, either, but she wanted real *something*. Real emotion. A touch of panic, perhaps, such as the powerless feel.

Tickling was a good example. When we tickled Madeleine, she both wanted it and didn't want it. The ticklishness itself came out of her helplessness, that edge of not-wanting. She had tried tickling us, and we had writhed appropriately and gone he-he-he, but she had been able to tell that we were faking it. We didn't feel helpless enough. We didn't feel *ambivalent*.

After thinking about this for a while, she came up with a substitute for tickling: licking. It wasn't a perfect solution, because in fact we still weren't ambivalent. We definitely did not want it. But at least our reaction was involuntary, like the laughter she had sparked in us long ago by putting pasta on her head. Now when she said, "If you kiss me, I'll kiss you," or when she came to us with glittering, avid eyes and said, "Let me kiss your hand," we were never sure what we might get. (She was smart enough to kiss us as often as she licked us.) She could sense our uneasiness and our reluctance to appear to reject her affection. The choice was entirely hers whether to relax us or repel us. And when she did lick, she was also, in a hidden way, sticking out her tongue at us, a rejection reflex analogous to the gagging she directed at Cora.

At the Hellion end of the spectrum stood the various transgression games, which like the helper fantasies tended toward wordy scenarios. Once Madeleine and I had constructed one, it would linger for weeks as a set piece she could cue with a word or gesture. For example, when she strode toward the couch with a backward glance of pure wickedness, I was supposed to don obliviousness like a coat of mail and erupt into this: "Gee, I'm so glad I just got the couch cleaned! That cost a lot of money, and I can't afford to do it again. So whatever you do, Madeleine, don't jump on the couch with those filthy muddy disgusting shoes you have on . . . Oh, no!!"

True, it was only a game, but its limits were alluringly vague. If it was all right to bounce on the couch in socks and pretend they were shoes (it was), wouldn't it also be all right to bounce on the couch in clean shoes and pretend they were dirty (it . . . sort of was, as long as the shoes were *very* clean), and then wouldn't it also be all right to bounce on the couch in dirty shoes and only pretend we cared about the couch getting dirty? (No, it wasn't.) But wasn't there something darkly satisfying in the way these games turned into fights, confirming all her worst fears and making her want to stick out her tongue at me and lick me until I ran away so she could finally live in peace by herself and then when I desperately needed someone to help me feed Bob the Rat she wouldn't be there and *wouldn't I be sorry?!*

Sometimes there was no pretense of a game at all, but simple, serious obnoxiousness. Theodore hit, but Madeleine's energies were verbal, so she struck with words. She might begin to talk as Cora was falling asleep, or when Pamela and I needed to discuss something, and she would speak louder and louder and nothing we said could shut her up, and when she ran out of thoughts she just shouted "Blah blah blah." I would tell her to leave the room and she would shout me down, so I would carry her into the playroom and close the door and she'd immediately come out again, still blathering at the top of her lungs.

Sometimes I could see it coming. She would be doing just what we wanted, and we would be telling her what a good girl she was, and I would find it easy to imagine her gorge rising at all this facile praise, this bare minimum of attention that we accorded her as we smugly got what we wanted, and contemplated our good parenting skills, and took her for granted. Here was the muttering stream of adult efficiency, just begging for a Katha-sized boulder.

Splash! Surprise!

And since Katha had shown her the way, Madeleine often *became* Katha when she wanted to cause trouble, effortlessly mimicking her. Pamela and I were deeply startled the first time she opened her mouth and Katha's voice emerged, exact in pitch, whine, and drawl. She even had Katha's body language right, a fastidious curling of the wrist, a coltish prancing away with heels kicked up high behind. It was uncannily like a spiritual posses-sion, the little devil Katha taking over our innocent girl. But of course that was doting parental nonsense. This was a true part of Madeleine, her doppelgänger, the anti-Madeleine, which, as it turned out, did not always have to be stillborn.

Like Zachary and Darius, she was the resolution of opposites. Her long name was even more capacious than she had thought.

∾ 13 ∾

MADELEINE knew the months now. She knew what my late August birthday meant. After haltingly dictating to Pamela a birthday card for me, she sailed fluently into another: "Soon it's Madeleine's birthday! Soon I will be three years old, in Sep-tember!"

Meanwhile, she worked on honing her sense of her place in the world. From "This way — home!" and "That way — *not* home!" and other clarifying oppositions, she was drawn to the general case, the world-halving sword she could carry every-where: the distinction between left and right. With the pacifier in her mouth, her hand behind her head, and her right and left hands correctly identified, she would now have all four corners of the earth covered.

So she practiced daily, asking us to confirm which foot or hand was which, and when she gave us directions to wherever she currently lived there were always heavily stressed references to right turns or left turns. It bothered her that she couldn't always remember the two sides correctly. I suppose we could have given her something like a bracelet as an aid, but it didn't occur to us, so she was forced to find the mnemonic on her own, which she triumphantly did. If she pictured us all in the car, she knew that the driver sat on the left.

She was intrigued by that other set of names for the four corners of the earth: east, west, north, and south. Standing in the living room and pointing, she sometimes got it right, sometimes not. Toward the kitchen was west. Toward the road was east. The road ran north-south. Brian and Susan lived to the south, Matt and company lived to the north. Since right and left always felt the same on her body, it seemed unreasonable to her that the four directions could be anywhere. Worse, not only was left not always east, even the road, which she now felt confident did not move, was not always east, since as soon as we crossed it, it was west.

She knew the number of our house and the name of our road. When we drove to town, we were going southeast. The sun rose in the east, she knew, and by our midmorning treks into town it always came straight through the windshield, blinding her. At least *this* was constant. Theodore lived farther on, south of town. Katha lived directly south of us, but not south of town. When we went to Katha's house, we turned south on our road, but when we went most other places, including Theodore's house, we turned briefly north, to get to the state road. On the way to town we passed the hospital, and then Amity's house. Amity was an eleven-year-old with a big dollhouse. Amity was going to come to Madeleine's birthday party.

New York was a state. Cousin Leah lived in California and Cousin Andrew in Minnesota. Grandma Peggy and Grandpa Al were in Boston, and Grandma Graydon and Grandpa Larry were in Washington, D.C. Madeleine could point to these places on our puzzle map. It took a day in the car to get to Boston or Washington, whereas you flew to California. To find Panama (where Theodore was moving in November), we had to get the globe off the piano. That was a long way away, and we wouldn't be seeing Theodore much anymore. We lived in America and the United States. Panama was in America, but not in the United States. Wolf, the good dog, lived in Washington, like Grandma Graydon and Grandpa Larry, but *his* Washington was over near California.

"It's kind of complicated," Madeleine said cheerfully. This was the phrase she employed when telling herself not to worry about something; it was beyond reasoning, like vowels.

She painted blue splotches on a piece of paper and told us it was a dragon. "You can get a ride. There's a button you can push and it will go up and down. I didn't want it to move away. I only see it a few times. I don't want it to go away or die or something."

She knew cars. By herself, she had learned to distinguish Ford Escorts (our car), Toyota Tercels (Katha's), Honda Civics (Theodore's). At first she had thought that all Toyota Tercels on the road contained a Katha, and she would beg us to follow them as they headed (surely) to some park or playground. Now she would merely maturely note, "That's like Katha's car." Then she would beg us to drive to Katha's house.

She knew she spoke English. She knew Theodore spoke German and his daycare woman, Nadine, spoke French, and a family we were helping to settle spoke Bosnian. She could correctly distinguish German, French, and Bosnian by their sound. She knew Katha spoke in "Katha's voice," and she knew we didn't like it.

She knew how to answer the phone. "Hello?" she would say. "Who is it? Do you want to talk to Mama or Daddy?" When my mother called and said something Madeleine didn't understand, she handed the receiver to me, explaining, "Grandma started to speak in Bosnian and confused up her words."

She had just figured out how to draw herself. Her head was huge, with huge eyes, and her hair was a broad scar of scribbles floating just above the scalp. Her body was tiny, indistinct. "I'm big!" she said, pointing to the big head. Pamela drew a picture of Madeleine in the same style. Madeleine took a look and said, "Where are my feet?" Pamela made them larger, but there wasn't enough room on the page to do anything about the body. Madeleine looked again and complained, "I'm short!"

She knew that couldn't be right. She stood against the kitchen door frame for another measurement.

She knew that Cora, as her little sister, would one day look up to her the way she (Madeleine) looked up to Zachary and Darius, and the way Gloria looked up to Frances in *Best Friends for Frances*. Emitting soft burbles and wet squeaks like a coffee machine, Cora lay in her bouncy chair and watched Madeleine bounce a ball, and Madeleine said, "Cora's watching me because she thinks that whatever I do is interesting."

She knew this placed a certain responsibility on her. When Frances refused to play ball with Gloria, making Gloria cry, Madeleine knew Frances was being mean. Her talk of regressing in peeing and pooping had recently acquired a new angle. "If I peed in my pants, I'd go into a room where nobody could see me and close two doors and lock them."

"Why?"

"Because I wouldn't want anybody to see me, because then they might think it's OK for them to pee in their pants." Heavy's the head that wears the halo.

When Katha hit Cora one day, Madeleine moved, it seemed instinctively, to her defense: "Don't hit my sister!"

In encouraging Madeleine to feel protective of Cora, we were working with the grain. She was the same tender girl who had cried for the fallen Will and the lovelorn Frog, and she generally wanted everyone to be happy. She had started to append jokes to the ends of the letters she dictated to us — "goodbye, banana"; "goodbye, swing set" — because it delighted her to think that she was leaving her correspondents laughing.

I've mentioned the subversive appeal of dramatic irony (as in *The Carrot Seed*, in which the parents thought erroneously that the boy would not be able to grow anything), and Madeleine even had a set phrase now, which she would chortle to me as she turned from a text just as its denizens headed down some wrong path for the umpteenth time: "Ofcourseweknowthat . . ." But in her make-believe she had combined this feeling of secret power with her helper fantasies, and so turned herself into something like a good fairy, or an evangelist, eternally bringing good news. What she alone knew was always something *wonderful* — say, that a candy bar was hidden in her hand — and all she had to do was reveal it to banish the sorrows of whichever doll or stuffed animal she imagined was grieving. The model for this, I think, was wrapping presents, which had thrilled her in recent months. To call out "Don't look, Daddy!" as I passed through the room a few days before a holiday evoked a whole complex of joys: to know something I didn't know; to revel in her own competence with the bright paper and ribbons, the tape and scissors; to think of the great day approaching and the likelihood that she, too, would get a present.

By being a good fairy, Madeleine could underpin her hope for greater fairies who would watch over her as she watched over her animals and (sometimes) her sister. She was not the world, but surely she reflected the world out of which she had precipitated, and it was comforting to imagine that good things lay hidden behind life's frequently troubling façade. Pamela and I were not perfect, nor entirely benevolent, but perfection and benevolence hovered somewhere behind us, shaped for now like Zachary and Darius, as it had once been shaped (and would be again) like Santa Claus.

Good fairies had to be valiant. Protecting Cora from Katha was easy, but what about monsters? Madeleine had us read to her over and over a poem called "I Eat Kids Yum Yum," which showed the way. In it, a girl chased off a monster by standing her ground and shouting back a capitalized variant on the beast's own threatening quatrain:

> I EAT MONSTERS BURP!
> THEY MAKE ME SQUEAL AND SLURP.
> IT'S TIME TO CHOMP AND TAKE A CHEW —
> AND WHAT I'LL CHEW IS YOU!

Our daughter giant now threw around herself the remembered tatters of this magic cloak and strode a step, perhaps two, into darkened rooms, all the braver for clearly being scared. She even tilted at the daddy giant. The damsel in distress, in this scenario, was her own mother. When Pamela and I had an argument, Madeleine apparently could tell from our tones of voice that I tended to browbeat my wife. Valiantly, honorably, she would enter the fray on Pamela's side, always throwing down the same gauntlet: "Mama, you're right! Daddy, you're wrong!" In ten years of marriage, Pamela had never found anything so effective for stopping me in my tracks.

Good fairies also had to be vigilant. Madeleine was acutely attuned to the sound of concern in either Pamela's or my voice. Our telephone conversations with friends in the mildest sorts of crises were carried on against the backdrop of Madeleine's choral "What happened? What happened?" There were also key words or phrases that acted like clarions, calling Madeleine from the next room ("What happened?") even when spoken softly and embedded in running text. One that I used all the time was "Oh no," and I was constantly looking up to find Madeleine standing in the doorway, twirling her hair and demanding explanations that for the most part ranged from a dropped spoon to a smear of jam on the newspaper. Another was "dead": dead end, dead ringer, dead tired. (Ding ding ding!) "Who's dead?"

In this connection, that old difficult word "sad" had gradually assumed tremendous mimetic power. Just hearing the word made Madeleine sad, and pronouncing it herself was worse. She never wanted Pamela to sing "My Favorite Things," a song with no unpleasant crib/lullaby associations, because of the line "when I'm feeling SAD." When we tried one day to read a new book to her, *The Little Engine That Could*, everything went fine until the text conceded that the dolls and toys on the stranded train, unable to attract the help of the big engines rushing by, were SAD. The word might as well have punched Madeleine in the nose: she burst into tears.

Sadness in books hit her the hardest for the same reasons it does most adults: because she could understand that world more or less completely, and her relationship with fictional characters was uncomplicated. But although her response to real events was more muted, her instinct was still to offer comfort, even when she barely understood what had happened. When a friend of ours had a miscarriage, all she gleaned from our explanations (which she insisted on as soon as we had hung up the phone) was that a baby was involved, and someone was sad. The next morning we found her trying to cheer up a whole crowd of imaginary miscarried babies by jumping with them on the couch.

Madeleine the Vigilant: she didn't just want everyone to be happy, she wanted everyone to be safe and accounted for.

When friends left our house, she ran to the front window. Would they turn north or south? Would they hit the mailbox? (Katha's father had done that once.) She would watch them drive out of sight. Why had they gone that way?

"Because they live . . ."

She usually knew the answer, but liked to hear me say it. It meant they were going home, where they belonged. Or if they turned the other way, I would have to speculate. "Maybe they first had to get so-and-so, and if they were going to the so-and-so store, they would have to go that way." Ahh, of course. And *then* they'd go home, right?

Assuredly.

As we climbed into our own car to visit friends, she would ask, "Do they know we're coming?" She imagined us arriving at an empty, locked house, abandoned toys tipped over in the grass. Oops, I would say. They've all gone to Panama.

"They know, hon."

Or when we headed, always in a hurry, for a plane or a puppet show: "Will they wait for us?" (Were they friends? Did they know we were coming?)

"No, they won't wait."

"Why not?" (Were they mean?)

"There are a lot of other people there. They can't make every-one wait just for us."

This comforted her. They weren't mean, they just had to think of everybody. She could understand that. But if they wouldn't wait . . . "Let's go, let's go!" she would urge us on.

And frequently, as we backed down the driveway: "Daddy, do you got your seat belt on?"

"Yes, hon." I remembered something I hadn't thought of in thirty years. When our family drove anywhere, back in those pre-seat-belt days, I used to check that everyone's door was locked. I imagined loved ones sliding out, screaming, on the curves.

The second dream Madeleine related to us was, like her first, about a car. She dreamed she got out of bed and saw Matt's family driving off. "You guys were still in bed." The family real-ized that Madeleine wanted to see them better, so they stopped. Madeleine checked that they were all strapped in and Rachel was in her car seat.

Whenever I drove, if I braked the tiniest bit harder than usual, or swerved a foot out of true, Madeleine would pipe up from the back, "What happened?" Wavering cyclists on the shoulder, cars waiting to enter whose drivers weren't looking at me, people who didn't use their turn signals — we discussed all of these things on our way into town. "Will the police give them a ticket?" Madeleine would ask. The police loomed large in her world. As enforcers, they appealed to her. It also spoke well of them that they "pulled" people, as she pulled her animals around in a cart behind her tricycle. She wondered if police cars had hooks on the back.

"No, hon, they pull people *over*, that's something different . . ."

But she was also afraid the police might someday give *me* a ticket. She already knew I wasn't perfect, but perhaps it discomfited her to imagine my inadequacies being tagged for public notice. Consequently, "ticket" was a loaded word, and at public events Pamela and I had gotten into the habit of heading off her cries of concern by saying in one breath, "We need to go get tickets, the *good* kind of tickets."

As we drove home at night, our attempts to help Madeleine fall asleep in the car involved a new twist. She seemed to have lost the uncanny, instinctive sense of direction she had displayed a year ago, replacing it with acquired knowledge: the sight of certain landmarks, the names of the roads. So when she seemed almost asleep, and we took the detour around the square-mile block, she didn't know precisely where we were, and would murmur, eyes closed, twirling her hair, "Are we on our road yet?" I suppose I could have said yes, but I hated to lie to her, so I kept repeating, when she asked again at each right-angle turn, "Not yet." She held on. With the last turn I would say, "Now we're on our road." Within two or three seconds she would be asleep.

Madeleine first obeyed rules instinctively, because for millions of years babies survived by copying their parents' avoidance of danger before they could understand it. Now, however, understanding was all. She urgently wanted to believe that Pamela and I were not sadistic ogres, so it was comforting to hear (and internalize, and respout) the reasons for her not always getting her way.

Why couldn't she eat as many sweets as she wanted? "Remember what happened to Liam!" she sang. That big, cherubic Papageno had wolfed down great slabs of cake and icecreambergs at his second birthday party and fifteen minutes later, in a spectacular coup de théâtre, had geysered it all over his howling mother, while his father and I sprinted for paper towels.

Why did she have to stand on a chair over to the side of the stove instead of right in front of it, where she could help stir the pot? As she climbed up on her chair, she would explain of her own accord, "You might fall and touch something hot. It's not safe." (It has occurred to me to wonder if the impersonal "you" in English derives from children echoing their parents' commands and logically generalizing them.)

And the most pressing question at the moment: why couldn't we get rid of Cora? One day Madeleine said she wanted to pretend to be Pamela, and Pamela should pretend to be Madeleine. "Say 'I don't want Cora around!'" Madeleine prompted, to get the ball rolling.

P: I don't like having Cora around all the time. Sometimes I want to be alone with you.
M: But I love Cora.
P: But sometimes I just want to eat her up.
M: But we can't eat her up!
P: Why not?
M: Because she's a person. She would start crying.
P: But she can't do anything.
M: But she will. She'll grow up and be twelve years old.
P: Is that going to happen soon?
M: No. That takes a long time.

In short, Madeleine's world had become reasonable. When you returned to a place, it was still there. September always followed August, and not the other way around. You got bigger and older, not smaller and younger. When you asked "What happened?" you were told what had happened, and you understood what had happened because what happened was understandable. Everything could be questioned because everything had an answer.

It may take a moment to appreciate how monumental a development this is. Madeleine now believed that her brain could confront the entire cosmos; that it could *contain* it. Reason was another word for that perfect benevolence that lay behind all things, which Pamela and I strove to embody, goodheartedly but fallibly. And since Madeleine's own reason was a drop from the oceanic Reason, she possessed within herself the ability, and the right, to measure us. This wasn't the make-believe parity of "helping" me wash diapers or of mutual tickling; this was real.

When, for example, during a business phone call, I sat absent-mindedly on one of our ancient cane chairs, Madeleine remembered they were off limits to heavy lummoxes like me and kept trying to break in. I thought she only wanted to get on the phone and say hello, so I signaled to Pamela, who tried to explain to her that this was an important call and not a friend, but Madeleine rose up, yelling "No! No!" She was a witness and she must speak. Pamela finally yelled back, and Madeleine ran crying out of the room, unwilling to watch the catastrophe, and when I hung up and bellowed *"What?"* she returned and pealed right back at me: I was sitting on the cane chair! I wasn't supposed to do that! "Oh," Pamela and I both deflated. I hugged her, and together we inspected the chair and found that, in fact, I had broken some of the cane.

As the world around her made more and more sense, Madeleine puzzled increasingly over the one unreasonable blot that refused to go away: the existence of pain and death. Since I, and later Pamela, had lied to her about the possibility of our own deaths during her childhood, she didn't openly worry about us anymore, although there persisted a buried concern (down there with the buried truth, I suppose) that leaked out, for example, in her current obsession with a book about three owl babies who woke in the night to find their mother missing.

But her overt anxiety centered once more on those animals

whose mortality, like that of the bugs on the windowsills, was conspicuous. Disturbing examples came from illustrations. In an issue of *Ladybug* — a magazine that tended toward trite stock images — we ran across the standard bird-pulling-worm-from-ground picture. The worm had been given a vivid cartoon face, which looked distinctly worried.

"What's the bird going to do?" Madeleine asked.

"It's going to eat the worm."

"And the worm doesn't like that?"

"No, not much."

Madeleine pondered. "But if the worm says 'Ow,' then the bird will stop."

She waited for me to confirm this. "I . . . suppose it could happen," I said, with profound lameness.

That was the greatest rule, of course: First, do no harm. *Everyone Poops* ended with a diptych showing a chorus line of animals eating, followed by the same line viewed from behind, pooping. The eating line looked festive: the gorilla with its banana, the ungulate with its grass, the lion with its . . . eviscerated, bloody ungulate. This was the other shoe that had been waiting to drop for two years now. All those beaming animals she had grown up with, on her plates and bottles and mobile, saying "Hi, Madeleine!" and waving. They were her friends! They ate each other! Paddling around with Madeleine in *Ladybug's* warm, sudsy world, even I had found the dying worm's face a bit of a shock.

Worse: there was the *other* other shoe, which now dropped as well. "Chicken" meant the egg-layers out back, and it also referred to a white, al dente material we sometimes ate at friends' houses and in restaurants. (At home we were vegetarian.) Madeleine finally made the connection. Now she wanted the truth, and insisted that we line up the obscurantist words with their synonyms: pork and pig, beef and cow, venison and deer. (We didn't even want to get into lamb or veal.) For a couple of weeks she held up any suspiciously solid lump that she found on her plate and asked, "Is this meat?" and eventually decided that she wouldn't eat any of it. (She has now stuck to that resolve for more than a year, with two exceptions, which she acknowledges without embarrassment: the pork dumplings at the Chinese buffet and the chicken satay at the Thai restaurant. "Because they're so good," she says.)

She proposed to us (and to the world, if it was listening) that lions and tigers and so on could simply do what she had done and renounce eating meat. We explained that their stomachs would not allow them to do that. If they didn't eat meat, they would die. This seemed to strike Madeleine like that old logical contradiction of the man who always lies saying "I am lying." Antelopes got eaten by lions, and they didn't like that. If lions didn't eat antelopes, they starved to death, and they didn't like *that*. Madeleine kept cycling through these two propositions, looking for a flaw in the reasoning.

She had a great stake in the belief that children's conflicts always had a solution: share; take turns; be gentle. Perhaps the system often didn't work, but the *possibility* of a peaceable kingdom was there, and the road to it clear. She strove to solve the carnivore problem as well.

She was more disturbed by the lion's killing than the antelope's death. To drag a prey down and eat it when it didn't want to be eaten struck her as intolerably mean. Her first brainstorm was, Animals died of old age anyway, right? Right. So she gathered her stuffed animals together and took them on field trips in search of animals that had died quietly in their sleep. These she would feed to her hungry mama wolf. This solution might have satisfied her for some time, except that she wanted me to confirm that it was a viable one for real animals, and in the face of her seriousness I had to be honest. Or sort of honest. Instead of saying that lions and such were genetically programmed to *like* killing healthy young animals, I merely doubted that there was enough old, peacefully dead meat to go around.

Her second idea was prompted by a sight that traumatized her. One day down at the lake we saw a duck with a badly mutilated foot, floundering in the water and evidently starving. As a man waded toward it, we led Madeleine away so that she wouldn't see him wring its neck. She wept over the duck off and on all that day, and we tried to explain that sometimes an animal was in so much pain that it was better to be dead. By the next morning she had sealed up both of the cracks in Creation: now she imagined that the lions and tigers of this pain-wracked world could perhaps go around killing the animals that wanted to be killed. Again she asked me for confirmation, and again I reluctantly admitted that carnivorism didn't work that way. The broken expression that flitted across her face made my heart go out to her. It was the first time, I think, that I saw her discouraged.

Having just discovered Reason's empire, she had already run into its limits. In fact, there was *not* an answer to everything. At least, not within her or me. It was shortly after this that she began telling me she believed in God.

It always occurred this way: chancing upon the subject while discussing something else with her, I would emit my set phrase, "Some people believe in God, and some people don't. I don't."

"*I* do," she would say.

Once I had asked her whether she thought God was a he or a she, and what he/she looked like.

"It's a he," she said. "He has white hair." She pointed upward.

Now, I also tended to point upward when referring to my nonexistent Almighty, but I had not referred exclusively to God as a male, and I had never said anything at all about appearance.

I thought about this. A man, somewhere above us, with a white beard. Madeleine had first heard about God in our discussions of the baby Jesus, while we were learning carols. Was He up on the roof, then, with His reindeer? Would He one day come down the chimney, His sack filled with four-chambered stomachs for lions and immortality for all?

∾ 14 ∾

FOR MADELEINE's third birthday party, she would have three candles and three guests: Theodore, Katha, and Amity. For the party meal she had asked for cheese fondue, because she wanted to play with those long, sharp forks. She had picked out her ice cream cake and was going to help make the madeleines.

But the party was still two days away. Today was her actual birthday, and when she woke up we told her to look under her pillow. There she found a piece of paper with a clue, which Pamela read out: "On the thing that you bounce on / You will find a clue to pounce on."

Madeleine was stunned. In a recent issue of *Ladybug*, she had seen a cartoon about a birthday treasure hunt that began with a clue under a pillow. She had been much taken with the idea. Hidden good things — what she had always wanted to believe in. And now it was happening to her. There were three clues, each leading her to the next, and at the end was a wrapped box, a present from Pamela's parents: a wooden train set.

Any accurate description I might attempt here of Madeleine's happiness would seem overwritten. She writhed and squirmed and danced. Her voice couldn't contain what she felt, either, so it broke. Now she was old enough to anticipate, and she had anticipated the hell out of this day, living for the previous week in the washed-out present while the sunburst Moment approached. Now the Moment was here, and she could hardly believe it, and her disbelief was compounded by having seen this treasure hunt enacted in the pages of her magazine. (And perhaps this Moment, though ecstatic, was a tiny bit dulled by this disbelief. Perhaps it had paled to an afterimage of the fierce anticipatory daydreams of the last few days.)

Madeleine paid little attention to the train set. She wanted another treasure hunt.

In fact, there were two more presents, one from my parents and one from Pamela and me. But we gave Madeleine the impression, without actually saying so, that it was impossible for us to produce the second present until midafternoon. Enjoy this first one, we said. Make the day last.

She tried. We helped her put the train track together, and she played with it for a while. But she really wanted another treasure hunt. We read books to her. We cajoled. We had lunch. At last it was time for the second present, and Madeleine leaped and writhed and shouted. New clues — O Moment, once more! — and at the end of the hunt was a cash register, with a pop-out drawer and a real number display.

Another treasure hunt! she cried.

After dinner, we said. You don't want it to be over too soon, do you?

We bought groceries at Madeleine's Corner Store. The receipt roll in the cash register didn't work very well. But Madeleine liked it, and thanked Grandma Peggy when she called to say happy birthday.

We ate dinner. Treasure hunt! Madeleine shrieked.

This is the last one, we warned. Enjoy it. Be here now.

O Moment!

And it was over. The third present was a jewelry box, with a ballerina that twirled to a snippet from *Swan Lake*. Madeleine had been asking for something like this ever since seeing it in a book, and for a minute or two she was struck with reverence. She spoke to us in a soft voice, touching it, drinking it in.

Later (I can say in retrospect) she would get much pleasure from these three gifts. But tonight —

Another treasure hunt!

That's everything, we said. Happy birthday!

And so, after the sunburst, the cloudburst. Madeleine cried and screamed and kicked, and her voice broke again, this time from hoarseness, as she rubbed her vocal cords raw and set our ears ringing. During an exhausted lull I held her and talked about time passing. Things come to an end, I said. The more fun something is, the harder it is when it's over. If we had special days every day, they wouldn't be special, etc., etc.

Having regained some strength during this pause, she set off into wails again. Of course, if she had not raced forward through this day, if instead she had thrown out an anchor and tried to drag herself to a halt, nothing would have been different. We would have been shoved off the cliff at precisely the same moment, by the clock.

Things come to an end.

I couldn't really expect that to console her. Working through and around a few more screams, I got her to agree to another treasure hunt, which she understood would end in one of the presents she had already received. I wrote three new clues, and we went through them, and she found the un-new present in its bedraggled rewrapping. Then we ran the treasure hunt again, this time using the same clues. Then we did it a third time, everything the same. With each repetition the hunt grew less enjoyable, the treasure less valuable. We were muddying the experience, degrading it, to the point where it would not be so painful to let it go.

Finally, Madeleine was bored. Tomorrow would be a better day. She crawled into bed with us and fell asleep.

EPILOGUE

PAMELA AND I talk at night, wondering when Madeleine grew up, how it happened so fast. We know we aren't supposed to do that until she heads off to college, but our own nostalgia is already here, the first of a series of autumn moods that will pile up, layer on layer, as she leaves her various younger selves behind. And Cora is coming after, walking now, with a vocabulary of some fifty words, hurrying to keep up with her godlike older sister.

Madeleine is four years old. She still twirls her hair. A few months ago my father was gazing at her, and he said, apropos of nothing, "I used to do that all the time when I was a kid."

She never saw Zachary and Darius again after that one hour on the trampoline, but she still sometimes mentions them, and when an older girl asked her recently who these boys were that she was talking about, a look of pure puppy love came over her face, radiant and self-conscious, as she described them.

Theodore has been gone a long time, first in Panama and now in Washington, D.C. Katha is still Madeleine's best friend, and Madeleine is Katha's only friend. They play very well together, for long periods with no fights. Most of their fantasy collaborations involve kids doing naughty things. When she's not with Katha, Madeleine hugely enjoys stories she solicits from me that involve a good girl named Madeleine and her wicked, scheming double, Badeleine. Sadly, Katha will be moving to Vermont soon. We get out the atlas to see where it is.

It has now been more than two years since we sang Madeleine to sleep in her own room, but she still gets sad when she hears any of those old lullabies. She no longer remembers sleeping in the crib; she remembers only that the songs are sad, so she offers different reasons now. She tells me that "Hush Little Baby" is sad because everything in it gets broken, or fails to work. "Rock-a-bye Baby" is sad because the cradle falls out of the tree. And "Summertime" — which I tried to sing just yesterday and was asked to stop — why does "Summertime" make her sad? "Ohh," she said, deliberating with a sidelong squint, "it's about summer . . ."

She has forgotten her Christmas carols. She has forgotten the chicken that bit her foot and the two dogs that jumped up on her. In the car on the way to town, she often asks me for a story about when I was little, and I am struck by the sparseness of what I can recall. For my life before my third birthday, I have a single image: the fireworks over my head, and me crying into the grass.

Madeleine's earliest memory, for now, is of a dream she had about a year ago, when she was three and a half. It was prompted by a real event. Far away, in that other Washington, Wolf was dying. We got telephone calls, during which Madeleine asked, in the background, "What happened?" and afterward we explained to her that Wolf had lost all use of his back legs. Pamela's sister had to carry him everywhere. His mind was going, and he didn't understand what was happening to him, and he was unhappy. Pamela's sister had decided to put him to sleep.

"Sleep?"

We call it that, we said, because it feels to him like he's going to sleep. But he'll be dead.

That night, she dreamed her dream:

Wolf was lying on the kitchen floor. He was brown with red spots, to show that he was poisonous. Madeleine was in the kitchen with him, and she patted him. She said, "Good dog!" She picked him up and carried him. Then he died, and was buried.

But Madeleine said, "No!" She said, "Abracadabra!" She gave him the famous medicine, and she told him, "You never have to die."

BIBLIOGRAPHY

MADELEINE'S BOOKS

Anglund, Joan Walsh. *A Bedtime Book*. Simon and Schuster, New York, 1993.

Anno, Mitsumasa. *Anno's Counting Book*. HarperTrophy, New York, 1977.

Bemelmans, Ludwig. *Madeline*. Viking, New York, 1960.

———. *Madeline's Rescue*. Viking, New York, 1953.

Boynton, Sandra. *A to Z*. Simon and Schuster, New York, 1984.

Brandenberg, Franz. *Aunt Nina and Her Nephews and Nieces*. Illustrated by Aliki Brandenberg. Greenwillow Books, New York, 1983.

Brown, Margaret Wise. *Goodnight Moon*. Illustrated by Clement Hurd. HarperCollins, New York, 1991.

———. *The Runaway Bunny*. HarperCollins, New York, 1991.

Carle, Eric. *The Very Hungry Caterpillar*. Philomel Books, New York, 1987.

Castor, Père. *La Chèvre et les Biquets*. (The Goat and Her Kids.) Illustrated by Gerda Castor. Flammarion, Paris, 1958.

Cowley, Stewart. *Hide-and-Seek Puppies*. Illustrated by Kate Davies. Reader's Digest, 1991.

Day, Alexandra. *Carl Goes Shopping*. Farrar, Straus and Giroux, New York, 1989.

————. *Carl's Masquerade*. Farrar, Straus and Giroux, New York, 1992.

Dr. Seuss [Theodore Seuss Geisel]. *Green Eggs and Ham*. Beginner Books, New York, 1960.

————. *Horton Hears a Who!* Random House, New York, 1954.

Dyer, Jane. *Moo, Moo, Peekaboo!* Random House, New York, 1986.

Flack, Marjorie. *Angus and the Ducks*. The Bodley Head, London, 1933.

Gomi, Taro. *Everyone Poops*. Translated by Amanda Mayer Stinchecum. Kane/Miller Books, Brooklyn, New York, 1993.

Greenway, Shirley, and Oxford Scientific Films. *Color Me Bright*. Whispering Coyote Press, Halesite, New York, 1992.

Guback, Georgia. *The Carolers*. Greenwillow Books, New York, 1992.

Hazen, Barbara. *The Sorcerer's Apprentice*. Illustrated by Tomi Ungerer. Lancelot Press, New York, 1969.

Hill, Eric. *Where's Spot?* Putnam, New York, 1980.

Hines, Anna Grossnickle. *Big Like Me*. Greenwillow Books, New York, 1989.

Hoban, Russell. *Bedtime for Frances*. Illustrated by Garth Williams. Faber and Faber, London, 1963.

————. *Best Friends for Frances*. Illustrated by Lillian Hoban. Harper and Row, New York, 1969.

Johnson, Audean. *Soft as a Kitten*. Random House, New York, 1982.

Krauss, Ruth. *The Carrot Seed*. Illustrated by Crockett Johnson. HarperFestival, New York, 1993.

Kunhardt, Dorothy. *Pat the Bunny*. Western Publishing, Racine, Wis., 1991.

Landström, Olof and Lena. *Will's New Cap*. Translated by Richard E. Fisher. R & S Books, Stockholm, 1992.

Lee, Dennis. "I Eat Kids Yum Yum!," in *Talking Like the Rain*.

Edited by X. J. Kennedy and Dorothy M. Kennedy. Illustrated by Jane Dyer. Little, Brown, Boston, 1992.

Malecki, Maryann P., R.N. *Mom and Dad and I Are Having a Baby!* Penny Press, Seattle, 1982.

Meryl, Debra. *Baby's Peek-a-Boo Album*. Illustrated by True Kelley. Grosset and Dunlap, New York, 1989.

Milne, A. A. "Rice Pudding," in *When We Were Very Young*. E. P. Dutton, New York, 1924.

Moore, Clement Clarke. *The Night Before Christmas*. Illustrated by Tasha Tudor. Rand McNally, 1975.

Piper, Watty. *The Little Engine That Could*. Illustrated by George and Doris Hauman. Platt and Munk, New York, 1961.

Ricklen, Neil. *Baby's Zoo*. Simon and Schuster, New York, 1992.

Shott, Stephen. *Baby's World: A First Picture Catalog*. Dutton Children's Books, New York, 1990.

Velthuijs, Max. *Frog in Love*. Translated by Anthea Bell. Farrar, Straus and Giroux, New York, 1989.

Waddell, Martin. *Owl Babies*. Illustrated by Patrick Benson. Candlewick Press, Cambridge, Mass., 1975, 1992.

Wilder, Alec. *Lullabies and Night Songs*. Illustrated by Maurice Sendak. Edited by William Engvick. Harper and Row, New York, 1965.

Winter, Susan. *A Baby Just Like Me*. Dorling Kindersley, New York, 1994.

Zelinsky, Paul O. *The Wheels on the Bus*. Dutton Children's Books, New York, 1990.

MY BOOKS

Darwin, Charles. "A Biographical Sketch of an Infant," in *Mind: A Quarterly Review of Psychology and Philosophy* (London), vol. 2, no. 7, July 1877.

Diamond, Jared. *The Third Chimpanzee: The Evolution and Future of the Human Animal*. HarperCollins, New York, 1992.

Harrison, Fraser. *A Father's Diary*. Pantheon, New York, 1985.

Matthews, Gareth B. *Philosophy and the Young Child*. Harvard University Press, Cambridge, Mass., 1980.

Morris, Desmond. *Babywatching*. Crown, New York, 1992.

———. *The Naked Ape*. McGraw-Hill, New York, 1967.

Nilsson, Lennart, and Lars Hamberger. *A Child Is Born*. Translated by Clare James. Delacorte Press/Seymour Lawrence, New York, 1990.

Piaget, Jean. *The Origins of Intelligence in Children*. Translated by Margaret Cook. International Universities Press, New York, 1952.

———. *Play, Dreams and Imitation in Childhood*. Translated by C. Gattegno and F. M. Hodgson. Routledge and Kegan Paul, London, 1962.

Restak, Richard M., M.D. *The Infant Mind*. Doubleday, Garden City, New York, 1986.

Schatz, Marilyn. *A Toddler's Life: Becoming a Person*. Oxford University Press, New York, 1994.

A SELECTED LIST OF NON-FICTION
AVAILABLE IN VINTAGE

☐	DARK HEART	Nick Davies	£7.99
☐	THE VINTAGE BOOK OF FATHERS	Louise Guinness	£8.99
☐	THE WARRIOR'S HONOR	Michael Ignatieff	£7.99
☐	MAFIA WOMEN	Clare Longrigg	£6.99
☐	THE UNDERTAKING	Thomas Lynch	£5.99
☐	DOGS NEVER LIE ABOUT LOVE	Jeffrey Masson	£6.99
☐	A YEAR OF READING PROUST	Phyllis Rose	£7.99
☐	TOUCHING THE VOID	Joe Simpson	£7.99
☐	DIFFERENT FOR GIRLS	Joan Smith	£6.99
☐	PROMISCUITIES	Naomi Wolf	£7.99

* All Vintage books are available through mail order or from your local bookshop.
* Please send cheque/eurocheque/postal order (sterling only), Access, Visa, Mastercard, Diners Card, Switch or Amex:

☐☐☐☐☐☐☐☐☐☐☐☐☐☐☐☐

Expiry Date:_____Signature:_____

Please allow 75 pence per book for post and packing U.K.
Overseas customers please allow £1.00 per copy for post and packing.

ALL ORDERS TO:
Vintage Books, Books by Post, TBS Limited, The Book Service,
Colchester Road, Frating Green, Colchester, Essex CO7 7DW

NAME:_____

ADDRESS:_____

_____

_____

Please allow 28 days for delivery. Please tick box if you do not
wish to receive any additional information   ☐
Prices and availability subject to change without notice.